Writings in Exile

writings in exile

LEON TROTSKY

Edited by
Kunal Chattopadhyay and Paul Le Blanc

PLUTO PRESS

First published 2012 by Pluto Press
345 Archway Road, London N6 5AA

www.plutobooks.com

This collection copyright © Kunal Chattopadhyay and Paul Le Blanc 2012

The right of Kunal Chattopadhyay and Paul Le Blanc to be identified as
the authors of the introductions to this work has been asserted by them
in accordance with the Copyright, Designs and Patents Act 1988.

British Library Cataloguing in Publication Data
A catalogue record for this book is available from the British Library

ISBN   978 0 7453 3144 7   Hardback
ISBN   978 0 7453 3148 5   Paperback
ISBN   978 1 8496 4634 5   PDF eBook
ISBN   978 1 8496 4635 2   EPUB eBook
ISBN   978 1 8496 4636 9   Kindle eBook

Library of Congress Cataloging in Publication Data applied for

10   9   8   7   6   5   4   3   2   1

Designed and produced for Pluto Press by Chase Publishing Services Ltd
Typeset from disk by Stanford DTP Services, Northampton, England

CONTENTS

ACKNOWLEDGEMENTS

From both editors: This volume could not have been composed without the marvellous efforts and accomplishments of the Marxist Internet Archive and the Encyclopedia of Trotskyism On-Line – those who have created and sustained these resources deserve a global embrace for their immense achievement and contribution. We salute them.

From Paul Le Blanc: My first thanks go to my dearest friend Nancy Ferrari, who was gently but tenaciously insistent that I would not expire before this book saw the light of day.

I must acknowledge teachers, comrades, and mentors who helped me comprehend, through their own lives, the meaning of Trotsky's contributions. There are many, but among those who gave me special inspiration and encouragement are George Breitman, Frank and Sarah Lovell, Evelyn Sell, Morris Lewit, Ernest Mandel, Pierre Broué, and Dennis Brutus. My contact with, and the example of, Esteban Volkov has also been important to me. I have benefited over the years from the insights of my dear friend and intellectual soul-mate Tom Twiss. Pierre Rousset and Michael Löwy (and for that matter, my co-editor Kunal Chattopadhyay) have also helped shape my thinking on Trotsky's perspectives.

Of course, today's revolutionary socialists and activists – mostly younger than me (thank God) – have impacted powerfully on my ongoing development (with those in the International Socialist Organization, especially in Pittsburgh, deserving special mention). The global occupation and resistance movements are giving an especially vibrant confirmation of the continuing relevance of the revolutionary who told us about uneven and combined development, permanent revolution, and the masses of people who, uninvited, crash onto the stage of history.

From Kunal Chattopadhyay: My thanks go, first of all, to Soma Marik, with whom I have shared much of my life, my political and personal goals, and whose research has alerted me to what the reception of classical Marxism in today's world needs to be like.

I owe political and intellectual thanks to a wide range of people. My political development, in a country where revolutionary-democratic socialism has had a very limited exposure, was due in the first place to my father, the late professor Gautam Chattopadhyay, a CPI member who after the Twentieth CPSU Congress, in his own words, refused to accept any more that there was an infallible leader or a god for communists. My ideas about Trotsky's position in the history of Marxism have evolved in exchanges with the late Professor A. R. Desai, engagements both verbal and written with Paul Le Blanc and Michael Löwy, and with Sipra Sarkar, Sumit and Tanika Sarkar. Comrades of the Communist League/Inquilabi Communist Sangathan, the former Section of the Fourth International in India, to which I belonged between 1980 and 2003, notably Amar Jesani, Vibhuti Patel, Achin Vanaik, Rohit Prajapati, Trupti Shah and comrades of the organisation Radical Socialist, the organisation in which I am currently involved, have been very important for the context of my understanding of Trotsky, and for my writing about the contemporary meaning of his work.

A group of comrades with whom I have had sustained engagement and which has been entirely to my benefit are activists in the US organisation Solidarity, most of them Michigan-based, notably Peter Solenberger, Ron Lare, and Matt Siegfried. Without their constant encouragement my earlier work on Trotsky might not have been completed and published.

Countless activists, from my days as a student involved in the Democratic Students' Front, to activists in the anti-nuclear movement, the anti-globalisation/anti-Special Economic Zones struggles, and others who are fighting for independent peoples' movements against capitalism and all exploitative hierarchies, have shown the continued relevance of the revolutionary and democratic traditions of classical Marxism, especially of Trotsky's struggles for combined revolution, for opposition to fascism and to Stalinism and any other bureaucratic excrescence in the workers' movement, and have thereby made my own engagement with Trotsky more meaningful.

Part One:
Introductory Essay

1

LEON TROTSKY AND THE STRUGGLE FOR LIBERATION

Kunal Chattopadhyay and Paul Le Blanc

The quest for freedom, social justice, and democratic control by the masses of working people over the decisions and conditions that shape their lives – this characterised some of the most inspiring chapters of the twentieth century. It was punctuated by intense struggles associated with the Mexican Revolution, the Russian Revolution, the Chinese Revolution, European and Asian resistance movements against fascism, independence struggles throughout Africa and Asia complemented by revolutionary nationalist upsurges in Latin America, the Vietnamese revolution, the Cuban revolution, and more.[1]

At the same time, the twentieth century was an era of disappointed hopes, bitter exploitation and murderous war, racism and genocide, repressive bureaucracies, ruthless dictatorships, and the triumphant power of global business operations securing enormous profits for a few at the expense of the many. That has shaped the reality inherited by those of us making our way through the twenty-first century. One is reminded of a 22-year-old activist at the beginning of the twentieth century, in the backwaters of the Russian Empire, who wrote these brave, angry words:

> The nineteenth century has in many ways satisfied and has in even more ways deceived the hopes of the optimist … It has compelled him to transfer most of his hopes to the twentieth century … And now that century has come! What has it brought with it at the outset? … Hatred and murder, famine and blood … It seems as if the new century, this gigantic newcomer, were bent at the very moment of its appearance to drive the optimist into absolute pessimism and civic nirvana.

- Death to Utopia! Death to faith! Death to love! Death to hope! Thunders the twentieth century in salvos of fire and in the rumbling of guns.
- Surrender, you pathetic dreamer. Here I am, your long awaited twentieth century, your 'future.'
- No, replies the unhumbled optimist: You – you are only the *present*.[2]

These are the words of Lev Davidovich Bronstein – before he chose the revolutionary pseudonym *Trotsky*. Born in 1879, he was educated first in Odessa and then in Nikolayev, where he was influenced first by liberal relatives, and then by revolutionaries. Attracted to the revolutionary underground from 1896 to 1897, he first declared himself a Narodnik (radical populist), but then became a Marxist by the age of 19.

Leon Trotsky became one of the most impressive revolutionaries of the twentieth century, and his example and ideas have profoundly attracted successive generations of labour and socialist activists. He was certainly one of the finest writers associated with the Marxist movement. But Trotsky was also one of the central leaders of the Russian Revolution of October/November 1917, second only to Vladimir Ilyich Lenin when they led the revolutionary Bolshevik Party (soon to be renamed the Russian Communist Party) in the attempted creation of a radical workers' and peasants' republic that would be governed by democratic *soviets* (the Russian word for councils). It was Trotsky who became the organiser of the Red Army that defended the Soviet Republic in the face of civil war and foreign invasions, as well as a founder and leader of the Communist International. After Lenin's death in 1924, he became one of the foremost defenders of the original ideas and ideals of the 1917 Revolution and of the early Communist movement. He was compelled to carry out such a defence within the Communist movement that he had helped to create – against the bureaucratic tyranny that gave its own poisoned meaning to the word 'Communism' with the crystallisation of the Stalin dictatorship in the 1920s and 1930s.[3]

Although Trotsky was an original thinker, much of his theory and analysis stand as a creative elaboration – or in some cases a parallel development – of ideas that we can find in the contributions of Karl Marx, Rosa Luxemburg, and Lenin.[4] He is best known for his classic three-volume *History of the Russian Revolution* (1932–33), insightful elaborations of his distinctive 'theory of permanent revolution', and a critical analysis of the Stalin regime, *The Revolution Betrayed* (1936–37).[5] He also made substantial contributions in his analyses of fascism and anti-fascist strategies, in developing a 'transitional programme' for socialist revolution, and in employing Marxist theory to deal with a remarkable range of social, political, economic, and cultural realities.

The present collection of Trotsky's writings is drawn from the final phase of his life, from 1929 to 1940, when he lived in exile after his expulsion from the Soviet Union. We have excluded his major book-length works (since excerpts do not provide a full sense of his ideas), as well as all his pre-1929 writings. And yet we believe these selections, drawn from the rich pool of his mature shorter works, provide a comprehensive introduction to his essential theoretical and political perspectives. They were composed at a time in which Trotsky was engaged in an intense, heroic, desperate effort to recompose a revolutionary vanguard layer that could withstand the murderous policies of fascist and Stalinist tyrannies, the global economic collapse of the Great Depression, and a second world war – far more destructive than the first – that Trotsky could see approaching with terrifying velocity.

Despite the calamities engulfing humanity, there was some cause for hope. In this period, handfuls of dissident Communists were rallying to Trotsky from various countries.

- In the Soviet Union, there remained a sizeable number of seasoned Left Oppositionists (who would survive – and whose revolutionary potential would endure – until the Stalinist massacres of the late 1930s).
- Prominent militants were attracted from the substantial revolutionary movement of China, where Stalin's policies had resulted in the disastrous massacre of Chinese Communists in 1927.
- There was a significant cluster of seasoned working-class revolutionaries from the United States which formed the well-organised Communist League of America (going through various incarnations culminating in the Socialist Workers Party), in the process attracting a significant left-wing intellectual milieu, and publishing a steady stream of Trotskyist literature.

- Energetic young activists from France were able to provide Trotsky with much-needed personnel and material aid, and a vital forum for his ideas within the labour movement.
- In Germany a rich Marxist working-class tradition, combined with disillusionment over the Stalinisation of the massive German Communist Party, seemed to generate significant opportunities – although these would soon be closed off by the triumph of Hitler, whose victory had been facilitated by Stalin's myopic sectarianism.
- Clusters of tough-minded working-class activists and intellectuals in Britain had an impact far beyond their small numbers as they sought to renew the labour movement.
- In Spain key cadres in the Communist movement declared agreement with Trotsky's perspectives and built up an impressive cadre of militants.
- A small core of Jewish and English dissident Communists in South Africa laboured to reach out to exploited black Africans and working-class Afrikaaners with a unifying vision of revolutionary socialism.
- In Vietnam a sizeable movement sank roots in the Saigon working class, and in Ceylon a genuinely mass party of Trotskyists came to dominate the anti-colonialist left.
- Throughout Latin America Trotskyist currents also began to stir, and one of Trotsky's earliest supporters was the world-famous muralist of the Mexican Revolution, Diego Rivera.

As Trotsky and his closest comrades sought to draw such forces into a strong global network of revolutionaries – what he saw as 'the world party of socialist revolution' and which came to be known as the Fourth International – he devoted immense intellectual and literary energy into explaining what had been the classical heritage of revolutionary Marxism, the lessons of Lenin's Bolshevism, and the accumulation of experience and insight encompassed in the twentieth century's second and third decades. It was his hope that 'the spotless banner' of the Fourth International would be a rallying point for the radicalising masses emerging from the Second World War. The realities of the 1930s, fraught with greater violence and complication than even Trotsky had anticipated, prevented the potential of the Fourth International from being fully realised. There were disappointed hopes, divisions and splits, and innumerable frustrations. But incapable of despair, Trotsky never stopped, never recoiled from the struggle for socialism, never lost sight of the revolutionary possibilities.[6]

The writings in this volume are drawn from this incredibly complex and tumultuous period. In them we see Trotsky seeking to distil all that he knew into a concentration of revolutionary analysis, strategy, and tactics that could guide Marxist activists and insurgent workers in the life and death struggles of the 1930s – and of the immediate future.

At the conclusion of this introductory essay, we will want to consider the contemporary relevance of these remarkable writings. But first we should give more detailed attention to the biographical and historical contexts that gave rise to the ideas that Trotsky offers us here.

Before the Russian Revolution

Lev Davidovich Bronstein was the third child of David Bronstein, a Russified Jewish peasant and his wife Anna, residents of Yanovka, in present-day Ukraine. As a radicalising student, he was initially drawn to the revolutionary populists who saw the peasants as the primary revolutionary force in Russia, who might be inspired by acts of individual terrorism against hated symbols of authority. This was seen as culminating in a mass revolutionary upheaval that might enable Russia to make a detour around capitalism, developing its own distinctive form of socialism based partly on traditional peasant communes.

In contrast, the early Russian Marxists saw capitalism as inevitably taking hold of Russia, and they looked to the emerging urban working class as the force that would be the key to transforming Russia. The workers would form trade unions and other organisations to defend their rights in their work places and communities, just as had been the case in Western Europe, becoming the base for a mass socialist party – the Russian Social Democratic Labour Party, which actually came into being (more as an embryo and promise of what might be possible) in 1898. Marxists tended to see this workers' movement as playing a central role in a hoped-for democratic revolution that would overthrow the absolute monarchy and stultifying feudal vestiges of Tsarism. A democratic republic and the development of industrial capitalism, in the opinion of most Marxists, would set the stage for the future working-class socialist revolution.

Trotsky was won to Marxism under the influence of Alexandra Sokolovskaya. A major figure in the underground South Russian Workers' Union, he was arrested in 1898, imprisoned and then exiled to Siberia. In prison he married Alexandra, and their daughters, Nina and Zina, were born in exile. In Siberia, he became an influential Social Democratic figure. When the Marxist journal *Iskra* (the Spark) appeared, he felt a need to join in its work, and escaped with a forged passport and the pseudonym Trotsky, which became his surname for life. Alexandra remained behind, and the separation became permanent.

Trotsky made his way to London, where he met and was befriended by Vladimir Lenin, and worked with the *Iskra* editors, as a young and talented addition to their group. Personally, he was closest to older comrades Pavel Axelrod, Vera Zasulich and Julius Martov. In Paris, he met and married Natalya Sedova, and subsequently had two sons, Lev and Sergei. At the Second Congress of the Russian Social Democratic Labour Party, Trotsky held a Siberian mandate. A staunch defender of *Iskra*'s draft programme, he became known as 'Lenin's cudgel'. But in the later part of the congress, the *Iskra* group split, and Trotsky sided with Axelrod, Zasulich, and Martov. The incident, often portrayed as a struggle between democratic and authoritarian socialism, was actually a sentimental response to Lenin's businesslike proposal for a smaller Editorial Board for the party paper, excluding the relatively underperforming Axelrod, Zasulich, and Alexander Potresov, and including only three members – George Plekhanov, Lenin, and Martov. The original split between 'Bolsheviks' (majority-ites) and 'Mensheviks' (minority-ites) was thus not over fundamental principles. But what characterised Trotsky was the vehemence with which he attacked Lenin over these issues.

Soon after the Party Congress, Plekhanov broke with Lenin, and invited the minority, who had been boycotting party institutions, into the Editorial Board. Thus, it was not Lenin's authoritarianism but the minority's insistence on flouting democratic decisions that deepened the split. Trotsky, as part of the minority, joined the now Menshevik-dominated *Iskra*. But he quickly left the Mensheviks, partly because of Plekhanov's hostility to him, and partly because of emerging political differences. In 1904 his pamphlet appeared, *Our Political Tasks*, strongly criticising Lenin.

In 1905, when the revolution broke out in Russia, Trotsky was the first of the émigré intellectuals to return. Inside Russia, he collaborated with both the Bolsheviks and the Mensheviks. He wrote leaflets for the Bolshevik Central Committee and also influenced Menshevik activists in St Petersburg. After a general strike in October, when the Soviet of Workers' Deputies was formed in the capital, he became the guiding figure in it, and after the arrest of its first chair, Khrustalev-Nosar, he also became the chairperson, at the age of 26. After the defeat of the revolution he was tried and sentenced to Siberian exile, from which he escaped en route. At the beginning of 1905, in a number of essays, he had been arguing that the working class would play the leading role in the revolution. He also opposed strongly any alliance with the pro-capitalist liberals. After his arrest, he wrote a major essay, *Results and Prospects*. Subsequently, he wrote a brilliant account of the revolution, in a book entitled *1905*. In both writings, he developed his concept of permanent revolution.

In *the theory of permanent revolution*, we see the dynamic interplay of democracy and class struggle, the self-activity of the masses of labouring and oppressed people reaching for their own liberation within, while at the same time straining beyond, the context of global capitalism. Three elements can be found in Trotsky's theory: (a) the possibility and necessity under the right circumstances, of democratic and immediate struggles spilling over into the struggle for working-class political power, (b) culminating in a transitional period going in the direction of socialism, (c) which can be realised only through the advance of similar struggles around the world. In fact, these elements permeate Trotsky's orientation from his youth to his death.

Between 1907, when the revolutionary wave gave way to counter-revolution, and 1914, Trotsky remained outside the two major factions. He was the most influential 'conciliationist', seeking to keep the party united while also defending, against right-wing Mensheviks, the need for the underground party. This current was quite influential, and his role in it was reflected at the January 1910 meeting of the Central Committee, where a key resolution was drafted by him, as well as in the popularity of the Vienna-based *Pravda* edited by him. But when he refused to publicly criticise Mensheviks who had violated the party line, Lenin pressed for a break with him, and decided to launch a paper named *Pravda* inside Russia.

During the Balkan Wars, Trotsky served as a correspondent for a liberal Russian newspaper, an experience that served him well when he was Commissar for War. When the First World War broke out, he took a revolutionary anti-war stand, along with the majority of Russian Social Democrats. He participated in the first international meeting of anti-war Social Democrats at Zimmerwald, and drafted the Zimmerwald manifesto. He disagreed with Lenin on the call for 'revolutionary defeatism', arguing for anti-war formulations designed to draw broader working-class support in the struggle for peace. In Paris, he was the most influential figure of the internationalist daily *Nashe Slovo*. Expelled from France, and then from Spain, he went to the United States of America. There, he collaborated with Nikolai Bukharin in the journal *Novy Mir*.

Russian Revolution and Civil War

The outbreak of the February Revolution (March 8, by the Western calendar) in Russia found Trotsky in New York. Socialist agitation around International Women's Day in the capital city of Petrograd had 'got out of hand', leading to a mass working-class uprising – spearheaded by working women – that was joined by masses of soldiers (whom Trotsky later characterised as 'peasants in uniform'). The monarchy was swept away – replaced by democratic councils of the workers and soldiers (soviets) coexisting uneasily with a Provisional Government that had been quickly put together by conservative and liberal politicians, with the cooperation of some members of the Menshevik and Socialist-Revolutionary organisations.

Trotsky immediately urged the deepening of the revolution, the creation of soviets, and opposed any support to a Provisional Government made up of bourgeois-landlord 'liberals' and increasingly compromised moderate socialists. He reached

Petrograd in May 1917 and became the leader of a non-Bolshevik revolutionary organisation, the Inter-Borough Group (or Mezhraiontsii), made up of a number of veteran Marxists inclined to believe that a working-class revolution was now on the agenda. This was also Lenin's position. He insisted on no support for the Provisional Government, demanding 'peace, bread, land' (demands that the masses of people desired but that the Provisional Government could not deliver) and 'all power to the soviets'. In July, the Bolsheviks of Petrograd were involved in mass protests in which some of the demonstrators were carrying weapons. This was used as a pretext by the government, now headed by moderate socialist Alexander Kerensky, to violently suppress the demonstration, outlaw the Bolsheviks, and seek the arrest of their leaders. During the July Days, Trotsky, still not a member of the Bolshevik Party, wrote the statement on behalf of them. Following the July Days, he was arrested. Trotsky's group formally joined the Bolsheviks in the Sixth Party Congress, and Trotsky was elected to the Central Committee.

The repression of the revolutionary left inspired right-wing forces to rally around General Lavr Kornilov, with whom Kerensky had been allied. An impending military coup caused a panic-stricken Kerensky to release and arm the revolutionaries as part of a unified effort to block the coup. Within the soviets, the credibility of the Provisional Government rapidly deteriorated, and support grew for the Bolshevik demand of 'all power to the soviets'. Trotsky was subsequently elected chairperson of the Petrograd Soviet. In that capacity, he played the leading role in devising a strategy of soviet-led working-class and soldier insurrection against the Provisional Government in October/November 1917.

Governmental authority evaporated swiftly, and by the time Lenin reappeared from hiding to take charge, the Petrograd Soviet had in fact taken power in the capital. Functioning as military leader of the revolution, Trotsky led the resistance when Kerensky and the right wing tried to attack the city, defeating them at the battle of Pulkovo Heights. After this, he and Lenin united to oppose a call for diluting the struggle for Soviet power to a coalition government of socialist parties, not necessarily based on the Soviet system.

In the new Soviet Republic, Trotsky became the Peoples' Commissar for Foreign Affairs. He immediately published all secret treaties signed by the previous Russian governments with their wartime allies, which revealed publicly the imperialist plans of the allies. He also led the soviet delegation to the negotiations at Brest-Litovsk, with Germany.

The Bolsheviks had initially called for a general peace. But when the western powers did not respond to this call, the Germans made harsh demands, and divisions appeared among the Communists. Left Communists, like Nikolai Bukharin, proposed a revolutionary war to win over the German proletariat. Lenin suggested that revolutionary Russia must hold out for some time, and should therefore be willing to accept even a humiliating peace.

Trotsky agreed that war could not be waged, but wanted to avoid the charge of being German agents, and also thought that morally, it would be better if the new regime simply opted not to wage war, but without signing any formal peace treaty. In the government, the Left Socialist Revolutionaries, partners of the Bolsheviks, also called for revolutionary war. In the Central Committee, Lenin had seven votes, the Left Communists four, and Trotsky four. As a result, he held the balance, and initially his position was accepted. Trotsky also advocated using the negotiations to expose the German imperialist aims, to radicalise and rally the German working class. Trotsky turned the negotiations into an open forum for propaganda, shocking the traditionalist diplomats. Eventually, after prolonging the negotiations as long as possible, on 10 February 1918, Trotsky announced that the Soviet delegation was pulling out of the talks, declaring a situation of neither war nor peace. But when the Germans resumed the offensive, Trotsky and his supporters in the Central Committee had to take a position on whether to support war or peace, and they decided to support Lenin.

After the signing of the Treaty of Brest-Litovsk, Trotsky resigned from the position of Commissar for Foreign Affairs, becoming the People's Commissar of Army and Navy Affairs. The Red Army at that time was numerically small, did not possess many knowledgeable officers, and was beset with localism and the absence of a unified command structure. Recognising the problems, Trotsky took serious steps. He recruited a large number of ranking officers of the old army. Many of the Bolshevik leaders of the Red Army protested at this. At the same time, Trotsky was committed to building a revolutionary proletarian army, and this was reflected in the structural changes such as ensuring social equality between officers and soldiers, and ensuring the political loyalty of officers of the old army through the appointment of Communist Commissars to oversee the commanders.

Trotsky was also appointed chairman of the Supreme Military Council. The post of commander-in-chief was abolished, so Trotsky was in full control of the Red Army, responsible only to the government, which effectively meant the Communist Party leadership, after the Left Socialist Revolutionary Party left the government over Brest-Litovsk. His role was soon to be tested, with the onset of civil war and imperialist intervention. Trotsky went in for full-scale mobilisation, beginning first with the working class, mobilising a million men by October 1918. But both left-wing purists and factions round Stalin and Zinoviev attacked him. Trotsky's approach was vindicated by the successes of building the Red Army and defeating the enemy forces. But as he recognised later, his single-minded focus on defeating the enemy had earned him internal enmities.

With the victory of the Red Army assured in the civil war, Trotsky turned to internal affairs. Aware of the economic dislocations caused by war-induced compulsory statisation, often called War Communism, he proposed a degree of restoration of the market to help the peasants. When the party leadership turned down his proposal, he turned back to existing policies and was responsible, along with Lenin, for a further tightening of state control. In the winter of 1920–21 widespread dissensions broke out over the policies of War Communism, not only among the people in general but among the party leadership too. The central dispute was over the future role of the trade unions. The Workers Opposition wanted the unions to administer industry; Lenin and others wanted state management of factories, with the unions confined to traditional defence of working-class interests; Trotsky and his supporters favoured administration through unions representing the central state authority, arguing that in a workers' state there could not be oppositions between the trade unions and the state. Different factions were formed, and debates raged in the party.

As the Tenth Party Congress was to meet, armed uprising broke out in the Kronstadt garrison. Fearing a linking between Kronstadt and counter revolution, the regime suppressed the rebellion. Trotsky sided with Lenin, backing the ending of factional activities that had all these years characterised the Bolshevik Party, and also carrying out an economic retreat, involving freedom of trade for the peasants, financial accountability of industrial concerns, and with that the restoration of traditional roles for trade unions. But Trotsky lost a good deal of political influence at this Party Congress.

Struggle against Bureaucracy

The civil war had resulted in the collapse of soviet democracy, and the rise of bureaucratic tendencies. Politically, the ban on opposition parties and the ban on inner-party factions in the Bolshevik Party gave a great impetus to the bureaucratisation of the state and the ruling party. Both Trotsky and Lenin were gradually becoming aware of this. Lenin relied on the creation of new institutions, drawing in further workers and peasants, such as the Workers' and Peasants' Inspectorate or Rabkrin. But he also became aware by mid-1922 that a power struggle was involved, in which a triumvirate consisting of Stalin, Zinoviev, and Kamenev, was trying to break Trotsky's power and prestige. In a letter to Kamenev he responded angrily that he opposed this. From then till his final incapacity, he fought to evolve a collective leadership and gradually, to remove Stalin from the position of General Secretary. In this period, the partially recovered Lenin sought Trotsky's help in fighting Stalin, including over his heavy-handed nationalities policy. Trotsky did collaborate with Lenin. But he refused to accept the position of Deputy to Lenin in the Council of Peoples' Commissars, which would have made him the effective head of government in case of Lenin again falling ill. Moreover, he agreed to fight along with Lenin over the nationalities question, but when Lenin had another stroke before the Twelfth Party Congress, Trotsky held back from openly confronting Stalin. As a result, those fighting Stalin at the Congress were defeated.

However, by late 1923 Trotsky was seriously alarmed, especially when the GPU (the Soviet Union's secret police) chief, Dzerzhinsky, suggested that party members should report strikers to the GPU. This was when he wrote two letters to the Central Committee, asking for greater democracy. Reforms were promised, and Trotsky responded with an open letter detailing the direction they should take. This, however, served as the signal for a massive propaganda counterattack against Trotsky and his supporters. At this critical moment Trotsky fell ill and could take no personal part in the struggle. Those who did, like Pyatakov, Preobrazhenskii, and Radek, found Stalin using his organisational controls to ensure a stage-managed victory of the party leadership at the Party Conference in January 1924. This was followed by Lenin's death and the opening up of a long campaign against 'Trotskyism', calling it a semi-Menshevik tendency.

Later in 1924, Trotsky responded by writing a book-length introduction to a volume of his writings on 1917, giving it the title *The Lessons of October*. In this, he argued that even the most revolutionary party develops an inertia that has to be fought in time if a revolution is to succeed. This was clearly aimed at the triumvirate. A furious attack was launched on the book and on the theory of permanent revolution. A Lenin cult was promoted and Trotsky's past differences with Lenin shown as proof of his 'deviations' or opportunism.

Again ill, Trotsky was unable to respond and was condemned by the party leadership. He had to resign from his military position. In May 1925, he was given three posts: chairman of the Concessions Committee, head of the electro-technical board, and chairman of the scientific-technical board of industry. In these positions he concentrated on economic work, and eventually returned to a position he had developed originally in 1921–22, the need for a coordinated plan for the entire economy.

Meanwhile, the triumvirate broke up, and Zinoviev and Kamenev fought against a new majority in the Political Bureau, led by an alliance between Stalin and Bukharin. At the Fourteenth Party Congress, Zinoviev, Kamenev and their allies were completely routed. Trotsky had initially not taken part in the struggle. But he felt that Zinoviev's turnaround was due to the pressures of proletarian Leningrad. In 1926–27, the two oppositions, along with other opposition groups, joined hands to form the United Opposition. It was a significant force in the party. But by this time, Stalin had complete control. Opposition speakers in party meetings were whistled down. Oppositionists were subjected to various forms of repression. The main opposition statement, Platform of the Opposition, was not even allowed to be published.

The main arguments of the opposition included restoration of democracy in party and state, the move to a planned economy with a focus on industrialisation, improving the material condition of the workers, and active revolutionary internationalism. The Fifteenth Party Congress resolved that holding the views of the opposition were incompatible with party membership. Trotsky was expelled from the party, and shortly after that, exiled to Alma Ata. He worked to keep the opposition together, as Zinovievists started a process of recantation to get back into the party at any cost. Eventually, Stalin had him exiled from the Soviet Union altogether, sending him to Turkey, and subsequently depriving him of his Soviet citizenship.

Communist International

The developments inside the Soviet Union naturally had a powerful impact within the world Communist movement, which Lenin, Trotsky, and others had organised in 1919. This had been launched for the purpose of re-founding a revolutionary international organization. Trotsky wrote both the original call to revolutionary parties, and the manifesto of the founding congress. Despite his preoccupation with the civil war, he had played an active role in the Communist International, writing several of its manifestos and documents. He had been closely involved in the work of the European sections. After the disastrous 1921 March Action in Germany, he was a key Comintern leader who began to work out a strategy for communist work when the communists were a minority in the working-class movement, developing the working-class United Front tactics.[7]

In 1923, he advocated a course towards revolution in Germany, and its failure was the turning point in the bureaucracy's attacks on him in Soviet Union. From 1924, Stalin and Bukharin began to develop the theory of 'socialism in one country', according to which it was possible to build socialism within the Soviet Union, overturning traditional Marxist analysis, according to which it would need the productive forces of the advanced capitalist world to build socialism. Trotsky quickly came to see in this an abandonment of the world revolution. He also questioned the 'Bolshevization' of the Comintern by Zinoviev, the president of the

International, as a bureaucratic drive damaging the independence of the Communist Parties. By 1926, he was concentrating on the Chinese Revolution, which was being misled and eventually defeated through the Comintern advice for subordination of the workers and peasants to the bourgeoisie; and the Anglo-Russian trade union committee, a diplomatic alliance that was actually to help right-wing British trade unionists to defeat the General Strike of 1926. As a result of his criticisms of the Comintern policies he was removed from the Executive Committee of the Comintern in 1927.

In 1928, Trotsky appealed against his expulsion to the Sixth Congress of the Communist International, submitting a set of documents on the programme of the International, on the Chinese Revolution, and this had the effect of influencing some leading Communist activists, like James P. Cannon of the United States, who began the process of building Trotskyist oppositions in their parties.[8]

Exile, Opposition and Death

Trotsky was exiled from the Soviet Union in 1929. He found temporary shelter in Turkey, on the island of Prinkipo. But this cut him off from world politics. After some years he was able to move to France, but faced there the hostility of both the right-wing and the Stalinist Communist Party. He then received asylum in Norway, but when the Moscow show trials began, the Norwegian government gagged him for fear of Soviet reprisals if he was allowed to denounce the Soviet Union. In 1937 he was given shelter in Mexico by President Lázaro Cárdenas.

Trotsky had initially sought reform of the Communist Parties and the Communist International. In 1929–33, he focused on Germany, since it was an imperialist country with significant political instability, and both a powerful Communist Party and a growing fascist movement. But the passivity and sectarianism of the Communist Party contributed greatly to the Nazi seizure of power in 1933, despite the willingness shown by the German working class to fight. He was convinced that not only the Social Democratic Party, but also the Communist Party of Germany under Stalinist influence had completely betrayed the cause of the working class.[9] When the Communist International endorsed the line of the German party even after Hitler's seizure of power, he extended this analysis to the Comintern as well, and started calling for a new revolutionary international.

The developments inside the Soviet Union also compelled him to reassess Stalinism and the bureaucracy. In the 1920s, he had seen Stalin as heading a centre wing, while Bukharin, Rykov, and Tomsky were viewed as elements, whose victory might lead to capitalist restoration. By 1934, he was beginning to revise his assessment, a process that was completed with *The Revolution Betrayed* (1936). Trotsky argued that the bureaucracy was undermining the planned economy. He argued that what had been established in the Soviet Union was not a socialist economy but a contradictory system, and that eventually either the working class would have to carry out a supplementary revolution to throw out the bureaucracy and move to socialist democracy, or the bureaucracy would restore capitalism. However, he rejected the view that the bureaucracy was either a new class or a state capitalist class.

Trotsky's major political thrust, after 1933, was on bringing together a nucleus of revolutionary cadre to form a new revolutionary international. To do so, he also fought against the right-wing turn in the Comintern and its call for an anti-fascist 'popular front' that included 'democratic' bourgeoisie. In that era of reaction, his successes were limited, but the Fourth International that was formed in 1938 was crucial for the transmission of unfalsified classical Marxism, enriched by the analyses of events since 1917, to later generations.

Though Trotsky had written most of the major documents of the International, he was confined to Mexico, unable to travel anywhere. From 1936, Stalin had begun his final annihilation of the Bolshevik Party. Trotsky was depicted as the arch villain in each of the three frame-up trials. In an attempt to give him a fair hearing, an Independent Commission of Inquiry was set up, with noted philosopher John Dewey as chairman. This commission took evidence and prepared a report, published under the title 'Not Guilty'. Most of Trotsky's relatives inside the Soviet Union were killed, including his son Sergei. His daughter Zina committed suicide in the early 1930s, while his son Lev Sedov was killed by Stalinist agents in Paris. In Mexico, he had to live constantly under threat. Initially, he lived in the house of his artist friends Diego Rivera and Frida Kahlo but then he moved out and lived in his own house. The painter and Stalinist leader David Alfaro Siqueiros led an attack on his house in May 1940. Eventually, on 20 August, the Stalinist agent Ramon Mercader, who had infiltrated the Trotskyist movement under the pseudonym Jacson, managed to attack him with an ice-axe. Severely injured, Trotsky was admitted to hospital, and died on 21 August 1940.

Trotsky's Legacy

Trotsky made a number of important contributions to Marxist theory. Most noted is the theory of permanent revolution. This was the concept that under modern conditions of globally developed capitalism, present-day revolutions in backward countries would have a major proletarian participation, and potential proletarian hegemony. The working class would not be able to stop at the bourgeois democratic stage, but would deepen the revolution. How far the proletariat would be able to travel upon that road would depend upon the further course of events and not upon the designation of the revolution as 'bourgeois-democratic'. In this sense the revolution would be made permanent.

This theory was refined during the debates of the 1920s over 'Socialism in One Country'. At this stage, Trotsky argued that permanent revolution has three dimensions – the transformation of the bourgeois revolution into a proletarian revolution; the protracted work of economic and cultural transition; and the international spread of the revolution, since an isolated workers' state would not be able to hold out forever against a hostile capitalist world. Socialist revolutions must spread to other countries.

Apart from his analysis of Stalinism, Trotsky was one of the few Marxist thinkers to recognise the specificities of fascism, and produced a dialectical theory capturing both the mass movement nature of fascism and its close relationship with capitalism.

As a revolutionary Marxist, Trotsky was committed to building a revolutionary party. But his Leninism was distinctive, and his ideas on organisation incorporated many of his early conceptions. His defence of Leninist party building was certainly not an image of Stalinist substitutionism. He was also to be the foremost Bolshevik revolutionary who recognised the error in banning opposition parties and inner-party factions, calling for a restoration of soviet democracy and the right of the masses to choose which soviet parties should exist.

In fact, an understanding of the indissoluble link between democracy and socialism is an elemental feature of Trotsky's mature thought. This came through as he argued for a Communist-Socialist united front against Hitler in the early 1930s:

> In the course of many decades, the workers have built up within the bourgeois democracy by utilizing it, by fighting against it, their own strongholds and bases of proletarian democracy: the trade unions, the political parties, the educational and sports clubs, the cooperatives, etc. The proletariat cannot attain power within the formal limits of bourgeois democracy but can do so only by taking the road to revolution ... And these bulwarks of workers' democracy [which Hitler's Nazis were preparing to destroy] within the bourgeois state are absolutely essential for taking the revolutionary road.[10]

It also came through in his effort to mobilise Communists in the Soviet Republic of the mid-1920s against the bureaucratic onslaught represented by Stalin:

> We must not build socialism by the bureaucratic road, we must not create a socialist society by administrative orders; only by way of the greatest initiative, individual activity, persistence and resilience of the opinion of the many-millioned masses, who sense and know that the matter is their own concern ... socialist construction is possible only through the growth of genuine revolutionary democracy.[11]

We have noted that Trotsky sought to draw these revolutionary perspectives together in the program of the Fourth International, the worldwide network of revolutionary Marxists that he and his co-thinkers of the late 1930s sought to create before the world was drawn into the deadly conflagration of 1939–45. They were convinced that what they viewed as the second grand orchestration of imperialist slaughter would – even more than the first – generate radical and revolutionary upheavals, and that the Fourth International would necessarily play an essential role in these developments, helping to bring about, at long last, the triumph of socialism.

Trotsky and many of his comrades were killed before they could learn that the outcome of the Second World War would not be what they had anticipated. There was, as he predicted, an incredible wave of radicalisation and revolutionary upheaval. But contrary to expectations, the radicalised masses were not drawn into the ranks of the Fourth International. Instead, they were channelled into the larger, more traditional formations – into the exceedingly moderate socialism of the Social Democratic and Labour Parties, and into the Communist Parties that had been fatally corrupted by the policies and ethos of Stalinism.

Broad welfare state reforms initiated by the Social Democracy within the framework of Western European capitalism, and a new set of 'people's democracies' and 'workers' states' established through the auspices of Stalinism in Eastern Europe and Asia, seemed to give the old parties a new lustre and a new lease on life. Nor were most of the anti-colonial and radical nationalist struggles and revolutions sweeping through Asia, Africa, and Latin America following 'the spotless banner' held by the followers of Trotsky.

By the late 1950s and 1960s, however, accumulating problems, disappointments, and betrayals generated a widespread disillusionment with Social Democracy and Stalinism, giving rise to a youthful 'new left'. Within this global radicalising milieu it was Trotsky's ideas that found a new lease on life. Much of this radicalisation, however, was thwarted by a still resilient capitalism, and partially pushed back by a conservative neo-liberalism associated with the so-called 'revolutions' of such figures as Ronald Reagan and Margaret Thatcher.

The conservative counterattack made a special point of dismantling 'welfare state' reforms that many had assumed to be permanent. Social Democracy had neither effective resistance nor credible alternatives to offer in the face of this onslaught, and if anything seemed inclined to adapt to the conservative policies of cutbacks and privatisation. With the collapse of the USSR and most of the bureaucratically ruled states, which had presented themselves as 'actually-existing socialism' for so many years, the very word *socialism* seemed utterly discredited in the eyes of many.

Some ideologists proclaimed 'the end of history' – with the global and permanent consolidation of a more or less 'liberal democratic' capitalism. With the assistance of such media moguls as Rupert Murdoch, a virtual reality was constructed to lull masses of people into the conviction that all is well and shall remain well in this best of all possible worlds. Those inclined to disagree are trashed, ridiculed, demonised, and marginalised in this 'best of all possible' virtual worlds.[12] The problem with this is that reality exists – which has meant the unravelling of the perfect free market and its loyal governmental servants, and the evaporation of the 'end of history' utopia of the pro-capitalist ideologists. There is massive and growing discontent, accumulating protests, demands for 'global justice' and persistent assertions that 'another world is possible'. Tyrants have been toppled, and tyrannical realities sharply challenged by peaceful occupations, mass rallies and street battles. Mass struggles spreading from country to country make it clear that the oppressed people of the world, workers, students, unemployed youth, poor peasants, and others, will not alow themselves to be oppressed and exploited in silence.

The long years of identification between Stalinism and socialism have caused a significant rupture between contemporary struggles and the theoretical gains of the revolutionary movement of the twentieth century. But given the immense problems that we face, it is likely that growing numbers of activists – as they radicalise and get increasingly serious in their commitments – will want to consider whatever might be useful in the revolutionary traditions of the past.

Leon Trotsky was among the most important of the revolutionary socialists who fought, not only against capitalist exploitation and its spokespersons, but against the forces that distorted the struggles for human emancipation in the name of socialism itself. This is what makes it useful to read his writings today, when new generations of militants seek to build revolutionary struggles capable of bringing about a new and better world.

Notes

1. In different ways, these points are amply illustrated in Eric Hobsbawm's magisterial survey *The Age of Extremes: A History of the World, 1914–1991* (New York: Vintage Books, 1996) and Paul Mason's fast-paced blend of journalism and history, *Live Working or Die Fighting: How the Working Class Went Global* (London: Vintage Books, 2008). The issues are wrestled with somewhat differently in Paul Le Blanc, *Marx, Lenin and the Revolutionary Experience: Studies of Communism and Radicalism in the*

Age of Globalization (New York/London: Routledge, 2006). An invaluable resource can be found in Immanuel Ness et al., eds, *The International Encyclopedia of Revolution and Protest*, 8 vols. (Malden, MA, and Oxford: Wiley-Blackwell, 2009).

2. Isaac Deutscher, with George Novack, ed., *The Age of Permanent Revolution: A Trotsky Anthology* (New York: Dell Publishing Co., 1964), 40–1.

3. See David Mandel's outstanding entries on these matters in Ness et al., *The International Encyclopedia of Revolution and Protest*. A classic account of the Russian Revolution and Civil War can be found in William H. Chamberlin, *The Russian Revolution 1917–1921*, 2 vols (New York: Grosset and Dunlap, 1965). A more recent scholarly synthesis can be found in Rex A. Wade, *The Russian Revolution 1917*, second edition (Cambridge: Cambridge University Press, 2005). The Stalinist experience is surveyed in Roy Medvedev, *Let History Judge: The Origins and Consequences of Stalinism* (New York: Columbia University Press, 1989) and contextualised in Moshe Lewin, *The Soviet Century* (London: Verso, 2005). Trotsky's own writings during the civil war period can be found, with an interesting recent introduction by Slavoj Žižek, in *Terrorism and Communism* (London: Verso, 2007) and *How the Revolution Armed*, 5 vols (London: New Park Publications, 1979–81). His early struggle (1923–29) against the bureaucratic tyranny associated with Stalinism is documented in Leon Trotsky, *The Challenge of the Left Opposition*, 3 vols (New York: Pathfinder Press, 1975–81).

4. Trotsky's relationship to the larger Marxist tradition is explored in Michael Löwy, *The Politics of Combined and Uneven Development: The Theory of Permanent Revolution* (London: Verso, 1981) and Paul Le Blanc, *From Marx to Gramsci: A Reader in Revolutionary Marxist Politics* (Amherst, NY: Humanity Books, 1996).

5. These are arguably the three essential books written by Trotsky – *The History of the Russian Revolution* (Chicago: Haymarket Books, 2008); *The Permanent Revolution & Results and Prospects* (London: Socialist Resistance, 2007/Delhi: Aakar Books, 2006); and *The Revolution Betrayed* (Mineola, NY: Dover Publications, 2004/ Delhi, India: Aakar Books, 2006). A fine and meticulous study of the evolution of Trotsky's analysis of the crystallisation of the bureaucratic dictatorship in the Soviet Union has been provided in the substantial doctoral dissertation of Thomas Marshall Twiss, 'Trotsky and the Problem of Soviet Bureaucracy' (University of Pittsburgh, 2009).

6. A massive compendium with a Social Democratic twist is available in Robert J. Alexander, *International Trotskyism, 1929–1985: A Documented Analysis of the Movement* (Durham, NC: Duke University Press, 1991).

7. Trotsky's contributions to the first four congresses of the Communist International can be found in Leon Trotsky, *The First Five Years of the Communist International*, 2 vols (New York: Monad/Pathfinder, 1972). A succinct critical history of the Communist International's rise, early promise, and tragic degeneration is provided by Duncan Hallas, *The Comintern, A History of the Third International* (Chicago: Haymarket Books, 2008).

8. See Bryan Palmer, *James P. Cannon and the Origins of the American Revolutionary Left, 1890–1928* (Urbana and Chicago: University of Illinois

Press, 2007), and James P. Cannon, *The History of American Trotskyism: Report of a Participant* (New York: Pathfinder Press, 1972). Trotsky's major writings about the Sixth Congress have been published as Leon Trotsky, *The Third International After Lenin* (New York: Pathfinder Press, 1996).

9. Kunal Chattopadhyay, 'The Communist Party of Germany: The Theory of Social Fascism, and Hitler's Rise to Power', in *History: Journal of the Department of History*, University of Burdwan, 1998, 103–31, discusses both the Stalinist influence and its impact, and Trotsky's analysis, in some detail. Trotsky's own writings on the Nazi movement and the struggle against it in Germany have been anthologised in *The Struggle Against Fascism in Germany* (New York: Pathfinder Press, 1971).

10. Quoted in Kunal Chattopadhyay, *The Marxism of Leon Trotsky* (Kolkata [Calcutta], India: Progressive Publishers, 2006), p. 359; see Leon Trotsky, 'What Next?', in *The Struggle Against Fascism in Germany*, 158–9. Chattopadhyay's substantial work seeks to provide a comprehensive survey and exploration of Trotsky's thought, on the scale of Baruch Knei-Paz's *The Social and Political Thought of Leon Trotsky* (Oxford: Oxford University Press, 1978) – although with a sympathetic, rather than dismissive, approach to Trotsky's revolutionary commitments.

11. Quoted in Chattopadhyay, *The Marxism of Leon Trotsky*, 398, and Ernest Mandel, *Trotsky: A Study in the Dynamic of His Thought* (London: New Left Books, 1979), 137, note 7 (citing an article by Trotsky in *Izvestia*, 2 June 1925).

12. A classic statement of post-Cold War capitalist triumphalism can be found in Francis Fukuyama, *The End of History and the Last Man* (New York: Avon Books, 1992). Fact-laden considerations of the ephemeral nature of the much vaunted 'permanent' triumph of capitalism can be found in Walden Bello, *Dilemmas of Domination: The Unmaking of the American Empire* (New York: Henry Holt, 2005), and Naomi Klein, *The Shock Doctrine: The Rise of Disaster Capitalism* (New York: Henry Holt, 2007). A 'long view of history' suggesting the continuing relevance of Trotsky's thought can be found in Paul Le Blanc, 'Uneven and Combined Development and the Sweep of History: Focus on Europe' (www.internationalviewpoint.org/spip.php?article1125) in the online journal *International Viewpoint*.

Part Two:
Trotsky's Writings in Exile

Leon Trotsky, his wife Natalia Sedova, and his elder son Leon Sedov were expelled from the Soviet Union in 1929. The first land of exile was Turkey, where they set up residence on the isolated island of Prinkipo. In 1933 they were able to secure asylum in France, in the small town of Saint-Palais. Pressures from the Soviet regime and the Stalinist French Communist Party, plus ultra-right forces, soon caused Trotsky and Natalia to move to Norway by the middle of 1936 – but pressures from the neighbouring Stalin regime, as the purge trials were beginning (in which Trotsky was accused of masterminding anti-Soviet plots), made this untenable. At the beginning of 1937 – with the assistance of Diego Rivera – he was able to move to his final land of exile, in the Mexico City suburb of Coyoacán, where he met his death in 1940 at the hands of a Stalinist agent.

The aging revolutionary exile (50 when expelled, 61 when assassinated) maintained an intense schedule – in touch with co-thinkers and comrades throughout the world, constantly analysing world events, and developing an in-depth examination of how the Russian Revolution had been made and how it had degenerated. All of this was done from the standpoint of a sophisticated Marxist intellectual orientation and never-ceasing revolutionary socialist commitment.

All the time he was writing, writing, writing – such classic works as the autobiographical *My Life* (1929); a key theoretical explication, *The Permanent Revolution* (1930); the three-volume *History of the Russian Revolution* (1932–33); the incisive *Revolution Betrayed* (1936); an almost-completed biography of Stalin; portions of the never-completed biography of Lenin; but also much more that has been gathered into 14 English-language volumes edited under the masterful direction of George Breitman. The material presented here consists – with the exception of an excerpt from *The Revolution Betrayed* − of complete shorter works from this period of exile. Admirers and critics alike have found a richness, complexity, and passionate coherence in his revolutionary prose. Admirer and critic are combined in comments of ex-Trotskyist Irving Howe, reflecting on *The History of the Russian Revolution*: 'Anyone who surrenders to Trotsky's narrative powers must find this story exhilarating, but a critical intelligence is likely to want stops for question and debate, likely to suspect that the actuality was more chaotic than Trotsky allows.' Another ex-Trotskyist, James Burnham, breaking with Trotsky's revolutionary politics in an open letter, commented: 'I must stop awhile in wonder: at the technical perfection of the verbal structure you have created, the dynamic sweep of your rhetoric, the burning expression of your unconquerable devotion to the socialist ideal, the sudden, witty, flashing metaphors that sparkle through your pages.'[1]

Readers who do not share Howe's and Burnham's respective reformist and conservative end-points, remaining open to the revolutionary possibilities on which Trotsky insists, will of course find Trotsky's writings even more compelling. Historian Ian Thatcher, a relatively hostile 'Trotsky scholar', after a lengthy critique of Trotsky's account of the Russian Revolution, feels compelled to conclude: 'Measured against *The History of the Russian Revolution* most "modern" research does not seem so "modern" after all. Any student of 1917 would be foolish to overlook *The History of the Russian Revolution*. It is essential reading.' However, although he feels this account 'still forms our research agenda of the Russian Revolution', Thatcher complains that 'Trotsky was not … motivated to write … a textbook for future student use', but rather was seeking to provide 'a manual of sorts on how to make a revolution'.[2] Which is certainly true.

In the writings gathered here, then, one can find a sort of 'research agenda' for understanding the chaotic swirl of twentieth-century history. But more than this, one finds vibrant challenges, and perhaps vital resources, for those wanting not simply to understand the world but also to change it.

In considering these writings from Trotsky's years of final exile, one can find a number of essential points of continuity between his perspectives and those of others who went before − certainly Karl Marx and Frederick Engels, Rosa Luxemburg, Lenin, and others

– as well as many who came later, such as Antonio Gramsci. This is certainly true of what many consider to be the quintessentially Trotskyist contribution, the theory of permanent revolution.[3]

At the same time, within the evolving body of revolutionary Marxism, different revolutionaries came to certain insights and clarifications before others – this is a tradition that could be characterised as involving 'uneven and combined development'. Also, various Marxist revolutionaries gave a distinctive articulation to certain ideas: Gramsci's discussion of 'hegemony' and Luxemburg's description of the 'mass strike', for example, as well as Lenin's insights on the 'revolutionary party' and on the 'worker-peasant alliance' come to mind – and this list is hardly exhaustive. Many more essential contributions could be associated with each of these theorists – although rather than making them up out of whole cloth, they were, like Trotsky, simply drawing from the common pool of conceptualisations associated with revolutionary Marxism, giving them distinctive expression in the face of new experiences.

The obvious point should be added that Trotsky had the advantage of living longer than Marx and Engels, Luxemburg, and Lenin, and of having greater freedom and experience than Gramsci – which enabled him to make certain contributions not allowed to the others. Keeping all of this in mind, one could argue that Trotsky's 'defining features' – reflected in these writings – include the following:

1. his articulation of the theory of uneven and combined development and the related theory of permanent revolution;
2. his understanding of the Russian Revolution of 1917, reflected in his actions of that year and in his magnificent three-volume *History of the Russian Revolution*;
3. his articulation, as a leader of the Communist International, of the united front tactic (along with Lenin and others) to advance the genuine interests of the workers and oppressed;
4. his increasingly clear and profound critique, from 1923 onward, of the bureaucratic degeneration within the Soviet Republic, of the authoritarianism that accompanied it, and of the vicious 'revolution from above' that had such a devastating impact on the peasantry and working class

- and his retrieval of the concept of 'workers' democracy' (including, finally, the principle of political pluralism) that had been central to the revolutionary struggles of 1905 and 1917;

5. his defence of revolutionary internationalism against the deeply flawed notion of 'socialism in one country' – understanding, in the global political economy, the interlinked fates of the working classes and oppressed peoples of the early Soviet Union with those of the 'advanced' capitalist countries and with those in the 'underdeveloped' colonial and semi-colonial regions;

6. his analysis of the bureaucratic degeneration of the Soviet Union contained in *The Revolution Betrayed*, and his exposure of and opposition to the poisonous and murderous characteristics of Stalinism as reflected in the Moscow trials and massive repression in the Soviet Union in the late 1930s;

7. his analysis of fascism and his urgent call for a working-class united front to combat and defeat it;

8. his critique of the 'popular front' advanced by the Stalin-dominated Communist International beginning in 1935, with its inherent class collaborationism and its built-in dynamics of defeat;

9. his analysis of the underlying dynamics of the Second World War which – in contrast to perspectives prevalent within most of the left – provided the basis for a relatively clear understanding of post-war realities;[4]

10. his efforts – against overwhelming odds – to draw an international network of uncorrupted revolutionaries together into a Fourth International, armed with a 'transitional programme' designed to apply revolutionary Marxist perspectives to the current realities facing them.

Down through the years there have been small groups around the world that have sought to convert all of this into a dogmatic 'orthodoxy' – although this was alien to Trotsky's own critical method. He scathingly denounced efforts to devise a common set of 'Trotskyist' tactics to be applied 'from Paris to Honolulu'. Rather than constructing a special '-ism' that sets him apart, one could argue, it would be more useful to emphasise how connected his ideas are with those of the other revolutionaries we have mentioned. Yet it would be a mistake to minimise his distinctive contributions.

*   *   *

Trotsky's writings are available online through the Marxist Internet Archive, to which we are grateful for assistance in making available the materials utilised in this volume. For the Trotsky section of the Marxist Internet Archive, see www.marxists.org/archive/trotsky/index.htm.

The editors of this volume have made some clarifying insertions in brackets, in some cases adding informational footnotes as well. All footnotes from the editors are so identified, and any footnotes from Trotsky are also identified as such.

Notes

1. Irving Howe, *Leon Trotsky* (New York: Viking Press, 1978), 160; James Burnham, 'Science and Style', in Leon Trotsky, *In Defense of Marxism* (New York: Pathfinder Press, 1970), 187.
2. Ian D. Thatcher, *Trotsky* (London and New York: Routledge, 2003), 187.
3. This point is made in various ways in: Ernest Mandel, *The Place of Marxism in History* (Atlantic Highlands, NJ: Humanities Press, 1994); Paul Le Blanc, *From Marx to Gramsci: A Reader in Revolutionary Marxist Politics* (Amherst, NY: Humanity Books, 1996); Richard B. Day and Daniel Gaido, eds, *Witnesses to Permanent Revolution: The Documentary Record* (Leiden, Netherlands/Boston, MA: Brill, 2009).
4. This still-controversial point is argued in Ernest Mandel, *The Meaning of the Second World War* (London: Verso, 1986). Also see Chris Harman, *A People's History of the World* (London: Verso, 2008), 510–76.

2

FROM WORKERS' REVOLUTION TO BUREAUCRATIC DICTATORSHIP

The readings in this section focus on two related phenomena that were central to Trotsky's pre-exile experience: (1) the democratic and working-class uprising, fired by socialist aspirations, that was the Russian Revolution of 1917, which sought to establish rule by democratic councils (soviets) of the workers and peasants, and (2) the degeneration of this soviet regime into a bureaucratic, increasingly repressive and ultimately murderous tyranny personified by Josef Stalin (a reality that came to be known as Stalinism).

In 1932, Trotsky was provided a rare opportunity when he was invited by a Danish Social-Democratic student organization to give an address in Copenhagen on the fifteenth anniversary of the Russian Revolution. While the moderate socialist government of capitalist Denmark was willing to issue a visa for an eight-day visit, the King of Denmark insisted that it be for no longer – and that Danish radio not be permitted to broadcast what Trotsky had to say. Nonetheless, more than 2,000 people gathered to hear Trotsky's address, 'In Defence of October', which is presented here. Although a crowd of pro-Stalin Communists were present, intending to boo and hiss this 'traitor to the revolution', according to the Danish paper *Politken*, 'the moment Trotsky showed himself there was a deep silence – the sense of an historic personality and perhaps of a historic occasion'. In fact, this was the last large public meeting that Trotsky was able to address in person.[1]

'In Defence of October' combines not only an eloquent summary of his *History of the Russian Revolution* in which he had played a central role, but also brilliant expositions of two of his own contributions to Marxism – the theory of uneven and combined development, and the theory of permanent revolution.

In his 1932 speech, Trotsky insisted 'in the Soviet Union there is no socialism as yet', adding: 'The situation that prevails there is one of transition, full of contradictions, burdened with the heavy inheritance of the past, and in addition under the hostile pressure of the capitalistic states.' In fact, one of Trotsky's additional contributions to Marxism was the development of an historical materialist analysis of how and why this transitional society was evolving in an authoritarian direction inconsistent with the revolution's proclaimed goals and ideals. *The Revolution Betrayed* – from which excerpts are presented here, under the title 'Degeneration of the Soviet Regime' – provides an interpretive framework that continues to exercise powerful influence.

Apart from Trotsky's analysis, the most influential interpretation is that recently articulated – once again – by conservative historian Richard Pipes, who argues that the murderous totalitarian order associated with Stalin was actually what Lenin and his Bolsheviks had intended. According to Pipes, the revolutionary commitments of Lenin and his comrades were 'grounded in anger and driven by a craving for revenge' against what they perceived as an oppressive regime – yet their conception of what they were about would inevitably lead to even greater oppression. Disagreeing with Marx's faith in the revolutionary mission of the working class, according to Pipes, Lenin was convinced that 'revolutionary zeal had to be brought to it from the outside by a party of tightly organized professional revolutionaries'. In fact, Pipes informs us, Lenin's party never 'recruited many workers, being composed of intellectuals'. Stalin, Pipes assures us, 'was a faithful disciple and the rightful heir of Soviet Russia's founder', carrying out Lenin's will in imposing 'three related objectives: to build a powerful industrial base, to collectivize agriculture, and to impose on the nation complete conformity'. A problem with this is that it runs counter to a considerable amount of research and evidence.[2]

The virtue of Trotsky's analysis of the rise of the bureaucratic-authoritarian regime under Stalin is that it is more consistent with what we actually know of the working-class movement of the Russian empire, of which Lenin's Bolsheviks – it has been documented (Pipes to the contrary notwithstanding) – were an organic and influential component. It is also consistent with more evidence arising from the 1917 revolution than Pipes is inclined to deal with. At the same time, even left-wing analyses more informed and sophisticated than what Pipes offers (coming from certain anarchist, left-communist, socialist, and liberal sources), analyses accepting much of what Trotsky has to say in *The Revolution Betrayed*, have been advanced since the 1930s, arguing that there *is* a basic continuity between Lenin's Bolshevism and Stalin's murderous regime.

Trotsky responded in his 1937 essay 'Stalinism and Bolshevism', at a time when Stalin's murderous purges were in full throttle. He begins with a critique of an argument by Austrian ex-Communist Willi Schlamm, who temporarily was aligned with the deposed Russian moderate-reformer Alexander Kerensky (but would emigrate to the United States and evolve into a right-wing ideologue associated with the magazine *National Review*). Soon going far beyond Schlamm – considering criticisms prevalent among various socialists, left-communists, and anarchists – Trotsky digs deep into the objective causes of the revolution's degeneration (also critically commenting on the Bolshevik 'emergency measure' of eliminating all opposition parties), and concludes that 'certainly Stalinism "grew out" of Bolshevism, not logically, however, but dialectically; not as a revolutionary affirmation but as a Thermidorian negation. It is by no means the same.'

By 'Thermidor' Trotsky was making an analogy with developments within the French Revolution of 1789–94. From 1789 to 1793, according to influential interpretations of French history, there was a leftward swing – pushing increasingly in the direction of 'rule by the people' and challenges to wealthy and powerful elites – which was overthrown and reversed in the revolutionary month of Thermidor, 1794. The Thermidorian regime, called the Directory, was a corrupt, anti-democratic, relatively conservative force that allowed some of the former revolutionaries to benefit at the expense of the more consistent and radical revolutionary elements, and at the expense of the masses of people. This was consistent with what he saw as developing in the Soviet Union under the Stalin regime.[3]

Not surprisingly, Trotsky was especially concerned that Soviet workers become clear on the sharp difference between Stalinism and the original goals, ideals, and perspectives of revolutionary Bolshevism. This is clear in one of the last pieces of writing that he produced, his 1940 'Letter to the Workers of the USSR', in which he calls on them to re-establish their own power by carrying out the revolutionary overthrow of the bureaucratic dictatorship that was responsible for persecuting, arresting, and destroying millions of people – revolutionaries, workers, peasants, and others. 'The world revolution shall reinvigorate the Soviet working class', he predicted. 'It is necessary to prepare for this hour by stubborn, systematic revolutionary work.' Such revolutionary optimism, after so many Bolshevik cadres had been wiped out, was seen by one experienced former follower, Albert Glotzer, as highlighting a contradiction in the thought of the aging Trotsky: 'Trotsky's repetitious forecast of the certain overthrow of Hitler and Stalin by revolutionary working classes of Germany and Russia violated his own teachings, which were that such a social upheaval – where the working class was disorganized and lacked leadership – was not possible, even if the nation's ruling elite fell apart.'4

But it is hardly the case that Trotsky believed in the inevitability of a working-class revolution in the Soviet Union. He predicted that the failure of such a development, however, would mean the eventual re-establishment of capitalism there – a prediction which came to pass. It is also worth emphasising that Trotsky saw the possibility of the Soviet Union experiencing another workers' revolution and moving forward to socialism as being intimately related to the development of the world revolution. He was confident that the Second World War would generate a global revolutionary upsurge, as had been the case with the First World War. This global link also relates to the theory of permanent revolution.

Trotsky's theory of permanent revolution, has three components (1) the possibility and necessity, under the right circumstances, of democratic and immediate struggles spilling over into the struggle for working-class political power, (2) culminating in a transitional period going in the direction of socialism, (3) which can be realised only through the advance of similar struggles around the world. It was his conviction that it would not be possible to create a socialist democracy in an economically underdeveloped country such as Russia surrounded by a hostile capitalist world. In fact, a working-class revolution in one country would inevitably generate counter-revolutionary responses in surrounding countries – with efforts to repress the revolution. At the same time, it would inspire the workers and oppressed of countries throughout the world.

Realities unfolded differently than Trotsky had hoped – but, one can argue, not completely differently. His examination of the Soviet experience, from the 1917 workers' revolution to the consolidation of bureaucratic dictatorship, helps to illuminate not only what happened in history, but also the dynamics of global development and perhaps future possibilities.[5]

Notes

1. Victor Serge and Natalia Sedova Trotsky, *The Life and Death of Leon Trotsky* (New York: Basic Books, 1975), 188; Isaac Deutscher, *The Prophet Outcast, Trotsky: 1929–1940* (London, New York: Oxford University Press, 1963), 183–5.
2. Richard Pipes, *Communism* (New York: Random House/Modern Library, 2003), 29, 31, 35, 57. For several of many examples of research containing evidence contradicting key points of Pipes's interpretation – and of similar interpretations that first became popular during the Cold War – see: Moshe Lewin, *The Making of the Soviet System: Essays on the Interwar History of Russia* (New York: Pantheon Books, 1985), and *The Soviet Century* (London: Verso, 2005); Daniel Kaiser, ed., *The Workers' Revolution in Russia, 1917: The View from Below* (Cambridge, UK: Cambridge University Press, 1987); Rex A. Wade, *The Russian Revolution, 1917* (Cambridge: Cambridge University Press, 2000); Lars Lih, *Lenin Rediscovered: 'What Is To Be Done?' in Context* (Chicago: Haymarket Books, 2008); Kevin Murphy, *Revolution and Counter-revolution: Class Struggle in a Moscow Metal Factory* (Chicago: Haymarket Books, 2007); Paul Le Blanc, *Lenin and the Revolutionary Party*, new edition (Amherst, NY: Humanity Books, 1993).
3. An example of this interpretation of the French Revolution can be found in Albert Mathiez's 1921 work *The French Revolution* (London: Williams and Norgate, 1927), 487–510. See also Georges Lefebvre, *The French Revolution*, 2 vols (New York: Columbia University Press, 1962), vol. 2, 131–82. For a fine and quite detailed study of the development of Trotsky's analysis of the Soviet Union's bureaucratic regime, see the doctoral dissertation of Thomas Marshall Twiss, 'Trotsky and the Problem of Soviet Bureaucracy' (University of Pittsburgh, 2009).
4. Albert Glotzer, *Trotsky, Memoir and Critique* (Buffalo, NY: Prometheus Books, 1989), 315.
5. See Paul Le Blanc, 'Uneven and Combined Development and the Sweep of History', *International Viewpoint* (2005), online at www.internationalviewpoint.org/spip.php?article1125; also Bill Dunn and Hugo Radice, eds, *100 Years of Permanent Revolution, Results and Prospects* (London: Pluto Press, 2006), and Marcel van der Linden, *Western Marxism and the Soviet Union* (Chicago: Haymarket Books, 2009).

In Defence of October*

A speech delivered in Copenhagen, Denmark, in November 1932

The first time that I was in Copenhagen was at the International Socialist Congress, and I took away with me the kindest recollections of your city. But that was over a quarter of a century ago. Since then, the water in the Ore-Sund and in the fjords has changed over and over again. And not the water alone. The war has broken the backbone of the old European continent. The rivers and seas of Europe have washed down not a little blood. Mankind and particularly European mankind has gone through severe trials, has become more sombre and more brutal. Every kind of conflict has become more bitter. The world has entered into the period of the great change. Its extreme expressions are war and revolution.

Before I pass on to the theme of my lecture, the revolution, I consider it my duty to express my thanks to the organisers of this meeting, the organisation of social democratic students. I do this as a political adversary. My lecture, it is true, pursues historic scientific and not political lines. I want to emphasise this right from the beginning. But it is impossible to speak of a revolution, out of which the Soviet Republic arose, without taking up a political position. As a lecturer I stand under the banner as I did when I participated in the events of the revolution.

Up to the war, the Bolshevik Party belonged to the Social Democratic International. On 4 August 1914, the vote of the German social democracy for the war credits put an end to this connection once and for all, and opened the period of uninterrupted and irreconcilable struggle of Bolshevism against social democracy. Does this mean that the organisers of this assembly made a mistake in inviting me to lecture? On this point the audience will be able to judge only after my lecture. To justify my acceptance of the kind invitation to present a report on the Russian Revolution, permit me to point to the fact that during the 35 years of my political life the question of the Russian Revolution has been the practical and theoretical axis

* Trotsky Internet Archive (www.marxists.org/archive/trotsky/1932/11/oct.htm# poincare), with revisions by the editors.

of my thought and of my actions. The four years of my stay in Turkey were principally devoted to historical elaboration of the problems of the Russian Revolution. Perhaps this fact gives me a certain right to hope that I will succeed in part at least in helping not only friends and sympathisers, but also opponents, better to understand many features of the revolution which before had escaped their attention. At all events, the purpose of my lecture is to help to understand. I do not intend to conduct propaganda for the revolution, nor to call upon you to join the revolution. I intend to explain the revolution.

Let us begin with some elementary sociological principles which are doubtless familiar to you all, but as to which we must refresh our memory in approaching so complicated a phenomenon as the revolution.

The Materialist Conception of History

Human society is an historically-originated collaboration in the struggle for existence and the assurance of the maintenance of the generations. The character of a society is determined by the character of its economy. The character of its economy is determined by its means of productive labour.

For every great epoch in the development of the productive forces there is a definite corresponding social regime. Every social regime until now has secured enormous advantages to the ruling class.

It is clear, therefore, that social regimes are not eternal. They arise historically, and then become fetters on further progress. 'All that arises deserves to be destroyed.'

But no ruling class has ever voluntarily and peacefully abdicated. In questions of life and death, arguments based on reason have never replaced the arguments of force. This may be sad, but it is so. It is not we that have made this world. We can do nothing but take it as it is.

The Meaning of Revolution

Revolution means a change of the social order. It transfers the power from the hands of a class which has exhausted itself into those of another class, which is in the ascendant. Insurrection constitutes the sharpest and most critical moment in the struggle for power of two classes. The insurrection can lead to the real victory of the revolution and to the establishment of a new order only when it is based on a progressive class, which is able to rally around it the overwhelming majority of the people.

As distinguished from the processes of nature, a revolution is made by human beings and through human beings. But in the course of revolution, too, men act under the influence of social conditions which are not freely chosen by them but are handed down from the past and imperatively point out the road which they must follow. For this reason, and only for this reason, a revolution follows certain laws.

But human consciousness does not merely passively reflect its objective conditions. It is accustomed to react actively to them. At certain times this reaction assumes a tense, passionate, mass character. The barriers of right and might are overthrown. The active intervention of the masses in historical events is in fact the most indispensable element of a revolution.

But even the stormiest activity can remain in the stage of demonstration or rebellion, without rising to the height of a revolution. The uprising of the masses must lead to the overthrow of the domination of one class and to the establishment of the domination of another. Only then have we achieved a revolution. A mass uprising is no isolated undertaking, which can be conjured up any time one pleases. It represents an objectively-conditioned element in the development of a revolution, just as a revolution represents an objectively-conditioned process in the development of society. But if the necessary conditions for the uprising exist, one must not simply wait passively, with open mouth; as Shakespeare says: 'There is a tide in the affairs of men which taken at the flood, leads on to fortune.'

In order to sweep away the outlived social order, the progressive class must understand that its hour has struck and set before itself the task of conquering power. Here opens the field of conscious revolutionary action, where foresight and calculation combine with will and courage. In other words: here opens the field of action of the party.

The *Coup d'État*

The revolutionary party unites within itself the flower of the progressive class. Without a party which is able to orientate itself in its environment, appreciate the progress and rhythm of events and early win the confidence of the masses, the victory of the proletarian revolution is impossible. These are the reciprocal relations between the objective and the subjective factors of insurrection and revolution.

In disputations, particularly theological ones, it is customary, as you know, for the opponents to discredit scientific truth by driving it to an absurdity. This method is called in logic Reductio ad absurdum. We shall start from an absurdity so as to approach the truth with all the greater safety. In any case, we cannot complain of lack of absurdities. Let us take one of the most recent, and crude.

The Italian writer Malaparte, who is something in the nature of a Fascist theoretician – there are such, too – not long ago, launched a book on the technique of the *coup d'état*. Naturally, the author devotes a not inconsiderable number of pages of his 'investigation' to the October upheaval.

In contradistinction to the 'strategy' of Lenin which was always related to the social and political conditions of Russia in 1917, 'the tactics of Trotsky', in Malaparte's words, 'were, on the contrary, not at all limited by the general conditions of the country'. This is the main idea of the book! Malaparte compels Lenin and Trotsky, in the pages of his book, to carry on numerous dialogues, in which both participants together show as much profundity of mind as Nature put at the disposal of Malaparte alone. In answer to Lenin's considerations of the social and political prerequisites of the upheaval, Malaparte has his alleged Trotsky say, literally, 'Your strategy requires far too many favourable circumstances; the insurrection needs nothing, it is self-sufficing.' You hear: 'The insurrection needs nothing!' That is precisely the absurdity which must help us to approach the truth. The author repeats persistently, that, in the October Revolution, it was not the strategy of Lenin but the tactics of Trotsky which won the victory. These tactics, according to his words, are a menace even now to the peace of the states of Europe. 'The strategy of Lenin' I quote word for word, 'does not constitute any immediate danger for the Governments of Europe. But the tactics of Trotsky do constitute an actual and consequently a permanent danger to them.' Still more concretely, 'Put Poincaré [President of France] in the place of Kerensky [reformist President of Russia who was overthrown] and the Bolshevik *coup d'état* of October, 1917 would have been just as successful.' It is hard to believe that such a book has been translated into several languages and taken seriously.

We seek in vain to discover what is the necessity altogether of the historically-conditioned strategy of Lenin, if 'Trotsky's tactics' can fulfil the same tasks in every situation. And why are successful revolutions so rare, if only a few technical recipes suffice for their success?

The dialogue between Lenin and Trotsky presented by the fascist author is in content, as well as in form, an insipid invention, from beginning to end. Of such inventions there are not a few floating around the world. For example, in Madrid, there has been printed a book, *La Vida del Lenin (The Life of Lenin)* for which I am as little responsible as for the tactical recipes of Malaparte. The Madrid weekly, *Estampa*, published in advance whole chapters of this alleged book of Trotsky's on Lenin, which contain horrible desecrations of the life of that man whom I valued and still value incomparably higher than anyone else among my contemporaries.

But let us leave the forgers to their fate. Old Wilhelm Liebknecht, the father of the unforgettable fighter and hero Karl Liebknecht, liked to say, 'A revolutionary politician must provide himself with a thick skin.'* Doctor Stockmann [in Ibsen's play *Enemy of the People*] even more expressively recommended that anyone who proposed to act in a manner contrary to the opinion of society should refrain from putting on new trousers. We will take note of the two good pieces of advice and proceed.

The Causes of October

What questions does the October Revolution raise in the mind of a thinking man?

---

* Wilhelm Liebknecht, a comrade of Marx, was one of the early leaders of the German Social Democratic Party. Karl Liebknecht was a leader of the revolutionary wing of the German socialist movement, and with Rosa Luxemburg was arrested and killed after the abortive uprising of 1919. – Editors

- Why and how did this revolution take place? More correctly, why did the proletarian revolution conquer in one of the most backward countries in Europe?
- What have been the results of the October Revolution? And finally:
- Has the October Revolution stood the test?

The first question, as to the causes, can now be answered more or less exhaustively. I have attempted to do this in great detail in my *History of the Revolution*. Here I can only formulate the most important conclusions.

The Law of Uneven Development

The fact that the proletariat reached power for the first time in such a backward country as the former Tsarist Russia seems mysterious only at a first glance; in reality it is fully in accord with historical law. It could have been predicted, and it was predicted. Still more, on the basis of the prediction of this fact the revolutionary Marxists built up their strategy long before the decisive events.

The first and most general explanation is: Russia is a backward country, but only a part of world economy, only an element of the capitalist world system. In this sense Lenin solved the enigma of the Russian Revolution with the lapidary formula, 'The chain broke at its weakest link.'

A crude illustration: the Great War, the result of the contradictions of world imperialism, drew into its maelstrom countries of different stages of development, but made the same claims on all the participants. It is clear that the burdens of the war would be particularly intolerable for the most backward countries. Russia was the first to be compelled to leave the field. But to tear itself away from the war, the Russian people had to overthrow the ruling classes. In this way the chain of war broke at its weakest link.

Still, war is not a catastrophe coming from outside like an earthquake, but, as old Clausewitz said, the continuation of politics by other means. In the last war, the main tendencies of the imperialistic system of 'peace' time only expressed themselves more crudely. The higher the general forces of production, the tenser the competition on the world markets, the sharper the antagonisms and the madder the race for armaments, so much the more difficult it became for the weaker participants. That is precisely why the backward countries assumed the first places in the succession of collapse. The chain of world capitalism always tends to break at its weakest link.

If, as a result of exceptional unfavourable circumstances – for example, let us say, a successful military intervention from the outside or irreparable mistakes on the part of the Soviet government itself – capitalism should arise again on the immeasurably wide Soviet territory, its historical inadequacy would at the same time have inevitably arisen and such capitalism would in turn soon become the victim of the same contradictions which caused its explosion in 1917. No tactical recipes could have called the October Revolution into being, if Russia had not carried it within its body. The revolutionary party in the last analysis can claim only the role of an obstetrician, who is compelled to resort to a caesarean operation.

One might say in answer to this: 'Your general considerations may adequately explain why old Russia had to suffer shipwreck, that country where backward capitalism and an impoverished peasantry were crowned by a parasitic nobility and a decaying monarchy. But in the simile of the chain and its weakest link there is still missing the key to the real enigma: How could a socialist revolution succeed in a backward country? History knows of more than a few illustrations of the decay of countries and civilisations accompanied by the collapse of the old classes for which no progressive successors had been found. The breakdown of old Russia should, at first sight have changed the country into a capitalist colony rather than into a Socialist state.

This objection is very interesting. It leads us directly to the kernel of the whole problem. And yet, this objection is erroneous; I might say, it lacks internal symmetry. On the one hand, it starts from an exaggerated conception of the phenomenon of historical backwardness in general.

Living beings, including man, of course, go through similar stages of development in accordance with their ages. In a normal five-year-old child, we find a certain correspondence between the weight, size and the internal organs. But it is quite otherwise with human consciousness. In contrast with anatomy and physiology, psychology, both individual and collective, is distinguished by exceptional capacity of absorption, flexibility and elasticity; therein consists the aristocratic advantage of man over his nearest zoological relatives, the apes. The absorptive and flexible psyche confers on the so-called social 'organisms', as distinguished from the real, that is biological organisms, an exceptional variability of internal structure as a necessary condition for historical progress. In the development of nations and states, particularly capitalist ones, there is neither similarity nor regularity. Different stages of civilisation, even polar opposites, approach and intermingle with one another in the life of one and the same country.

The Law of Combined Development

Let us not forget that historical backwardness is a relative concept. There being both backward and progressive countries, there is also a reciprocal influencing of one by the other; there is the pressure of the progressive countries on the backward ones; there is the necessity for the backward countries to catch up with the progressive ones, to borrow their technology and science, etc. In this way arises the combined type of development: features of backwardness are combined with the last word in world technique and in world thought. Finally the countries historically backward, in order to escape their backwardness, are often compelled to rush ahead of the others.

The flexibility of the collective consciousness makes it possible under certain conditions to achieve the result, in the social arena, which in individual psychology is called 'overcoming the consciousness of inferiority'. In this sense we can say that the October Revolution was an heroic means whereby the people of Russia were able to overcome their own economic and cultural inferiority.

But let us pass over from these historico-philosophic, perhaps somewhat too abstract, generalisations, and put up the same question in concrete form, that is within the cross-section of living economic facts. The backwardness of Russia expressed itself most clearly at the beginning of the twentieth century in the fact that industry occupied a small place in that country in comparison with the peasantry. Taken as a whole, this meant a low productivity of the national labour. Suffice it to say that on the eve of the war, when Tsarist Russia had reached the peak of its well-being, the national income was eight to ten times lower than in the United States. This expresses numerically the 'amplitude' of its backwardness if the word 'amplitude' can be used at all in connection with backwardness.

At the same time however, the law of combined development expressed itself in the economic field at every step, in simple as well as in complex phenomena. Almost without highways, Russia was compelled to build railroads. Without having gone through the European artisan and manufacturing stages, Russia passed directly to mechanised production. To jump over intermediate stages is the way of backward countries.

While peasant agriculture often remained at the level of the seventeenth century, Russia's industry, if not in scope, at least in type, reached the level of progressive countries and in some respects rushed ahead of them. It suffices to say that gigantic enterprises, with over a thousand workers each, employed in the United States less than 18 per cent of the total number of industrial workers. In Russia it was over 41 per cent. This fact is hard to reconcile with the conventional conception of the economic backwardness of Russia. It does not on the other hand, refute this backwardness, but dialectically complements it.

The same contradictory character was shown by the class structure of the country. The finance capital of Europe industrialised Russian economy at an accelerated tempo. The industrial bourgeoisie forthwith assumed a large-scale capitalistic and anti-popular character. The foreign stock-holders moreover, lived outside of the country. The workers, on the other hand, were naturally Russians. Against a numerically weak Russian bourgeoisie, which had no national roots, there stood confronting it a relatively strong proletariat with strong roots in the depths of the people.

The revolutionary character of the proletariat was furthered by the fact that Russia in particular, as a backward country, under the compulsion of catching up with its opponents, had not been able to work out its own social or political conservatism. The most conservative country of Europe, in fact of the entire world, is considered, and correctly, to be the oldest capitalist country –

England. The European country freest of conservatism would in all probability be Russia.

But the young, fresh, determined proletariat of Russia still constituted only a tiny minority of the nation. The reserves of its revolutionary power lay outside of the proletariat itself – in the peasantry, living in half-serfdom; and in the oppressed nationalities.

The Peasantry

The subsoil of the revolution was the agrarian question. The old feudal monarchic system became doubly intolerable under the conditions of the new capitalist exploitation. The peasant communal areas amounted to some 140 million *dessiatines*. But 30,000 large landowners, whose average holdings were over 2,000 *dessiatines*, owned altogether 70 million *dessiatines*, that is as much as some 10 million peasant families or 50 million of peasant population. These statistics of land tenure constituted a ready-made programme of agrarian revolt.

The nobleman, Bokorin, wrote in 1917 to the dignitary, Rodsianko, the Chairman of the last municipal Duma: 'I am a landowner and I cannot get it into my head that I must lose my land, and for an unbelievable purpose to boot, for the experiment of the socialist doctrine.' But it is precisely the task of revolutions to accomplish that which the ruling classes cannot get into their heads.

In Autumn 1917, almost the whole country was the scene of peasant revolts. Of the 642 departments of old Russia, 482, that is 77 per cent, were affected by the movements! The reflection of the burning villages lit up the arena of the insurrections in the cities.

But you may argue the war of the peasants against the landowners is one of the classic elements of bourgeois revolution, and not at all of the proletarian revolution!

Perfectly right, I reply – so it was in the past. But the inability of capitalist society to survive in an historically backward country was expressed precisely in the fact that the peasant insurrections did not drive the bourgeois classes of Russia forward but on the contrary, drove them back for good into the camp of reaction. If the peasantry did not want to be completely ruined there was nothing else left for it but to join the industrial proletariat. This revolutionary joining of the two oppressed classes was foreseen by the genius of Lenin and prepared for him long before.

Had the agrarian question been courageously solved by the bourgeoisie, the proletariat of Russia would not, obviously, have been able to arrive at the power in 1917. But the Russian, bourgeoisie, covetous and cowardly, too late on the scene, prematurely a victim of senility, dared not lift a hand against feudal property. But thereby it delivered the power to the proletariat and together with it the right to dispose of the destinies of bourgeois society.

In order for the Soviet state to come into existence, it was consequently necessary for two factors of a different historical nature to collaborate: the peasant war, that is to say, a movement which is characteristic of the dawn of bourgeois development, and the proletarian insurrection, or uprising which announces the decline of the bourgeois movement. There we have the combined character of the Russian Revolution.

Once let the Bear – the peasant – stand up on his hind feet, he becomes terrible in his wrath. But he is unable to give conscious expression to his indignation. He needs a leader. For the first time in the history of the world, the insurrectionary peasants found a faithful leader in the person of the proletariat.

Four million workers in industry and transport leading a hundred million peasants. That was the natural and inevitable reciprocal relations between proletariat and peasantry in the revolution.

The National Question

The second revolutionary reserve of the proletariat was formed by the oppressed nationalities, who moreover were also predominantly peasants. Closely allied with the historical backwardness of the country is the extensive character of the development of the state, which spread out like a grease spot from the centre at Moscow to the circumference. In the East, it subjugated the still more backward peoples, basing itself upon them, in order to stifle the more developed nationalities of the West. To the 70 million Great Russians, who constituted the main mass of the population were added gradually some 90 millions of other races.

In this way arose the empire, in whose composition the ruling nationality made up only 43 per cent of the population, while the remaining 57 per cent, consisted of nationalities of varying degrees of civilisation and legal deprivation. The national pressure was incomparably cruder than in the neighbouring states, and not only than those beyond the western frontier, but beyond the eastern one too. This conferred on the national problem an enormous explosive force.

The Russian liberal bourgeoisie was not willing in either the national or the agrarian question, to go beyond certain amelioration's of the regime of oppression and violence. The 'democratic' governments of Miliukov and Kerensky, which reflected the interests of the great Russian bourgeoisie and bureaucracy actually hastened to impress upon the discontented nationalities in the course of the eight months of their existence: 'You will obtain what you can get by force.'

The inevitability of the development of the centrifugal national movements had been early taken into consideration by Lenin. The Bolshevik Party struggled obstinately for years for the right of self-determination for nations, that is, for the right of full secession. Only through this courageous position on the national question could the Russian proletariat gradually win the confidence of the oppressed peoples. The national independence movement as well as the agrarian movement, necessarily turned against the official democracy, strengthened the proletariat, and poured into the stream of the October upheaval.

The Permanent Revolution

In these ways the riddle of the proletarian upheaval in an historically backward country loses its veil of mystery.

Marxist revolutionaries predicted, long before the events, the march of the revolution and the historical role of the young Russian proletariat. I may be permitted to repeat here a passage from a work of my own in 1905.

> In an economically backward country the proletariat can arrive at power earlier than in a capitalistically advanced one ...
>
> The Russian Revolution creates the conditions under which the power can (and in the event of a successful revolution must) be transferred to

the proletariat, even before the policy of bourgeois liberalism receives the opportunity of unfolding its genius for government to its full extent.

The destiny of the most elementary revolutionary interest of the peasantry ... is bound up with the destiny of the whole revolution, that is, with the destiny of the proletariat. The proletariat, once arrived at power, will appear before the peasantry as the liberating class.

The proletariat enters into the government as the revolutionary representative of the nation, as the acknowledged leader of the people in the struggle with absolutism and the barbarism of serfdom.

The proletarian regime will have to stand from the very beginning for the solution of the agrarian question, with which the question of the destiny of tremendous masses of the population of Russia is bound up.

I have taken the liberty of quoting these passages as evidence that the theory of the October Revolution which I am presenting today is no casual improvisation and was not constructed ex-post facto under the pressure of events. No, in the form of a political prognosis it preceded the October upheaval by a long time. You will agree that a theory is in general valuable only in so far as it helps to foresee the course of development and influence it purposively. Therein, in general terms, is the invaluable importance of Marxism as a weapon of social historical orientation. I am sorry that the narrow limits of the lecture do not permit me to enlarge upon the above quotation materially. I will therefore content myself with a brief resume of the whole work which dates from 1905.

In accordance with its immediate tasks, the Russian Revolution is a bourgeois revolution. But the Russian bourgeoisie is anti-revolutionary. The victory of the revolution is therefore possible only as a victory of the proletariat. But the victorious proletariat will not stop at the programme of bourgeois democracy: it will go on to the programme of socialism. The Russian Revolution will become the first stage of the Socialist world revolution.

This was the theory of permanent revolution formulated by me in 1905 and since then exposed to the severest criticism under the name of 'Trotskyism'.

To be more exact, it is only a part of this theory. The other part, which is particularly timely now, states:

The present productive forces have long outgrown their national limits. A socialist society is not feasible within national boundaries. Significant as the economic successes of an isolated workers' state may be, the programme of 'Socialism in one country' is a petty-bourgeois utopia. Only a European and then a world federation of socialist republics can be the real arena for a harmonious socialist society.

Today, after the test of events, I see less reason than ever to discard this theory.

Prerequisites for October

After all that has been said above, is it still worthwhile to recall the fascist writer Malaparte, who ascribes to me tactics which are independent of strategy and amount to a series of technical recipes for insurrection, applicable in all latitudes and longitudes? It is a good thing that the name of the luckless theoretician of the *coup d'état* makes it easy to distinguish him from the victorious practitioner of the *coup d'état*; no one therefore runs the risk of confusing Malaparte with Bonaparte.

Without the armed insurrection of 7 November 1917, the Soviet state would not be in existence. But the insurrection itself did not drop from heaven. A series of historical prerequisites were necessary for the October Revolution.

1. The rotting away of the old ruling classes – the nobility, the monarchy, the bureaucracy.
2. The political weakness of the bourgeoisie, which had no roots in the masses of the people.
3. The revolutionary character of the agrarian question.
4. The revolutionary character of the problem of the oppressed nationalities.
5. The significant social burdens weighing on the proletariat.

To these organic preconditions must be added certain highly important connected conditions.

6. The revolution of 1905 was the great school or in Lenin's phrase, 'the dress rehearsal' of the revolution of 1917. The soviets as the irreplaceable organisational form of the proletarian united front in the revolution were created for the first time in the year 1905.

7. The imperialist war sharpened all the contradictions, tore the backward masses out of their immobility, and thus prepared the grandiose scale of the catastrophe.

The Bolshevik Party

But all these conditions, which fully sufficed for the outbreak of the revolution, were insufficient to assure the victory of the proletariat in the revolution. For this victory one condition more was necessary.

8. The Bolshevik Party

When I enumerate this condition last in the series, I do it only because it follows the logical sequence, and not because I assign the last place in the order of importance to the party.

No, I am far from such a thought. The liberal bourgeoisie can seize power and has seized it more than once as the result of struggles in which it took no part; it possesses organs of seizure which are admirably adapted to the purpose. But the working masses are in a different position; they have long been accustomed to give, and not to take. They work, are patient as long as they can be, hope, lose patience, rise up and struggle, die, bring victory to others, are betrayed, fall into despondency, bow their necks, and work again. Such is the history of the masses of the people under all regimes. To be able to take the power firmly and surely into its hands the proletariat needs a party, which far surpasses other parties in the clarity of its thought and in its revolutionary determination.

The Bolshevik Party, which has been described more than once and with complete justification as the most revolutionary party in the history of mankind was the living condensation of the modern history of Russia, of all that was dynamic in it. The overthrow of Tsarism had long been recognised as the necessary condition for the development of economy and culture. But for the solution of this task, the forces were insufficient. The bourgeoisie feared the revolution. The intelligentsia tried to bring the peasant to his feet. The *muzhik* [peasant], incapable of generalising his own miseries and his aims, left this appeal unanswered. The intelligentsia armed itself with dynamite. A whole generation was wasted in this struggle.

On 1 March 1887, Alexander Ulyanov carried out the last of the great terrorist plots. The attempted assassination of Alexander III failed. Ulyanov and the other participants were executed. The attempt to make chemical preparation take the place of a revolutionary class, came to grief. Even the most heroic intelligentsia is nothing without the masses. Ulyanov's younger brother Vladimir, the future Lenin, the greatest figure of Russian history, grew up under the immediate impression of these facts and conclusion. Even in his early youth he placed himself on the foundations of Marxism and turned his face toward the proletariat. Without losing sight of the village for a moment he sought the way to the peasantry through the workers. Inheriting from his revolutionary predecessors their capacity for self-sacrifice, and their willingness to go to the limit, Lenin, at an early age, became the teacher of the new generation of the intelligentsia and of the advanced workers. In strikes and street fights, in prisons and in exile, the workers received the necessary tempering. They needed the searchlight of Marxism to light up their historical road in the darkness of absolutism.

Among the émigrés the first Marxist group arose in 1883. In 1898 at a secret meeting, the foundation of the Russian Social Democratic Workers Party was proclaimed (we all called ourselves Social Democrats in those days). In 1903 occurred the split between Bolsheviks and Mensheviks, and in 1912 the Bolshevik faction finally became an independent party.

It learned to recognise the class mechanics of society in its struggles during the events of twelve years (1905–17). It educated groups equally capable of initiative and of subordination. The discipline of its revolutionary action was based on the unity of its doctrine, on the tradition of common struggles and on confidence in its tested leadership.

Such was the party in 1917. Despised by the official 'public opinion' and the paper thunder of the intelligentsia press, it adapted itself to the movement of the masses. It kept firmly in hand the lever of control in the factories and regiments. More and more the peasant masses turned toward it. If we understand by 'nation' not the privileged heads, but the majority of the people, that is, the workers and peasants, then the Bolsheviks became during the course of 1917 a truly national Russian Party.

In September, 1917, Lenin who was compelled to keep in hiding gave the signal, 'The crisis is ripe, the hour of insurrection has approached.' He was right. The ruling classes faced with the problems of the war, the land and liberation, had got into inextricable difficulties. The bourgeoisie positively lost its head. The democratic parties, the Mensheviks and Social Revolutionaries [left-wing populists], dissipated the last remaining bit of confidence of the masses in them by their support of the imperialist war, by their policy of compromise and concessions to the bourgeois and feudal property owners. The awakened army no longer wanted to fight for the alien aims of imperialism. Disregarding democratic advice, the peasantry smoked the landowners out of their estates. The oppressed nationalities of the far boundaries rose up against the bureaucracy of Petrograd. In the most important workers' and soldiers' soviets the Bolsheviks were dominant. The ulcer was ripe. It needed a cut of the lancet.

Only under these social and political conditions was the insurrection possible. And thus it also became inevitable. But there is no playing around with insurrection. Woe to the surgeon who is careless in the use of the lancet! Insurrection is an art. It has its laws and its rules.

The party faced the realities of the October insurrection with cold calculation and with ardent resolution. Thanks to this, it conquered almost without victims. Through the victorious soviets the Bolsheviks placed themselves at the head of a country which occupies one sixth of the surface of the globe.

The majority of my present listeners, it is to be presumed, did not occupy themselves at all with politics in 1917. So much the better. Before the young generation lies much that is interesting, if not always easy. But the representatives of the old generation in this hall will certainly remember well how the seizure of power by the Bolsheviks was received: as a curiosity, as a misunderstanding, as a scandal; most often as a nightmare which was bound to disappear with the first rays of dawn. The Bolsheviks would last 24 hours, a week, month, year. The period had to be constantly lengthened. The rulers of the whole world armed themselves up against the first workers' state: civil war was stirred up, interventions again and again, blockade. So passed year after year. Meantime, history has recorded 15 years of existence of the Soviet power.

Can October be Justified?

'Yes', some opponents will say, 'the adventure of October has shown itself to be much more substantial than many of us thought. Perhaps it was not even quite an "adventure". Nevertheless, the question retains its full force. Have the dazzling promises which the Bolsheviks proclaimed on the eve of the Revolution been fulfilled?'

Before we answer the hypothetical opponent let us note that the question in and of itself is not new. On the contrary, it followed right at the heels of the October Revolution, since the day of its birth.

The French journalist, Claude Anet, who was in Petrograd during the revolution, wrote as early as 27th October, 1917:

> The maximalists (which was what the French called the Bolsheviks at that time) have seized power and the great day has come. At last, I say to myself, I shall behold the realisation of the socialist Eden which has been promised us for so many years ... Admirable adventure! A privileged position!

And so on and so forth. What sincere hatred was behind the ironical salutation! The very morning after the capture of the Winter Palace, the reactionary journalist hurried to register his claim for a ticket of admission to Eden. Fifteen years have passed since the revolution. With all the greater absence of ceremony our enemies reveal their malicious joy over the fact that the land of the Soviets, even today, bears but little resemblance to a realm of general well-being. Why then the revolution and why the sacrifice?

Permit me to express the opinion that the contradictions, difficulties, mistakes and insufficiency of the Soviet regime are no less familiar to me than to anyone. I, personally, have never concealed them, whether in speech or in writing. I have believed and I still believe that revolutionary politics, as distinguished from conservative, cannot be built up on concealment. 'To speak out that which is' must be the highest principle of the workers' state.

But in criticism, as well as in creative activity, perspective is necessary. Subjectivism is a poor adviser, particularly in great questions. Periods of time must be commensurate with the tasks, and not with individual caprices. Fifteen years! How long is that in the life of one man! Within that period not a few of our generation were borne to their graves and those who remain have added innumerable grey hairs. But these same 15 years – what an insignificant period in the life of a people! Only a minute on the clock of history.

Capitalism required centuries to establish itself in the struggle against the Middle Ages, to raise the level of science and technique, to build railroads, to make use of electric current. And then? Then humanity was thrust by capitalism into the hell of wars and crises.

But Socialism is allowed by its enemies, that is, by the adherents of capitalism, only a decade and a half to install on earth Paradise, with all modern improvements. Such obligations were never assumed by us.

The processes of great changes must be measured by scales which are commensurate with them. I do not know if the Socialist society will resemble the biblical Paradise. I doubt it. But in the Soviet Union there is no Socialism as yet. The situation that prevails there is one of transition, full of contradictions, burdened with the heavy inheritance of the past and in addition is under the hostile pressure of the capitalistic states. The October Revolution has proclaimed the principles of the new society. The Soviet Republic has shown only the first stage of its realisation. Edison's first lamp was very bad. We must learn how to discern the future.

But the unhappiness that rains on living men! Do the results of the revolution justify the sacrifice which it has caused? A fruitless question, rhetorical through and through; as if the processes of history admitted of a balance sheet accounting! We might just as well ask, in view of the difficulties and miseries of human existence, 'Does it pay to be born altogether?' To which Heine wrote: 'And the fool expects an answer' ... Such melancholy reflections haven't hindered mankind from being born and from giving birth. Even in these days of unexampled world crisis, suicides fortunately constitute an unimportant percentage. But peoples never resort to suicide. When their burdens are intolerable they seek a way out through revolution.

Besides, who are they who are indignant over the victims of the social upheaval? Most often those who have paved the way for the victims of the imperialist war, and have glorified or, at least, easily accommodated themselves to it. It is now our turn to ask, 'Has the war justified itself? What has it given us? What has it taught?'

The reactionary historian, Hippolyte Taine, in his eleven-volume pamphlet against the great French Revolution, describes, not without malicious joy, the sufferings of the French people in the years of the dictatorship of the Jacobins and afterward. The worst off were the lower classes of the cities, the plebeians, who as 'sans-culottes' had given of their best for the Revolution. Now they or their wives stood in line throughout cold nights to return empty-handed to the extinguished family hearth. In the tenth year of the revolution, Paris was poorer than before it began. Carefully selected, artificially pieced-out facts serve Taine as justification for his destructive verdict against the revolution. Look, the plebeians wanted to be dictators and have precipitated themselves into misery!

It is hard to conceive of a more uninspired piece of moralising. First of all, if the revolution precipitated the country into misery the blame lay principally on the ruling classes who drove the people to revolution. Second, the great French Revolution did not exhaust itself in hungry lines before bakeries. The whole of modern France, in many respects the whole of modern civilisation, arose out of the bath of the French Revolution!

In the course of the Civil War in the United States in the '60s of the past century, 500,000 men were killed. Can these sacrifices be justified?

From the standpoint of the American slaveholder and the ruling classes of Great Britain who marched with them – no! From the standpoint of the Negro or of the British working man – absolutely. And from the standpoint of the development of humanity as a whole there can be no doubt whatever. Out of the Civil War of the '60s came the present United States with its unbounded practical initiative, its rationalised technique, its economic energy. On these achievements of Americanism, humanity will build the new society.

The October Revolution penetrated deeper than any of its predecessors into the Holy of Holies of society – into the property relations. So much the longer time is necessary to reveal the creative consequences of the revolution in all spheres of life. But the general direction of the upheaval is already clear: the Soviet

Republic has no reason whatever to bow its head before the capitalists accusers and speak the language of apology.

In order to appreciate the new regime from the stand-point of human development, one must first answer the question, 'How does social progress express itself and how can it be measured?'

The Balance Sheet of October

The deepest, the most objective and the most indisputable criterion says: progress can be measured by the growth of the productivity of social labour. From this angle the estimate of the October Revolution is already given by experience. The principle of socialistic organisation has for the first time in history shown its ability to record results in production unheard of in a short space of time.

The curve of the industrial development of Russia expressed in crude index numbers is as follows, taking 1913, the last year before the war as 100. The year 1920, the highest point of the civil war, is also the lowest point in industry – only 25, that is to say, a quarter of the pre-war production. In 1925 it rose to 75, that is, three-quarters of the pre-war production; in 1929 about 200, in 1932: 300, that is to say, three times as much as on the eve of the war.

The picture becomes even more striking in the light of the international index. From 1925 to 1932 the industrial production of Germany has diminished one and a half times, in America twice, in the Soviet Union it has increased four-fold. These figures speak for themselves.

I have no intention of denying or concealing the seamy side of the Soviet economy. The results of the industrial index are extraordinarily influenced by the unfavourable development of agriculture, that is to say, in the domain which essentially has not yet risen to Socialist methods, but at the same time had been led on the road to collectivisation with insufficient preparation, bureaucratically rather than technically and economically. This is a great question, which however goes beyond the limits of my lecture.

The index numbers cited require another important reservation. The indisputable and, in their way, splendid results of Soviet industrialisation demand a further economic checking-up from the stand-point of the mutual adaptation of the various elements of the economy, their dynamic equilibrium and consequently their productive capacity. Here great difficulties and even set backs are inevitable. Socialism does not arise in its perfected form from the Five-Year Plan like Minerva from the head of Jupiter, or Venus from the foam of the sea. Before it are decades of persistent work, of mistakes, corrections, and reorganisation. Moreover, let us not forget that socialist construction in accordance with its very nature can only reach perfection on the international arena. But even the most favourable economic balance sheet of the results so far obtained could reveal only the incorrectness of the preliminary calculations, the faults of planning and errors of direction. It could in no way refute the empirically firmly established fact – the possibility, with the aid of socialist methods, of raising the productivity of collective labour to an unheard of height. This conquest, of world historical importance, cannot be taken away from us by anybody or anything.

After what has been said it is scarcely worthwhile to spend time on the complaints that the October Revolution has brought Russia to the downfall of its civilisation. That is the voice of the disquieted ruling houses and salons. The feudal bourgeois 'civilisation' overthrown by the proletarian upheaval was only barbarism with decorations *à la* Talmi (costume jewelry). While it remained inaccessible to the Russian people, it brought little that was new to the treasury of mankind.

But even with respect to this civilisation, which is so bemoaned by the white émigrés, we must put the question more precisely – in what sense has it been destroyed? Only in one sense: the monopoly of a small minority in the treasures of civilisation has been done away with. But everything of cultural value in the old Russian civilisation has remained untouched. The 'Huns' of Bolshevism have shattered neither the conquests of the mind nor the creations of art. On the contrary, they carefully collected the monuments of human creativeness and arranged them in model order. The culture of the monarchy, the nobility and the bourgeoisie has now become the culture of the historic museums.

The people visit these museums eagerly. But they do not live in them. They learn. They construct. The fact alone that the October Revolution taught the Russian people, the dozens of peoples of

Tsarist Russia, to read and write stands immeasurably higher than the whole former hot-house Russian civilisation.

The October Revolution has laid the foundations for a new civilisation which is designed, not for a select few, but for all. This is felt by the masses of the whole world. Hence their sympathy for the Soviet Union which is as passionate as once was their hatred for Tsarist Russia.

Human language is an irreplaceable instrument not only for giving names to events, but also for their valuation. By filtering out that which is accidental, episodic, artificial, it absorbs into itself that which is essential, characteristic, of full weight. Notice with what sensibility the languages of civilised nations have distinguished two epochs in the developments of Russia. The culture of the nobility brought into world currency such barbarisms as Tsar, Cossack, pogrom, *nagaika*. You know these words and what they mean. The October Revolution introduced into the language of the world such words as Bolshevik, Soviet, *kolkhoz*, Gosplan, *piatiletka*.* Here practical linguistics holds its historical supreme court!

The most profound meaning of the revolution, but the hardest to submit to immediate measurement, consists in the fact that it forms and tempers the character of the people. The conception of the Russian people as slow, passive, melancholy, mystical, is widely spread and not accidental. It has its roots, in the past. But in Western countries up to the present time those far reaching changes which have been introduced into the character of the people by the revolution, have not been sufficiently considered. Could it be otherwise?

Every man with experience of life can recall the picture of some youth that he has known, receptive, lyrical, all too susceptible, who later becomes suddenly under the influence of a powerful moral impetus, stronger, better balanced and hardly recognisable. In the developments of a whole nation, such moral transformations are wrought by the revolution.

---

* Tsar is an absolute monarch; Cossack represented the fierce repressive forces defending the Tsar; pogroms were violent and often murderous assaults on communities of ethnic minorities (generally Jews); *nagaika* was a short, thick whip (also called a knout). Bolsheviks were uncompromising revolutionaries, soviets were democratic councils; *kokholz*, Gosplan, *piatiletka* were associated with economic planning and development (collective farm, State Planning Commission, and Five-Year Plan respectively). – Editors

The February insurrection against the autocracy, the struggle against the nobility, against the imperialist war, for peace, for land, for national equality, the October insurrection, the overthrow of the bourgeoisie and of those parties which supported it, or sought agreements with the bourgeoisie, three years of civil war on a front of 5,000 miles, the years of blockade, hunger, misery, and epidemics, the years of tense economic reconstruction, of new difficulties and renunciations – these make a hard but good school. A heavy hammer smashes glass, but forges steel. The hammer of the revolution is forging the steel of the people's character.

'Who will believe', wrote a Tsarist general, Zalweski, with indignation shortly after the upheaval, 'that a porter or a watchman suddenly becomes a chief justice, a hospital attendant the director of the hospital, a barber an office-holder, a corporal a commander-in-chief, a day-worker a mayor, a locksmith the director of a factory?'

'Who will believe it?' But it had to be believed. They could do nothing else but believe it, when the corporals defeated the generals, when the mayor – the former day-worker – broke the resistance of the old bureaucracy, the wagon greaser put the transportation system into order, the locksmith as director put the industrial equipment into working condition. 'Who will believe it?' Let anyone only try not to believe it.

For an explanation of the extraordinary persistence which the masses of the people of the Soviet Union are showing throughout the years of the revolution, many foreign observers rely, in accord with ancient habit, on the 'passivity' of the Russian character. Gross anachronism! The revolutionary masses endure privations patiently but not passively. With their own hands they are creating a better future and are determined to create it at any cost. Let the enemy class only attempt to impose his will from outside on these patient masses! No, better, he should not try!

The Revolution and its Place in History

Let me now, in closing, attempt to ascertain the place of the October Revolution, not only in the history of Russia but in the history of the world. During the year of 1917, in a period of eight months, two historical curves intersect. The February upheaval

– that belated echo of the great struggles which had been carried out in the past centuries on the territories of Holland, England, France, nearly all over Continental Europe – takes its place in the series of bourgeois revolutions. The October Revolution proclaimed and opened the domination of the proletariat. World capitalism suffered its first great defeat on the Russian territory. The chain broke at its weakest link. But it was the chain that broke, and not only the link.

Capitalism has outlived itself as a world system. It has ceased to fulfil its essential function: the raising of the level of human power and human wealth. Humanity cannot remain stagnant at the level which it has reached. Only a powerful increase in productive force and a sound, planned, that is, socialist organisation of production and distribution can assure humanity – all humanity – of a decent standard of life and at the same time give it the precious feeling of freedom with respect to its own economy. Freedom in two senses – first of all man will no longer be compelled to devote the greater part of his life to physical toil. Second, he will no longer be dependent on the laws of the market, that is, on the blind and obscure forces which work behind his back. He will build his economy freely, according to plan, with compass in hand. This time it is a question of subjecting the anatomy of society to the X-ray through and through, of disclosing all its secrets and subjecting all its functions to the reason and the will of collective humanity. In this sense, socialism must become a new step in the historical advance of mankind. Before our ancestor, who first armed himself with a stone axe, the whole of nature represented a conspiracy of secret and hostile forces. Since then, the natural sciences hand in hand with practical technology, have illuminated nature down to its most secret depths. By means of electrical energy, the physicist passes judgement on the nucleus of the atom. The hour is not far when science will easily solve the task of alchemists, and turn manure into gold and gold into manure. Where the demons and furies of nature once raged, now reigns over more courageously the industrious will of man.

But while he wrestled victoriously with nature, man built up his relations to order men blindly almost like the bee or the ant. Slowly and very haltingly he approached the problems of human society.

The Reformation represented the first victory of bourgeois individualism in a domain which had been ruled by dead tradition. From the church, critical thought went on to the state. Born in the struggle with absolutism and the medieval estates, the doctrine of the sovereignty of the people and of the rights of man and the citizen grew stronger. Thus arose the system of parliamentarianism. Critical thought penetrated into the domain of government administration. The political rationalism of democracy was the highest achievement of the revolutionary bourgeoisie.

But between nature and the state stands economic life. Technical science liberated man from the tyranny of the old elements – earth, water, fire, and air – only to subject him to its own tyranny. Man ceased to be a slave to nature to become a slave to the machine, and, still worse, a slave to supply and demand. The present world crisis testifies in especially tragic fashion how man, who dives to the bottom of the ocean, who rise up to the stratosphere, who converses on invisible waves from the Antipodes, how this proud and daring ruler of nature remains a slave to the blind forces of his own economy. The historical task of our epoch consists in replacing the uncontrolled play of the market by reasonable planning, in disciplining the forces of production, compelling them to work together in harmony and obediently serve the needs of mankind. Only on this new social basis will man be able to stretch his weary limbs and – every man and every woman, not only a selected few – become a citizen with full power in the realm of thought.

The Future of Man

But this is not yet the end of the road. No, it is only the beginning. Man calls himself the crown of creation. He has a certain right to that claim. But who has asserted that present-day man is the last and highest representative of the species Homo Sapiens? No, physically as well as spiritually he is very far from perfection, prematurely born biologically, with feeble thought, and has not produced any new organic equilibrium.

It is true that humanity has more than once brought forth giants of thought and action, who tower over their contemporaries like summits in a chain of mountains. The human race has a right to be proud of its Aristotle, Shakespeare, Darwin, Beethoven, Goethe, Marx, Edison, and Lenin. But why are they so rare? Above all, because almost without exception they came out of the middle and upper classes. Apart from rare exceptions, the sparks of genius in the suppressed depths of the people are choked before they can burst into flame. But also because the processes of creating, developing and educating a human being have been and remain essentially a matter of chance, not illuminated by theory and practice, not subjected to consciousness and will.

Anthropology, biology, physiology, and psychology have accumulated mountains of material to raise up before mankind in their full scope the tasks of perfecting and developing body and spirit. Psychoanalysis, with the inspired hand of Sigmund Freud, has lifted the cover of the well which is poetically called the 'soul'. And what has been revealed? Our conscious thought is only a small part of the work of the dark psychic forces. Learned divers descend to the bottom of the ocean and there take photographs of mysterious fishes. Human thought, descending to the bottom of its own psychic sources must shed light on the most mysterious driving forces of the soul and subject them to reason and to will.

Once he has done with the anarchic forces of his own society man will set to work on himself, in the pestle and retort of the chemist. For the first time mankind will regard itself as raw material, or at best as a physical and psychic semi-finished product. Socialism will mean a leap from the realm of necessity into the realm of freedom in this sense also, that the man of today, with all his contradictions and lack of harmony, will open the road for a new and happier race.

Degeneration of the Soviet Regime*

We have defined the Soviet Thermidor as a triumph of the bureaucracy over the masses. We have tried to disclose the historic conditions of this triumph. The revolutionary vanguard of the proletariat was in part devoured by the administrative apparatus and gradually demoralized, in part annihilated in the civil war, and in part thrown out and crushed. The tired and disappointed

---

* Excerpts from *The Revolution Betrayed* (New York: Doubleday, and Doran and Co., 1937), 105–7, 112–14, 254–6.

masses were indifferent to what was happening on the summits. These conditions, however, are inadequate to explain why the bureaucracy succeeded in raising itself above society and getting its fate firmly into its own hands. Its own will to this would in any case be inadequate; the arising of a new ruling stratum must have deep social causes.

The victory of the Thermidorians over the Jacobins in the 18th century was also aided by the weariness of the masses and the demoralization of the leading cadres, but beneath these essentially incidental phenomena a deep organic process was taking place. The Jacobins rested upon the lower petty bourgeoisie lifted by the great wave. The revolution of the 18th century, however, corresponding to the course of development of the productive forces, could not but bring the great bourgeoisie to political ascendancy in the long run. The Thermidor was only one of the stages in this inevitable process. What similar social necessity found expression in the Soviet Thermidor? We have tried already in one of the preceding chapters to make a preliminary answer to the question why the gendarme triumphed. We must now prolong our analysis of the conditions of the transition from capitalism to socialism, and the role of the state in this process. Let us again compare theoretic prophecy with reality. 'It is still necessary to suppress the bourgeoisie and its resistance,' wrote Lenin in 1917, speaking of the period which should begin immediately after the conquest of power, 'but the organ of suppression here is now the majority of the population, and not the minority as had heretofore always been the case ... In that sense the state is beginning to *die away*.' In what does this dying away express itself? Primarily in the fact that 'in place of special institutions of a privileged minority (privileged officials, commanders of a standing army), the majority itself can directly carry out' the functions of suppression. Lenin follows this with a statement axiomatic and unanswerable: 'The more universal becomes the very fulfillment of the functions of the state power, the less need is there of this power.' The annulment of private property in the means of production removes the principal task of the historic state – defense of the proprietary privileges of the minority against the overwhelming majority.

The dying away of the state begins, then, according to Lenin, on the very day after the expropriation of the expropriators – that is, before the new regime has had time to take up its economic and cultural problems. Every success in the solution of these problems means a further step in the liquidation of the state, its dissolution in the socialist society. The degree of this dissolution is the best index of the depth and efficacy of the socialist structure. We may lay down approximately this sociological theorem: The strength of the compulsion exercised by the masses in a workers' state is directly proportional to the strength of the exploitive tendencies, or the danger of a restoration of capitalism, and inversely proportional to the strength of the social solidarity and the general loyalty to the new regime. Thus the bureaucracy – that is, the 'privileged officials and commanders of the standing army' – represents a special kind of compulsion which the masses cannot or do not wish to exercise, and which, one way or another, is directed against the masses themselves ...

The basis of bureaucratic rule is the poverty of society in objects of consumption, with the resulting struggle of each against all. When there is enough goods in a store, the purchasers can come whenever they want to. When there is little goods, the purchasers are compelled to stand in line. When the lines are very long, it is necessary to appoint a policeman to keep order. Such is the starting point of the power of the Soviet bureaucracy. It 'knows' who is to get something and who has to wait.

A raising of the material and cultural level ought, at first glance, to lessen the necessity of privileges, narrow the sphere of application of 'bourgeois law', and thereby undermine the standing ground of its defenders, the bureaucracy. In reality the opposite thing has happened: the growth of the productive forces has been so far accompanied by an extreme development of all forms of inequality, privilege and advantage, and therewith of bureaucratism. That too is not accidental.

In its first period, the Soviet regime was undoubtedly far more equalitarian and less bureaucratic than now. But that was an equality of general poverty. The resources of the country were so scant that there was no opportunity to separate out from the masses of the population any broad privileged strata. At the same time the 'equalizing' character of wages, destroying personal interestedness, became a brake upon the development of the productive forces. Soviet economy had to lift itself from its poverty to a somewhat higher level before fat deposits of privilege became possible. The present state of production is still far from guaranteeing all necessities to everybody. But it is already adequate to give significant privileges to a minority, and convert inequality into a whip for the spurring on of the majority. That is the first reason why the growth of production has so far strengthened not the socialist, but the bourgeois features of the state.

But that is not the sole reason. Alongside the economic factor dictating capitalist methods of payment at the present stage, there operates a parallel political factor in the person of the bureaucracy itself. In its very essence it is the planter and protector of inequality. It arose in the beginning as the bourgeois organ of a workers' state. In establishing and defending the advantages of a minority, it of course draws off the cream for its own use. Nobody who has wealth to distribute ever omits himself. Thus out of a social necessity there has developed an organ which has far outgrown its socially necessary function, and become an independent factor and therewith the source of great danger for the whole social organism.

The social meaning of the Soviet Thermidor now begins to take form before us. The poverty and cultural backwardness of the masses has again become incarnate in the malignant figure of the ruler with a great club in his hand. The deposed and abused bureaucracy, from being a servant of society, has again become its lord. On this road it has attained such a degree of social and moral alienation from the popular masses, that it cannot now permit any control over either its activities or its income.

The bureaucracy's seemingly mystic fear of 'petty speculators, grafters, and gossips' thus finds a wholly natural explanation. Not yet able to satisfy the elementary needs of the population, the Soviet economy creates and resurrects at every step tendencies to graft and speculation. On the other side, the privileges of the new aristocracy awaken in the masses of the population a tendency to listen to anti-Soviet 'gossips' – that is, to anyone who, albeit in a whisper, criticizes the greedy and capricious bosses. It is a question, therefore, not of spectres of the past, not of the remnants of what no longer exists, not, in short, of the snows of yesteryear, but of new, mighty, and continually reborn tendencies to personal accumulation. The first still very meager wave of prosperity in the country, just because of its meagerness, has not weakened, but strengthened, these centrifugal tendencies. On the other hand, there has developed simultaneously a desire of the unprivileged to slap the grasping hands of the new gentry. The social struggle again grows sharp. Such are the sources of the power of the bureaucracy. But from those same sources comes also a threat to its power ...

To define the Soviet regime as transitional, or intermediate, means to abandon such finished social categories as *capitalism* (and therewith 'state capitalism') and also *socialism*. But besides being completely inadequate in itself, such a definition is capable of producing the mistaken idea that from the present Soviet regime only a transition to socialism is possible. In reality a backslide to capitalism is wholly possible. A more complete definition will of necessity be complicated and ponderous.

The Soviet Union is a contradictory society halfway between capitalism and socialism, in which: (a) the productive forces are still far from adequate to give the state property a socialist character; (b) the tendency toward primitive accumulation created by want breaks out through innumerable pores of the planned economy; (c) norms of distribution preserving a bourgeois character lie at the basis of a new differentiation of society; (d) the economic growth, while slowly bettering the situation of the toilers, promotes a swift formation of privileged strata; (e) exploiting the social antagonisms, a bureaucracy has converted itself into an uncontrolled caste alien to socialism; (f) the social revolution, betrayed by the ruling party, still exists in property relations and in the consciousness of the toiling masses; (g) a further development of the accumulating contradictions can as well lead to socialism as back to capitalism; (h) on the road to capitalism the counter-revolution would have to break the resistance of the workers; (i) on the road to socialism the workers would have to overthrow the bureaucracy. In the last analysis, the question will be decided by a struggle of living social forces, both on the national and the world arena.

Doctrinaires will doubtless not be satisfied with this hypothetical definition. They would like categorical formulae: yes – yes, and no – no. Sociological problems would certainly be simpler, if social phenomena had always a finished character. There is nothing more dangerous, however, than to throw out of reality, for the sake of logical completeness, elements which today violate your scheme and tomorrow may wholly overturn it. In our analysis, we have above all avoided doing violence to dynamic social formations which have had no precedent and have no analogies. The scientific task, as well as the political, is not to give a finished definition to an unfinished process, but to follow all its stages, separate its progressive from its reactionary tendencies, expose their mutual relations, foresee possible variants of development, and find in this foresight a basis for action.

Stalinism and Bolshevism[*]

Reactionary epochs like ours not only disintegrate and weaken the working class and isolate its vanguard but also lower the general ideological level of the movement and throw political thinking back to stages long since passed through. In these conditions the task of the vanguard is, above all, not to let itself be carried along by the backward flow: it must swim against the current. If an unfavourable relation of forces prevents it from holding political positions it has won, it must at least retain its ideological positions, because in them is expressed the dearly paid experience of the past. Fools will consider this policy 'sectarian'. Actually it is the only means of preparing for a new tremendous surge forward with the coming historical tide.

The Reaction Against Marxism and Bolshevism

Great political defeats provoke a reconsideration of values, generally occurring in two directions. On the one hand the true vanguard, enriched by the experience of defeat, defends with tooth and nail the heritage of revolutionary thought and on this basis strives to educate new cadres for the mass struggle to come. On the other hand the routinists, centrists and dilettantes, frightened by defeat, do their best to destroy the authority of the revolutionary tradition and go backwards in their search for a 'New World'.

One could indicate a great many examples of ideological reaction, most often taking the form of prostration. All the literature of the Second and Third Internationals, as well as of their satellites of the London Bureau, consists essentially of such examples. Not a suggestion of Marxist analysis. Not a single

---

[*]   From Trotsky Internet Archive (www.marxists.org/archive/trotsky/1937/08/stalinism. htm), with revisions by the editors.

serious attempt to explain the causes of defeat. About the future, not one fresh word. Nothing but clichés, conformity, lies and above all solicitude for their own bureaucratic self-preservation. It is enough to smell ten words from some Hilferding or Otto Bauer to know this rottenness. The theoreticians of the Comintern are not even worth mentioning. The famous Dimitrov is as ignorant and commonplace as a shopkeeper over a mug of beer. The minds of these people are too lazy to renounce Marxism: they prostitute it. But it is not they that interest us now. Let us turn to the 'innovators'.

The former Austrian Communist, Willi Schlamm, has devoted a small book to the Moscow trials, under the expressive title, *The Dictatorship of the Lie*. Schlamm is a gifted journalist, chiefly interested in current affairs. His criticism of the Moscow frame-up, and his exposure of the psychological mechanism of the 'voluntary confessions', are excellent. However, he does not confine himself to this: he wants to create a new theory of socialism that would insure us against defeats and frame-ups in the future. But since Schlamm is by no means a theoretician and is apparently not well acquainted with the history of the development of socialism, he returns entirely to pre-Marxist socialism, and notably to its German, that is to its most backward, sentimental and mawkish variety. Schlamm denounces dialectics and the class struggle, not to mention the dictatorship of the proletariat. The problem of transforming society is reduced for him to the realisation of certain 'eternal' moral truths with which he would imbue mankind, even under capitalism. Willi Schlamm's attempts to save socialism by the insertion of the moral gland is greeted with joy and pride in Kerensky's review, *Novaya Rossia* (an old provincial Russian review now published in Paris); as the editors justifiably conclude, Schlamm has arrived at the principles of true Russian socialism, which a long time ago opposed the holy precepts of faith, hope and charity to the austerity and harshness of the class struggle. The 'novel' doctrine of the Russian 'Social Revolutionaries' represents, in its 'theoretical' premises, only a return to the pre-March (1848!) Germany.* However, it would

---

* The reference here is to utopianism and other varieties of socialism preceding the publication of the Communist Manifesto. – Editors

be unfair to demand a more intimate knowledge of the history of ideas from Kerensky than from Schlamm. Far more important is the fact that Kerensky, who is in solidarity with Schlamm, was, while head of the government, the instigator of persecutions against the Bolsheviks as agents of the German general staff: organised, that is, the same frame-ups against which Schlamm now mobilises his moth-eaten metaphysical absolutes.

The psychological mechanism of the ideological reaction of Schlamm and his like, is not at all complicated. For a while these people took part in a political movement that swore by the class struggle and appealed, in word if not in thought, to dialectical materialism. In both Austria and Germany the affair ended in a catastrophe. Schlamm draws the wholesale conclusion: this is the result of dialectics and the class struggle! And since the choice of revelations is limited by historical experience and … by personal knowledge, our reformer in his search for the word falls on a bundle of old rags which he valiantly opposes not only to Bolshevism but to Marxism as well.

At first glance Schlamm's brand of ideological reaction seems too primitive (from Marx … to Kerensky!) to pause over. But actually it is very instructive: precisely in its primitiveness it represents the common denominator of all other forms of reaction, particularly of those expressed by wholesale denunciation of Bolshevism.

'Back to Marxism'?

Marxism found its highest historical expression in Bolshevism. Under the banner of Bolshevism the first victory of the proletariat was achieved and the first workers' state established. No force can now erase these facts from history. But since the October Revolution has led to the present stage of the triumph of the bureaucracy, with its system of repression, plunder and falsification – the 'dictatorship of the lie', to use Schlamm's happy expression – many formalistic and superficial minds jump to a summary conclusion: one cannot struggle against Stalinism without renouncing Bolshevism. Schlamm, as we already know, goes further: Bolshevism, which degenerated into Stalinism, itself grew out of Marxism; consequently one cannot fight Stalinism while remaining on the foundation of Marxism. There are others, less consistent but more numerous, who say on the contrary: 'We must return Bolshevism to Marxism.' How? To *what* Marxism? Before Marxism became 'bankrupt' in the form of Bolshevism it has already broken down in the form of social democracy, Does the slogan 'Back to Marxism' then mean a leap over the periods of the Second and Third Internationals ... to the First International? But it too broke down in its time. Thus in the last analysis it is a question of returning to the collected works of Marx and Engels. One can accomplish this historic leap without leaving one's study and even without taking off one's slippers. But how are we going to go from our classics (Marx died in 1883, Engels in 1895) to the tasks of a new epoch, omitting several decades of theoretical and political struggles, among them Bolshevism and the October Revolution? None of those who propose to renounce Bolshevism as an historically bankrupt tendency has indicated any other course. So the question is reduced to the simple advice to study *Capital*. We can hardly object. But the Bolsheviks, too, studied *Capital* and not badly either. This did not however prevent the degeneration of the Soviet state and the staging of the Moscow trials. So what is to be done?

Is Bolshevism Responsible for Stalinism?

Is it true that Stalinism represents the legitimate product of Bolshevism, as all reactionaries maintain, as Stalin himself avows, as the Mensheviks, the anarchists, and certain left doctrinaires considering themselves Marxist believe? 'We have always predicted this' they say, 'Having started with the prohibition of other socialist parties, the repression of the anarchists, and the setting up of the Bolshevik dictatorship in the Soviets, the October Revolution could only end in the dictatorship of the bureaucracy. Stalin is the continuation and also the bankruptcy of Leninism.'

The flaw in this reasoning begins in the tacit identification of Bolshevism, October Revolution and Soviet Union. The historical process of the struggle of hostile forces is replaced by the evolution of Bolshevism in a vacuum. Bolshevism, however, is only a political tendency closely fused with the working class but not identical with it. And aside from the working class there exist in the Soviet Union a hundred million peasants, diverse nationalities, and a heritage of oppression, misery and ignorance. The state built up by the Bolsheviks reflects not only the thought and will of Bolshevism but also the cultural level of the country, the social composition of the population, the pressure of a barbaric past and no less barbaric world imperialism. To represent the process of degeneration of the Soviet state as the evolution of pure Bolshevism is to ignore social reality in the name of only one of its elements, isolated by pure logic. One has only to call this elementary mistake by its true name to do away with every trace of it.

Bolshevism, in any case, never identified itself either with the October Revolution or with the Soviet state that issued from it. Bolshevism considered itself as one of the factors of history, its 'conscious' factor – a very important but not decisive one. We never sinned on historical subjectivism. We saw the decisive factor – on the existing basis of productive forces – in the class struggle, not only on a national scale but on an international scale.

When the Bolsheviks made concessions to the peasant tendency, to private ownership, set up strict rules for membership of the party, purged the party of alien elements, prohibited other parties, introduced the NEP [New Economic Policy], granted enterprises as concessions, or concluded diplomatic agreements with imperialist governments, they were drawing partial conclusions from the basic fact that had been theoretically clear to them from the beginning: that the conquest of power, however important it may be in itself, by no means transforms the party into a sovereign ruler of the historical process. Having taken over the state, the party is able, certainly, to influence the development of society with a power inaccessible to it before; but in return it submits itself to a ten times greater influence from all other elements in society. It can, by the direct attack by hostile forces, be thrown out of power. Given a more drawn-out tempo of development, it can degenerate internally while holding on to power. It is precisely this dialectic of the historical process that is not understood by those sectarian logicians who try to find in the decay of the Stalinist bureaucracy a crushing argument against Bolshevism.

In essence these gentlemen say: the revolutionary party that contains in itself no guarantee against its own degeneration is bad. By such a criterion Bolshevism is naturally condemned: it has no talisman. But the criterion itself is wrong. Scientific thinking demands a concrete analysis: how and why did the party degenerate? No one but the Bolsheviks themselves have, up to the present time, given such an analysis. To do this they had no need to break with Bolshevism. On the contrary, they found in its arsenal all they needed for the explanation of its fate. They drew this conclusion: certainly Stalinism 'grew out' of Bolshevism, not logically, however, but dialectically; not as a revolutionary affirmation but as a Thermidorian negation. It is by no means the same.

Bolshevism's Basic Prognosis

The Bolsheviks, however, did not have to wait for the Moscow trials to explain the reasons for the disintegration of the governing party of the USSR. Long ago they foresaw and spoke of the theoretical possibility of this development. Let us remember the prognosis of the Bolsheviks, not only on the eve of the October Revolution but years before. The specific alignment of forces in the national and international field can enable the proletariat to seize power first in a backward country such as Russia. But the same alignment of forces proves beforehand that *without a more or less rapid victory of the proletariat in the advanced countries* the worker's government in Russia will not survive. Left to itself the Soviet regime must either fall or degenerate. More exactly; it will first degenerate and then fall. I myself have written about this more than once, beginning in 1905. In my *History of the Russian Revolution* (cf. *Appendix* to the last volume: 'Socialism in One Country') are collected all the statements on the question made by the Bolshevik leaders from 1917 until 1923. They all amount to the following: without a revolution in the West, Bolshevism will be liquidated either by internal counter-revolution or by external intervention, or by a combination of both. Lenin stressed again and again that the bureaucratisation of the Soviet regime was not a technical question, but the potential beginning of the degeneration of the workers' state.

At the Eleventh Party Congress in March 1922, Lenin spoke of the support offered to Soviet Russia at the time of the NEP by certain bourgeois politicians, particularly the liberal professor Ustrialov. 'I am for the support of the Soviet power in Russia', said Ustrialov, although he was a Cadet, a bourgeois, a supporter of intervention – 'because it has taken the road that will lead it back to an ordinary bourgeois state.' Lenin prefers the cynical voice of the enemy to 'sugary communistic nonsense'. Soberly and harshly he warns the party of danger: 'We must say frankly that the things Ustrialov speaks about are possible. History knows all sorts of metamorphoses. Relying on firmness of convictions, loyalty and other splendid moral qualities is anything but a serious attitude in politics. A few people may be endowed with splendid moral qualities, but historical issues are decided by vast masses, which, if the few don't suit them, may at times, treat them none too politely.' In a word, the party is not the only factor of development and on a larger historical scale is not the decisive one.

'One nation conquers another', continued Lenin at the same congress, the last in which he participated ... 'this is simple and intelligible to all. But what happens to the culture of these nations? Here things are not so simple. If the conquering nation is more cultured than the vanquished nation, the former imposes its culture on the latter, but if the opposite is the case, the vanquished nation imposes its culture on the conqueror. Has not something like this happened in the capital of the RSFSR? Have the 4,700 Communists (nearly a whole army division, and all of them the very best) come under the influence of an alien culture?'

This was said in 1922, and not for the first time. History is not made by a few people, even 'the best'; and not only that: these 'best' can degenerate in the spirit of an alien, that is, a bourgeois culture. Not only can the Soviet state abandon the way of socialism, but the Bolshevik Party can, under unfavourable historic conditions, lose its Bolshevism.

From the clear understanding of this danger issued the Left Opposition, definitely formed in 1923. Recording day by day the symptoms of degeneration, it tried to oppose to the growing Thermidor the conscious will of the proletarian vanguard. However, this subjective factor proved to be insufficient. The 'gigantic masses' which, according to Lenin, decide the outcome of the struggle, become tired of internal privations and of waiting too long for the world revolution. The mood of the masses declined. The bureaucracy won the upper hand. It cowed the revolutionary vanguard, trampled upon Marxism, prostituted the Bolshevik Party. Stalinism conquered. In the form of the Left Opposition,

Bolshevism broke with the Soviet bureaucracy and its Comintern. This was the real course of development. To be sure, in a formal sense Stalinism did issue from Bolshevism. Even today the Moscow bureaucracy continues to call itself the Bolshevik Party. It is simply using the old label of Bolshevism the better to fool the masses. So much the more pitiful are those theoreticians who take the shell for the kernel and appearance for reality. In the identification of Bolshevism and Stalinism they render the best possible service to the Thermidorians and precisely thereby play a clearly reactionary role.

In view of the elimination of all other parties from the political field the antagonistic interests and tendencies of the various strata of the population, to a greater or lesser degree, had to find their expression in the governing party. To the extent that the political centre of gravity has shifted from the proletarian vanguard to the bureaucracy, the party has changed its social structure as well as its ideology. Owing to the tempestuous course of development, it has suffered in the last 15 years a far more radical degeneration than did the social democracy in half a century. The present purge draws between Bolshevism and Stalinism not simply a bloody line but a whole river of blood. The annihilation of all the older generation of Bolsheviks, an important part of the middle generation which participated in the civil war, and that part of the youth that took up most seriously the Bolshevik traditions, shows not only a political but a thoroughly physical incompatibility between Bolshevism and Stalinism. How can this not be seen?

Stalinism and 'State Socialism'

The anarchists, for their part, try to see in Stalinism the organic product, not only of Bolshevism and Marxism but of 'state socialism' in general. They are willing to replace Bakunin's patriarchal 'federation of free communes' by the modern federation of free Soviets. But, as formerly, they are against centralised state power. Indeed, one branch of 'state' Marxism, social democracy, after coming to power became an open agent of capitalism. The other gave birth to a new privileged caste. It is obvious that the source of evil lies in the state. From a wide historical viewpoint, there is a grain of truth in this reasoning. The state as an apparatus of coercion is an undoubted source of political and moral infection. This also applies, as experience has shown, to the workers' state. Consequently it can be said that Stalinism is a product of a condition of society in which society was still unable to tear itself out of the straitjacket of the state. But this position, contributing nothing to the elevation of Bolshevism and Marxism, characterises only the general level of mankind, and above all – the relation of forces between the proletariat and the bourgeoisie. Having agreed with the anarchists that the state, even the workers' state, is the offspring of class barbarism and that real human history will begin with the abolition of the state, we have still before us in full force the question: what ways and methods will lead, *ultimately*, to the abolition of the state? Recent experience bears witness that they are anyway not the methods of anarchism.

The leaders of the Spanish Federation of Labour (CNT), the only important anarchist organisation in the world, became, in the critical hour, bourgeois ministers. They explained their open betrayal of the theory of anarchism by the pressure of 'exceptional circumstances'. But did not the leaders of German social democracy produce, in their time, the same excuse? Naturally, civil war is not peaceful and ordinary but an 'exceptional circumstance'. Every serious revolutionary organisation, however, prepares precisely for 'exceptional circumstances'. The experience of Spain has shown once again that the state can be 'denied' in booklets published in 'normal circumstances' by permission of the bourgeois state, but the conditions of revolution leave no room for the denial of the state: they demand, on the contrary, the conquest of the state. We have not the slightest intention of blaming the anarchists for not having liquidated the state with the mere stroke of a pen. A revolutionary party, even having seized power (of which the anarchist leaders were incapable in spite of the heroism of the anarchist workers), is still by no means the sovereign ruler of society. But all the more severely do we blame the anarchist theory, which seemed to be wholly suitable for times of peace, but which had to be dropped rapidly as soon as the 'exceptional circumstances' of the … revolution had begun. In the old days there were certain generals – and probably are now – who considered that the most harmful thing for an army was war. Little better are those revolutionaries who complain that revolution destroys their doctrine.

Marxists are wholly in agreement with the anarchists in regard to the final goal: the liquidation of the state. Marxists are 'state-ist' only to the extent that one cannot achieve the liquidation of the state simply by ignoring it. The experience of Stalinism does not refute the teaching of Marxism but confirms it by inversion. The revolutionary doctrine which teaches the proletariat to orient itself correctly in situations and to profit actively by them, contains of course no automatic guarantee of victory. But victory is possible only through the application of this doctrine. Moreover, the victory must not be thought of as a single event. It must be considered in the perspective of an historical epoch. The workers' state – on a lower economic basis and surrounded by imperialism – was transformed into the gendarmerie of Stalinism. But genuine Bolshevism launched a life and death struggle against the gendarmerie. To maintain itself Stalinism is now forced to conduct a direct *civil war* against Bolshevism under the name of 'Trotskyism', not only in the USSR but also in Spain. The old Bolshevik Party is dead but Bolshevism is raising its head everywhere.

To deduce Stalinism from Bolshevism or from Marxism is the same as to deduce, in a larger sense, counter-revolution from revolution. Liberal, conservative and later reformist thinking has always been characterised by this cliché. Due to the class structure of society, revolutions have always produced counter-revolutions. Does not this indicate, asks the logician, that there is some inner flaw in the revolutionary method? However, neither the liberals nor reformists have succeeded, as yet, in inventing a more 'economical' method. But if it is not easy to rationalise the living historic process, it is not at all difficult to give a rational interpretation of the alternation of its waves, and thus by pure logic to deduce Stalinism from 'state socialism', fascism from Marxism, reaction from revolution, in a word, the antithesis from the thesis. In this domain as in many others anarchist thought is the prisoner of liberal rationalism. Real revolutionary thinking is not possible without dialectics.

The Political 'Sins' of Bolshevism as the Source of Stalinism

The arguments of the rationalists assume at times, at least in their outer form, a more concrete character. They do not deduce

Stalinism from Bolshevism as a whole but from its political sins.* The Bolsheviks – according to Gorter, Pannekoek, certain German 'Spartacists' and others – replaced the dictatorship of the proletariat with the dictatorship of the party; Stalin replaced the dictatorship of the party with the dictatorship of the bureaucracy, the Bolsheviks destroyed all parties except their own; Stalin strangled the Bolshevik Party in the interests of a Bonapartist clique. The Bolsheviks compromised with the bourgeoisie; Stalin became its ally and support. The Bolsheviks recognised the necessity of participation in the old trade unions and in the bourgeois parliament; Stalin made friends with the trade union bureaucracy and bourgeois democracy. One can make such comparisons at will. For all their apparent effectiveness they are entirely empty.

The proletariat can take power only through its vanguard. In itself the necessity for state power arises from the insufficient cultural level of the masses and their heterogeneity. In the revolutionary vanguard, organised in a party, is crystallised the aspiration of the masses to obtain their freedom. Without the confidence of the class in the vanguard, without support of the vanguard by the class, there can be no talk of the conquest of power. In this sense the proletarian revolution and dictatorship are the work of the whole class, but only under the leadership of the vanguard. The Soviets are only the organised form of the tie between the vanguard and the class. A revolutionary content can be given this form only by the party. This is proved by the positive experience of the October Revolution and by the negative experience of other countries (Germany, Austria, finally, Spain). No one has either shown in practice or tried to explain articulately on paper how the proletariat can seize power without the political leadership of a party that knows what it wants. The fact that this party subordinates the Soviets politically to its

---

* One of the outstanding representatives of this type of thinking is the French author of the book on Stalin, B. Souvarine. The factual and documentary side of Souvarine's work is the product of long and conscientious research. However, the historical philosophy of the author is striking in its vulgarity. To explain all subsequent historical mishaps he seeks inner flaws of Bolshevism. The influence of the real conditions of the historical process on Bolshevism are nonexistent for him. Even Taine with his theory of 'milieu' is closer to Marx than Souvarine is. *[Footnote by Trotsky. The book in question is Boris Souvarine*, Stalin: A Critical Study of Bolshevism *(New York: Longman Greens and Co., 1939). – Editors]*

leaders has, in itself, abolished the Soviet system no more than the domination of the conservative majority has abolished the British parliamentary system.

As far as the *prohibition* of other Soviet parties is concerned, it did not flow from any 'theory' of Bolshevism but was a measure of defence of the dictatorship on a backward and devastated country, surrounded by enemies on all sides. For the Bolsheviks it was clear from the beginning that this measure, later completed by the prohibition of factions inside the governing party itself, signalised a tremendous danger. However, the root of the danger lay not in the doctrine or the tactics but in the material weakness of the dictatorship, in the difficulties of its internal and international situation. If the revolution had triumphed, even if only in Germany, the need of prohibiting the other Soviet parties would have immediately fallen away. It is absolutely indisputable that the domination of a single party served as the juridical point of departure for the Stalinist totalitarian regime. The reason for this development lies neither in Bolshevism nor in the prohibition of other parties as a temporary war measure, but in the number of defeats of the proletariat in Europe and Asia.

The same applies to the struggle with anarchism. In the heroic epoch of the revolution the Bolsheviks went hand in hand with genuinely revolutionary anarchists. Many of them were drawn into the ranks of the party. The author of these lines discussed with Lenin more than once the possibility of allotting the anarchists certain territories where, with the consent of the local population, they would carry out their stateless experiment. But civil war, blockade, and hunger left no room for such plans. The Kronstadt insurrection? But the revolutionary government could naturally not 'present' to the insurrectionary sailors the fortress which protected the capital only because the reactionary peasant-soldier rebellion was joined by a few doubtful anarchists. The concrete historical analysis of the events leaves not the slightest room for legends, built up on ignorance and sentimentality, concerning Kronstadt, Makhno and other episodes of the revolution.

There remains only the fact that the Bolsheviks from the beginning applied not only conviction but also compulsion, often to a most severe degree. It is also indisputable that later the bureaucracy which grew out of the revolution monopolised the system of compulsions in its own hands. Every stage of development, even such catastrophic stages as revolution and counter-revolution, flows from the preceding stage, is rooted in it and carries over some of its features. Liberals, including the Webbs, have always maintained that the Bolshevik dictatorship represented only a new edition of Tsarism. They close their eyes to such 'details' as the abolition of the monarchy and the nobility, the handing over of the land to the peasants, the expropriation of capital, the introduction of the planned economy, atheist education, and so on. In exactly the same way liberal anarchist thought closes its eyes to the fact that the Bolshevik Revolution, with all its repressions, meant an upheaval of social relations in the interests of the masses, whereas Stalin's Thermidorian upheaval accompanies the reconstruction of Soviet society in the interest of a privileged minority. It is clear that in the identification of Stalinism with Bolshevism there is not a trace of socialist criteria.

Questions of Theory

One of the most outstanding features of Bolshevism has been its severe, exacting, even quarrelsome attitude towards the question of doctrine. The 26 volumes of Lenin's works will remain forever a model of the highest theoretical conscientiousness. Without this fundamental quality Bolshevism would never have fulfilled its historic role. In this regard Stalinism, coarse, ignorant and thoroughly empirical, is its complete opposite.

The Opposition declared more than ten years ago in its programme: 'Since Lenin's death a whole set of new theories has been created, whose only purpose is to justify the Stalin group's sliding off the path of the international proletarian revolution.' Only a few days ago an American writer, Liston M. Oak, who has participated in the Spanish Revolution, wrote: 'The Stalinists are in fact today the foremost revisionists of Marx and Lenin – Bernstein did not dare go half as far as Stalin in revising Marx.' This is absolutely true. One must add only that Bernstein actually felt certain theoretical needs: he tried conscientiously to establish a correspondence between the reformist practices of social democracy and its programme. The Stalinist bureaucracy, however, not only had nothing in common with Marxism but is in general foreign to any doctrine or system whatsoever. Its 'ideology' is thoroughly permeated with police subjectivism, its practice is the empiricism of crude violence. In keeping with its essential interests the caste of usurpers is hostile to any theory: it can give an account of its social role neither to itself nor to anyone else. Stalin revises Marx and Lenin not with the theoretician's pen but with the heel of the GPU (the USSR's secret police).

Questions of Morals

Complaints of the 'immorality' of Bolshevism come particularly from those boastful nonentities whose cheap masks were torn away by Bolshevism. In petty bourgeois, intellectual, democratic, 'socialist', literary, parliamentary and other circles, conventional values prevail, or a conventional language to cover their lack of values. This large and motley society for mutual protection – 'live and let live' – cannot bear the touch of the Marxist lancet on its sensitive skin. The theoreticians, writers and moralists, hesitating between different camps, thought and continue to think that the Bolsheviks maliciously exaggerate differences, are incapable of 'loyal' collaboration and by their 'intrigues' disrupt the unity of the workers' movement. Moreover, the sensitive and touchy centrist has always thought that the Bolsheviks were 'slandering' him – simply because they carried through to the end for him his half-developed thoughts: he himself was never able to. But the fact remains that only that precious quality, an uncompromising attitude towards all quibbling and evasion, can educate a revolutionary party which will not be taken unawares by 'exceptional circumstances'.

The moral qualities of every party flow, in the last analysis, from the historical interests that it represents. The moral qualities of Bolshevism, self-renunciation, disinterestedness, audacity, and contempt for every kind of tinsel and falsehood – the highest qualities of human nature! – flow from revolutionary intransigence in the service of the oppressed. The Stalinist bureaucracy imitates also in this domain the words and gestures of Bolshevism. But when 'intransigence' and 'flexibility' are applied by a police apparatus in the service of a privileged minority they become a force of demoralisation and gangsterism. One can feel only contempt for these gentlemen who identify the revolutionary heroism of the Bolsheviks with the bureaucratic cynicism of the Thermidorians.

Even now, in spite of the dramatic events in the recent period, the average philistine prefers to believe that the struggle between Bolshevism ('Trotskyism') and Stalinism concerns a clash of personal ambitions, or, at best, a conflict between two 'shades' of Bolshevism. The crudest expression of this opinion is given by Norman Thomas, leader of the American Socialist Party: 'There is little reason to believe', he writes (*Socialist Review*, September 1937, p. 6), 'that if Trotsky had won (!) instead of Stalin, there would be an end of intrigue, plots, and a reign of fear in Russia.' And this man considers himself ... a Marxist. One would have the same right to say: 'There is little reason to believe that if instead of Pius XI, the Holy See were occupied by Norman I, the Catholic Church would have been transformed into a bulwark of socialism.' Thomas fails to understand that it is not a question of antagonism between Stalin and Trotsky, but of an antagonism between the bureaucracy and the proletariat. To be sure, the governing stratum of the USSR is forced even now to adapt itself to the still not wholly liquidated heritage of revolution, while preparing at the same time through direct civil war (bloody 'purge' – mass annihilation of the discontented) a change of the social regime. But in Spain the Stalinist clique is already acting openly as a bulwark of the bourgeois order against socialism. The struggle against the Bonapartist bureaucracy is turning before our eyes into class struggle: two worlds, two programmes, two moralities. If Thomas thinks that the victory of the socialist proletariat over the infamous caste of oppressors would not politically and morally regenerate the Soviet regime, he proves only that for all his reservations, shufflings and pious sighs he is far nearer to the Stalinist bureaucracy than to the workers. Like other exposers of Bolshevik 'immorality', Thomas has simply not grown to the level of revolutionary morality.

The Traditions of Bolshevism and the Fourth International

The 'lefts' who tried to skip Bolshevism in their return to Marxism generally confined themselves to isolated panaceas: boycott of parliament, creation of 'genuine' Soviets. All this could still seem extremely profound in the heat of the first days after the war. But now, in the light of most recent experience, such 'infantile diseases' have no longer even the interest of a curiosity. The Dutchmen Gorter and Pannekoek, the German 'Spartacists', the Italian Bordigists, showed their independence from Bolshevism only by artificially inflating one of its features and opposing it to the rest. But nothing has remained either in practice or in theory of these 'left' tendencies: an indirect but important proof that Bolshevism is the *only* possible form of Marxism for this epoch.

The Bolshevik Party has shown in action a combination of the highest revolutionary audacity and political realism. It established for the first time the correspondence between the vanguard and the class which alone is capable of securing victory. It has proved by experience that the alliance between the proletariat and the oppressed masses of the rural and urban petty bourgeoisie is possible only through the political overthrow of the traditional petty bourgeois parties. The Bolshevik Party has shown the entire world how to carry out armed insurrection and the seizure of power. Those who propose the abstraction of the Soviets from the party dictatorship should understand that only thanks to the party dictatorship were the Soviets able to lift themselves out of the mud of reformism and attain the state form of the proletariat. The Bolshevik Party achieved in the civil war the correct combination of military art and Marxist politics. Even if the Stalinist bureaucracy should succeed in destroying the economic foundations of the new society, the experience of planned economy under the leadership of the Bolshevik Party will have entered history for all time as one of the greatest teachings of mankind. This can be ignored only by sectarians who, offended by the bruises they have received, turn their backs on the process of history.

But this is not all. The Bolshevik Party was able to carry on its magnificent 'practical' work only because it illuminated all its steps with theory. Bolshevism did not create this theory: it was furnished by Marxism. But Marxism is a theory of movement, not of stagnation. Only events on such a tremendous historical scale could enrich the theory itself. Bolshevism brought an invaluable contribution to Marxism in its analysis of the imperialist epoch as an epoch of wars and revolutions; of bourgeois democracy in the era of decaying capitalism; of the correlation between the general strike and the insurrection; of the role of the party, Soviets, and trade unions in the period of proletarian revolution;

in its theory of the Soviet state, of the economy of transition, of fascism and Bonapartism in the epoch of capitalist decline; finally in its analysis of the degeneration of the Bolshevik Party itself and of the Soviet state. Let any other tendency be named that has added anything essential to the conclusions and generalisations of Bolshevism. Theoretically and politically Vandervelde, De Brouckere, Hilferding, Otto Bauer, Leon Blum, Zyromski, not to mention Major Attlee and Norman Thomas, live on the tattered leftovers of the past.* The degeneration of the Comintern is most crudely expressed by the fact that it has dropped to the theoretical level of the Second International. All the varieties of intermediary groups (Independent Labour Party of Great Britain, POUM and their like) adapt every week new haphazard fragments of Marx and Lenin to their current needs. Workers can learn nothing from these people.

Only the founders of the Fourth International, who have made their own the whole tradition of Marx and Lenin, take a serious attitude towards theory. Philistines may jeer that 20 years after the October victory the revolutionaries are again thrown back to modest propagandist preparation. The big capitalists are, in this question as in many others, far more penetrating than the petty bourgeois who imagine themselves 'socialists' or 'communists'. It is no accident that the subject of the Fourth International does not leave the columns of the world press. The burning historical need for revolutionary leadership promises to the Fourth International an exceptionally rapid tempo of growth. The greatest guarantee of its further success lies in the fact that it has not arisen away from the great historical road, but has organically grown out of Bolshevism.

28 August 1937

Letter to the Workers of the USSR†
(May 1940)

Greetings to the Soviet workers, collective farmers, soldiers of the Red Army and sailors of the Red Navy! Greetings from distant

---

* Trotsky is referring here to various leading personalities in the 1930s of the Socialist International (i.e., the social democratic Second International). – Editors
† From Trotsky Internet Archive (www.marxists.org/archive/trotsky/1940/05/workers. htm).

Mexico where I found refuge after the Stalinist clique had exiled me to Turkey and after the bourgeoisie had hounded me from country to country!

Dear Comrades! The lying Stalinist press has been maliciously deceiving you for a long time on all questions, including those which relate to myself and my political co-thinkers. You possess no workers' press; you read only the press of the bureaucracy, which lies systematically so as to keep you in darkness and thus render secure the rule of a privileged parasitic caste.

Those who dare raise their voices against the universally hated bureaucracy are called 'Trotskyists,' agents of a foreign power; branded as spies – yesterday it was spies of Germany, today it is spies of England and France – and then sent to face the firing squad. Tens of thousands of revolutionary fighters have fallen before the muzzles of GPU Mausers in the USSR and in countries abroad, especially in Spain. All of them were depicted as agents of fascism. Do not believe this abominable slander! Their crime consisted of defending workers and peasants against the brutality and rapacity of the bureaucracy. The entire Old Guard of Bolshevism, all the collaborators and assistants of Lenin, all the fighters of the October Revolution, all the heroes of the Civil War, have been murdered by Stalin. In the annals of history Stalin's name will forever be recorded with the infamous brand of Cain!

Revolution was not Made for Bureaucrats

The October Revolution was accomplished for the sake of the toilers and not for the sake of new parasites. But due to the lag of the world revolution, due to the fatigue and, to a large measure, the backwardness of the Russian workers and especially the Russian peasants, there raised itself over the Soviet Republic and against its peoples a new oppressive and parasitic caste, whose leader is Stalin. The former Bolshevik Party was turned into an apparatus of the caste. The world organisation which the Communist International once was is today a pliant tool of the Moscow oligarchy. Soviets of Workers and Peasants have long perished. They have been replaced by degenerate Commissars, Secretaries and GPU agents.

But, fortunately, among the surviving conquests of the October Revolution are the nationalized industry and the collectivised Soviet economy. Upon this foundation Workers' Soviets can build a new and happier society. This foundation cannot be surrendered by us to the world bourgeoisie under any conditions. It is the duty of revolutionists to defend tooth and nail every position gained by the working class, whether it involves democratic rights, wage scales, or so colossal a conquest of mankind as the nationalisation of the means of production and planned economy. Those who are incapable of defending conquests already gained can never fight for new ones. Against the imperialist foe we will defend the USSR with all our might. However, the conquests of the October Revolution will serve the people only if they prove themselves capable of dealing with the Stalinist bureaucracy, as in their day they dealt with the Tsarist bureaucracy and the bourgeoisie.

Stalinism Endangers the Soviet Union

If Soviet economic life had been conducted in the interests of the people; if the bureaucracy had not devoured and vainly wasted the major portion of the national income; if the bureaucracy had not trampled underfoot the vital interests of the population, then the USSR would have been a great magnetic pole of attraction for the toilers of the world and the inviolability of the Soviet Union would have been assured. But the infamous oppressive regime of Stalin has deprived the USSR of its attractive power. During the war with Finland, not only the majority of the Finnish peasants but also the majority of the Finnish workers, proved to be on the side of their bourgeoisie. This is hardly surprising since they know of the unprecedented oppression to which the Stalinist bureaucracy subjects the workers of nearby Leningrad and the whole of the USSR. The Stalinist bureaucracy, so bloodthirsty and ruthless at home and so cowardly before the imperialist enemies, has thus become the main source of war danger to the Soviet Union.

The old Bolshevik Party and the Third International have disintegrated and decomposed. The honest and advanced revolutionists have organised abroad the Fourth International which has sections already established in most of the countries of the world. I am a member of this new International. In participating in this work I remain under the very same banner that I served together with you or your fathers and your older brothers in 1917 and throughout the years of the Civil War, the very same banner under which together with Lenin we built the Soviet state and the Red Army.

Goal of the Fourth International

The goal of the Fourth International is to extend the October Revolution to the whole world and at the same time to regenerate the USSR by purging it of the parasitic bureaucracy. This can be achieved only in one way: By the workers, peasants, Red Army soldiers and Red Navy sailors, rising against the new caste of oppressors and parasites. To prepare this uprising, a new party is needed – a bold and honest revolutionary organisation of the advanced workers. The Fourth International sets as its task the building of such a party in the USSR.

Advanced workers! Be the first to rally to the banner of Marx and Lenin which is now the banner of the Fourth International! Learn how to create, in the conditions of Stalinist illegality, tightly fused, reliable revolutionary circles! Establish contacts between these circles! Learn how to establish contacts through loyal and reliable people, especially the sailors, with your revolutionary co-thinkers in bourgeois lands! It is difficult, but it can be done.

The present war will spread more and more, piling ruins on ruins, breeding more and more sorrow, despair and protest, driving the whole world toward new revolutionary explosions. The world revolution shall reinvigorate the Soviet working masses with new courage and resoluteness and shall undermine the bureaucratic props of Stalin's caste. It is necessary to prepare for this hour by stubborn systematic revolutionary work. The fate of our country, the future of our people, the destiny of our children and grandchildren are at stake.

Down With Cain Stalin and his Camarilla!
Down With the Rapacious Bureaucracy!

Long Live the Soviet Union, the Fortress of the Toilers!
Long Live the World Socialist Revolution!

Fraternally,
LEON TROTSKY
May 1940

WARNING! Stalin's press will of course declare that this letter is transmitted to the USSR by 'agents of imperialism'. Be forewarned that this, too, is a lie. This letter will reach the USSR through reliable revolutionists who are prepared to risk their lives for the cause of socialism. Make copies of this letter and give it the widest possible circulation. *L.T.*

3

WORKERS' UNITED FRONT: AGAINST FASCISM AND REFORMISM

Trotsky – along with Lenin and others in the early Communist International in the early 1920s – developed the tactical orientation of the *united front*, although there were certainly practical examples of this in previous years – registered, for instance, in Lenin's writings on Russia's 1905 revolutionary upsurge, and described in detail in Trotsky's account *1905*. The key conceptions of the united front were (a) the revolutionary organisation prioritising the defence and advance of working-class interests by building a broad front of unified struggle among a number of organisations associated with the workers and their allies, (b) while maintaining the independence, integrity, and ability to articulate its revolutionary perspectives, (c) at the same time developing and demonstrating in action the capacities of the revolutionary organisation to contribute to the workers' struggle, and (d) through its fighting example, its clear revolutionary programme, and the realities bearing out the validity of that programme, winning greater mass support and predominance in the struggle. In this, they were applying the classic Marxist notion that struggles for reforms (improvements in the here-and-now) should be combined with an active commitment to overthrowing the capitalist here-and-now, replacing it with working-class rule and socialism.[1]

In the period 1917–19, Lenin, Trotsky, and the other revolutionaries who formed the Communist International broke from the mass socialist organisations (Social Democratic and labour parties) which had shown themselves to be non-revolutionary – preferring the accumulation of reforms within capitalist society to the working-class overthrow of that society (the term for this being 'reformism').[2] They were hopeful that the newly-organised revolutionary Communist forces would be able to win working-class majorities and lead the workers and oppressed to victory in a number of countries. Yet the global wave of insurgencies, following the First World War, failed to triumph, and capitalist and reactionary forces throughout the world – more resilient than anticipated – mounted a counter-offensive not simply against Communists, but against the working-class movement, and the living standards of workers in general. In the face of this situation, Lenin, Trotsky, and other leading figures in the Communist International, fought to win their comrades (some inclined toward isolated revolutionary 'purity' and veering toward impatient revolutionary adventures) to the united front tactic, which included building alliances with mass reformist organisations, including the mass Social Democratic parties from which many of them had broken.[3]

After Lenin's death, and the defeat of Trotsky and the Left Opposition, the Communist International under Stalin at first veered toward a more thoroughgoing collaboration with working-class reformists (for example, the leaders of the British trade union movement) and, in less capitalistically developed countries such as China, with powerful pro-capitalist forces such as the Guomindang (Kuomintang) led by General Chiang Kai-shek. This turned out badly: the British trade union allies sold out the 1926 general strike and became vociferously anti-communist; Chiang Kai-shek's soldiers turned against the Chinese Communists, slaughtering them and destroying their organisations. With the Great Depression of 1929, it seemed that the end of capitalism might be on the agenda. True, there was the growth of mass movements of the extreme right, the Italian fascists and their German cousins under Nazi leader Adolf Hitler, but it seemed to Stalin and his co-thinkers that such elements, tied in to defending some variant of the capitalist status quo, could not endure in the face of the global capitalist crisis. The workers and oppressed masses – seeking solutions – would move to the left. The biggest obstacle, according to Stalin and his co-thinkers, consisted of the reformists, the Social Democrats, and any other socialist forces not part of the Communist mainstream. They argued that the reformists and Social Democrats, also defenders of some variant of the capitalist status quo, were 'twins' of the fascists, and the main fire of Communists should be directed against these 'social fascists'. If the growing Nazi movement took power in Germany, it would soon prove itself unable to cope with the situation. Leaders of Germany's sizeable Communist Party boasted: 'After Hitler – our turn!'[4]

In the face of the growing threat of the Nazis coming to power, Trotsky urgently appealed for a working-class united front between the massive German Communist Party and the even more massive German Social-Democratic Party. Together the two substantially outnumbered the Nazis and would have been capable of destroying this threat – if the rejection of united action by both Communist and Social-Democratic leaders could be overcome. Trotsky foresaw that both organizations and much else would be destroyed if Hitler came to power. On the other hand, the success of a united front struggle against Hitler would then create a situation in which the German working-class could come to power and move toward socialism, ending the isolation of the Soviet Union and setting an example for workers elsewhere to do likewise. 'The United Front for Defense', an open letter to German Social Democratic workers (obviously meant to be read by Communist workers as well) was one of many polemics and appeals analyzing the Nazi threat and calling for a united struggle of Communist and Social Democrats. The letter contains a frank critique of the policies of the German Social Democratic Party, but also an elaboration on the necessity and meaning of the united front.

German Social Democrats and Communists failed to mobilise to prevent the disaster, and Hitler took power with the connivance of the conservatives and capitalists. The formal name of the Nazis was the National Socialist German Workers Party – a deceptively left-sounding label for an organisation blending super-patriotism, cheap populism, glorification of militarism, a pervasive anti-Semitism and racialism, and an aggressive anti-Marxism into a heady and ultimately murderous mix. In 'What is National Socialism?' Trotsky offers a sophisticated revolutionary Marxist analysis of this development. Within a year, Hitler was able to consolidate his power at the expense of the German workers' movement, Communists and Social Democrats alike.[5]

By the time of the Seventh World Congress of the Communist International, the Stalin leadership had rallied to a new orientation articulated by George Dimitrov – the call for a People's Front, or popular front. According to Dimitrov, 'the toiling masses in a number of capitalist countries are faced with the necessity of making a definite choice, and of making it here today, not between proletarian dictatorship and bourgeois democracy, but between bourgeois democracy and fascism'. The new perspective called for wide-ranging and frankly class collaborationist alliances. It sought to defeat fascism by building electoral coalitions between Communists, Social Democrats, and pro-capitalist liberals, designed to establish governments that would favour reforms beneficial to the working class while developing a foreign policy that would involve an anti-fascist 'collective security' alliance of the 'capitalist democracies' with the Soviet Union against Germany, Italy and Japan. As E. H. Carr has demonstrated, the embrace of this policy – breaking formally and definitively with its revolutionary commitments – raised questions regarding the very purpose of the Communist International and actually represented the 'twilight of the Comintern' (which was, in fact, dissolved in 1943).[6]

Trotsky saw this dramatic reversion to reformism – promoting the struggle for reforms within capitalism to replace the struggle for a socialist alternative – as lethal. The flaws and crisis of 'democratic capitalism', as well as the inadequacy of reformism, generated a massive discontent that gave the Nazis their opportunity, he argued. A strategy based on providing more of the same would be handing a gift to fascism while thwarting possibilities of revolutionary action. The reformist strategy of the popular front stood in stark contrast to the working-class united front that Trotsky had been advocating. In a sense, it represented a rebirth of the old Menshevik worker-capitalist alliance of pre-1917 years – a fact that one of the leading Mensheviks, Theodore Dan, was later to acknowledge. It certainly had little to do with the conceptions elaborated in the Communist International in the era of Lenin and Trotsky.[7]

Radical labour insurgencies were generated throughout the world in reaction to the Great Depression and also in reaction to the threat of spreading fascism. In France and Spain, revolutionary possibilities seemed prevalent – and it was here that the application of the popular front strategy had special impact, forging successful electoral alliances between Communist, Socialist, and liberal capitalist parties. As Trotsky predicted, however, the resulting popular front governments proved neither to be durable nor capable of pushing back the global fascist upsurge. In the relatively new Spanish Republic, the liberal-Socialist-Communist government was targeted for overthrow by the military under General Francisco Franco, with powerful support from most of the big capitalists and landowners and a broad array of fascist, right-wing nationalist, and conservative elements. The attempted right-wing coup was blocked by a massive response from the working class – not only of the Socialist and Communist Parties, but also from the sizeable anarchist movement and the revolutionary POUM (Partido Obrero Unificación Marxista – Workers Party of Marxist Unification). The Spanish Civil War of 1936–39 provided a severe test for the popular front, to which even the anarchists and POUM offered critical support, although arguing that the war could be won only by advancing the revolutionary struggle. Nazi Germany and fascist Italy rushed to give massive aid to the right-wing insurgents, and the Soviet Union and Mexico gave more modest support to the Spanish Republic, which vainly appealed for aid from the 'capitalist democracies'.[8]

In many writings, including 'The Lessons of Spain: The Last Warning', reproduced here, Trotsky was uncompromisingly critical of the popular front and its supporters. He argued that the only hope was in a revolutionary push to replace the reform-capitalist regime with a workers' and peasants' regime, mobilizing for socialism. The anarchists and the POUM were not prepared to do this, and yet their continued revolutionary stance finally resulted in their violent repression. This was carried out by Communist-influenced forces of the republic, which were committed to demonstrating to the 'capitalist democracies' that the Spanish Republic should be supported not only as a bulwark against fascism but also as a bulwark against revolution. While a few (for example, Winston Churchill) were positively impressed, most pro-capitalist politicians even in the 'capitalist democracies' preferred to see the Spanish Republic – so dependent on support from the left-wing workers' movement – replaced by the even more reliable anti-revolutionaries led by Franco. And so it came to pass.

Notes

1. For example, see V. I. Lenin, 'A Militant Agreement for the Uprising', in *Revolution, Democracy, Socialism: Selected Writings*, ed. Paul Le Blanc (London: Pluto Press, 2008), 173–81; Leon Trotsky, *1905* (New York: Vintage Books, 1972).

2. Similar concerns had caused both Lenin and Trotsky – independently of each other – to break from the Menshevik faction of the Russian Social Democratic Labor Party (RSDLP) before the First World War. The Mensheviks believed that Russia's monarchy could only be overthrown by a worker-capitalist alliance, while Lenin's Bolshevik faction – refusing to subordinate the workers' struggle to the requirements of such collaboration with the class enemy of the workers – insisted on a worker-peasant alliance, that only such an alliance would be prepared to go all the way in overturning Russian tsarism. Trotsky was in basic agreement with this and joined the Bolsheviks when push came to shove in 1917. His own view was that such a struggle would bring the workers to political power, and that (with revolutions spreading to other lands) there should be a transition to socialism – his theory of permanent revolution. This orientation became that of the Bolsheviks and the early Communist movement.

3. See, for example, Leon Trotsky, 'On the United Front', in *The First Five Years of the Communist International*, vol. 2 (New York: Monad/Pathfinder, 1972), 91–109, Alfred Rosmer, *Moscow Under Lenin* (New York: Monthly Review Press, 1972), 146–52, John Riddell, ed., *Toward the United Front: Proceedings of the Fourth Congress of the Communist International, 1922* (Leiden/Boston: Brill, 2011).

4. See Duncan Hallas, *The Comintern* (Chicago: Haymarket Books, 2008).

5. Historical accounts can be found in Evelyn Anderson, *Hammer or Anvil: The Story of the German Working-Class Movement* (London: Victor Gollancz, 1945), 127–51, F. L. Carsten, *The Rise of Fascism* (Berkeley, CA: University of California Press, 1969), 82–159, and Donny Gluckstein, *The Nazis, Capitalism and the Working Class* (London: Bookmarks, 1999). David Beetham, ed., *Marxists in the Face of Fascism: Writings by Marxists on Fascism in the Inter-war Period* (Manchester: Manchester University Press, 1983) provides a richly diverse sampling of analyses. An invaluable resource can be found in Leon Trotsky, *The Struggle Against Fascism in Germany*, ed. Merry Maisel and George Breitman (New York: Pathfinder Press, 1971).

6. Georgi Dimitroff, *The United Front: The Struggle Against Fascism and War* (New York: International Publishers, 1938), 110; E. H. Carr, *Twilight of the Comintern, 1930–1935* (New York: Pantheon Books, 1982).

7. Theodore Dan, *The Origins of Bolshevism* (New York: Schocken Books, 1970), 406.

8. An outstanding and informative study can be found in Pierre Broué and Emile Témime, *The Revolution and the Civil War in Spain* (Chicago: Haymarket Books, 2008). See also Andy Durgan, *The Spanish Civil War* (New York: Palgrave Macmillan, 2007).

9. See *Leon Trotsky, The Spanish Revolution (1931–39)*, edited by Naomi Allen and George Breitman (New York: Pathfinder Press, 1973).

The United Front for Defence:
A Letter to a Social Democratic Worker*
(February 1933)

This pamphlet addresses itself to the Social Democratic workers, even though personally the author belongs to another party. The disagreements between Communism and Social Democracy run very deep. I consider them irreconcilable. Nevertheless, the course of events frequently puts tasks before the working class which imperatively demand the joint action of the two parties. Is such an action possible? Perfectly possible, as historical experience and theory attest: everything depends upon the conditions and the character of the said tasks. Now, it is much easier to engage in a joint action when the question before the proletariat is not one of taking the offensive for the attainment of new objectives, but of defending the positions already gained.

That is how the question is posed in Germany. The German proletariat is in a situation where it is retreating and giving up its positions. To be sure, there is no lack of windbags to cry that we are allegedly in the presence of a revolutionary offensive. These are people who obviously do not know how to distinguish their right from their left. There is no doubt that the hour of the offensive will strike. But today the problem is to arrest the disorderly retreat and to proceed to the regrouping of the forces for the defensive. In politics as in the military art, to understand a problem clearly is to facilitate its solution. To get intoxicated by phrases is to help the adversary. One must see clearly what is happening: the class enemy, that is, monopoly capital and large feudal property, spared by the November Revolution, is attacking along the whole front. The enemy is utilising two means with a different historical origin: first, the military and police apparatus prepared by all the preceding governments which stood on the ground of the Weimar Constitution; second, National Socialism, that is, the troops of the petty bourgeois counter-revolution that finance capital arms and incites against the workers.

* From Trotsky Internet Archive (www.marxists.org/archive/trotsky/germany/1933/330223.htm), with revisions by the editors.

The aim of capital and of the landowning caste is clear: to crush the organisations of the proletariat, to strip them of the possibility not only of taking the offensive but also of defending themselves. As can be seen, 20 years of collaboration of Social Democracy with the bourgeoisie have not softened by one iota the hearts of the capitalists. These individuals acknowledge but one law: the struggle for profit. And they conduct this struggle with a fierce and implacable determination, stopping at nothing and still less at their own laws.

The class of exploiters would have preferred to disarm and atomise the proletariat with the least possible expense, without civil war, with the aid of the military and police of the Weimar Republic. But it is afraid, and with good reason, that 'legal' means by themselves would prove to be insufficient to drive the workers back into a position where they will no longer have any rights. For this, it requires fascism as a supplementary force. But Hitler's party, fattened by monopoly capital, wants to become not a supplementary force, but the sole governing force in Germany. This situation occasions incessant conflicts between the governmental allies, conflicts which at times take on an acute character. The saviours can afford the luxury of engaging mutually in intrigues only because the proletariat is abandoning its positions without battle and is beating the retreat without plan, without system, and without direction. The enemy is unleashed to such a point that it does not constrain itself from discussing right in public where and how to strike the next blow: by frontal attack; by bearing down on the Communist left flank; by penetrating deeply at the rear of the trade unions and cutting off communications, etc. ... The exploiters whom it has saved discourse on the Weimar Republic as if it were some worn-out bowl; they ask themselves if it should still be utilised for a while or be thrown into the discard right away.

The bourgeoisie enjoys full freedom of manoeuvre, that is, the choice of means, of time, and of place. Its chiefs combine the arms of the law with the arms of banditry. The proletariat combines nothing at all and does not defend itself. Its troops are split up, and its chiefs discourse languidly on whether or not it is at all possible to combine forces. Therein lies the essence of the interminable discussions on the united front. If the vanguard workers do not become conscious of the situation and do not intervene peremptorily in the debate, the German proletariat may find itself crucified for years on the cross of fascism.

Is It Not Too Late?

It may be that here my Social Democratic interlocutor interrupts me and says, 'Don't you come too late to propagate the united front? What did you do before this?'

This objection would not be correct. This is not the first time that the question of a united front of defence against fascism is raised. I permit myself to refer to what I had the occasion to say on this subject in September 1930, after the first great success of the National Socialists. Addressing myself to the Communist workers, I wrote:

> The Communist Party must call for the defence of those material and moral positions which the working class has managed to win in the German state. This most directly concerns the fate of the workers' political organisations, trade unions, newspapers, printing plants, clubs, libraries, etc. Communist workers must say to their Social Democratic counterparts: 'The policies of our parties are irreconcilably opposed; but if the fascists come tonight to wreck your organisation's hall, we will come running, arms in hand, to help you. Will you promise us that if our organisation is threatened you will rush to our aid?' This is the quintessence of our policy in the present period. All agitation must be pitched in this key.
>
> The more persistently, seriously, and thoughtfully ... we carry on this agitation, the more we propose serious measures for defence in every factory, in every working-class neighbourhood and district, the less the danger that a fascist attack will take us by surprise, and the greater the certainty that such an attack will cement rather than break apart the ranks of the workers.

The pamphlet from which I take this extract was written two and a half years ago. There is not the slightest doubt today that if this policy had been adopted in time, Hitler would not be Chancellor at the present time and the positions of the German proletariat would be unassailable. But one cannot return to the past. As a result of the mistakes which were committed and the time which was allowed to pass, the problem of defence is posed today with infinitely greater difficulty: but the task remains just as before. Even right now it is possible to alter the relation of forces in favour of the proletariat. Towards this end, one must have a plan, a system, a combination of forces for the defence. But above all, one must have the will to defend himself. I hasten to add that he alone defends himself well who does not confine himself to the defensive but who, at the first occasion, is determined to pass over to the offensive.

What attitude does Social Democracy adopt towards this question?

A Non-Aggression Pact

The Social Democratic leaders propose to the Communist Party to conclude a 'non-aggression pact'. When I read this phrase for the first time in the *Vorwärts* [*Forward*, the official paper of the German Social Democratic Party], I thought it was an incidental and not very happy pleasantry. The formula of the non-aggression pact, however, is today in vogue and at the present time it is at the centre of all the discussions. The Social Democratic leaders are not lacking in tried-out and skilful policies. All the more reason for asking how they could have chosen such a slogan, which runs counter to their own interests.

The formula has been borrowed from diplomacy. The meaning of this type of pact is this: two states which have sufficient causes for war engage themselves for a determined period not to resort to the force of arms against each other. The Soviet Union, for example, has signed such a rigorously circumscribed pact with Poland. Assuming that a war were to break out between Germany and Poland, the said pact would in no way obligate the Soviet Union to come to the aid of Poland. Non-aggression and nothing more. In no way does it imply common action for defence; on the contrary, it excludes this action: without this, the pact would have a quite different character and would be called by a quite different name.

What sense then do the Social Democratic leaders give to this formula? Do the Communists threaten to sack the Social Democratic organisations? Or else is Social Democracy disposed to undertake a crusade against the Communists? As a matter of fact something entirely different is in question. If one wants to use the language of diplomacy, it would be in place to speak not of a non-aggression pact, but of a defensive alliance against a third party, that is, against fascism. The aim is not to halt or to exorcise an armed struggle between Communists and Social Democrats – there could be no question of a danger of war – but of combining the forces of the Social Democrats and the Communists against the attack with arms in hand that has already been launched against them by the National Socialists.

Incredible as it may seem, the Social Democratic leaders are substituting for the question of genuine defence against the armed actions of fascism, the question of the political controversy between Communists and Social Democrats. It is exactly as if one were to substitute for the question of how to prevent the derailment of a train, the question of the need for mutual courtesy between the travellers of the second and third classes.

The misfortune, in any case, is that the ill-conceived formula of a 'non-aggression pact' will not even be able to serve the inferior aim in whose name it is dragged in by the hair. The engagement assumed by two states not to attack each other in no way eliminates their struggle, their polemics, their intrigues, and their manoeuvres. The semi-official Polish journals, in spite of the pact, foam at the mouth when they speak of the Soviet Union. For its part, the Soviet press is far from making compliments to the Polish regime. The fact of the matter is that the Social Democratic leaders have steered a wrong course in trying to substitute a conventional diplomatic formula for the political tasks of the proletariat.

Organise the Defence Jointly; Do Not Forget the Past; Prepare for the Future

More prudent Social Democratic journalists translate their thought in this sense: they are not opponents of a 'criticism based upon facts', but they are against suspicions, insults, and calumnies. A very laudable attitude! But how is the limit to be found between permitted criticism and inadmissible campaigns? And where are the impartial judges? As a general rule, the criticism never pleases the criticised, above all when he can raise no objection to the essence of it.

The question of whether or not the criticism of the Communists is good or bad is a question apart. If the Communists and the Social Democrats had the same opinion on this subject, there wouldn't be two parties in the world, independent from each other. Let us concede that the polemic of the Communists is not worth much. Does that fact lessen the mortal danger of fascism or do away with the need for joint resistance?

However, let us look at the other side of the picture: the polemic of Social Democracy itself against Communism. The *Vorwärts* (I am simply taking the first copy at hand) publishes the speech which [Social Democratic spokesman Friedrich] Stampfer delivered on the subject of the non-aggression pact. In this same issue a cartoon has as its caption: *The Bolsheviks are signing a non-aggression pact with [Polish dictator Josef] Pilsudski, but they refuse to draw up a similar pact with Social Democracy.* Now, a cartoon is also a polemical 'aggression', and it so happens that this particular one is most unfortunate. The *Vorwärts* completely forgets the fact that a non-aggression treaty existed between the Soviets and Germany during the period when the Social Democrat [Hermann] Müller was at the head of the Reich government.

The *Vorwärts* of 15 February, on the same page, defends in the first column the idea of a non-aggression pact, and in the fourth column makes the accusation against the Communists that their factory committee at the Aschinger Company betrayed the interests of the workers during negotiations for the new wage scale. They openly use the word 'betrayed'. The secret behind this polemic (is it a criticism based on facts or a campaign of slander?) is very simple: new elections to the factory committee of the Aschinger Company were to take place at this time. Can we, in the interests of the united front asks the *Vorwärts*, put an end to attacks of this sort? In order for that to happen, the *Vorwärts* would have to stop being itself, that is, a Social Democratic journal. If the *Vorwärts* believes what it prints on the subject of the Communists, its first duty is to open the eyes of the workers to the faults, crimes, and 'betrayals' of the latter. How could it be otherwise? The need for a fighting agreement flows from the existence of two parties, but it does not do away with the fact. Political life goes on. Each party, even though it adopts the frankest attitude on the question of the united front cannot help thinking of its own future.

Adversaries Close Ranks in the Face of the Common Danger

Let us assume for the moment that a Communist member of the Aschinger Company factory committee declares to the Social Democratic member: 'Because the *Vorwärts* characterised my attitude on the question of the wage scale as an act of treason, I do not want to defend, together with you, my head and your neck from the fascist bullets.' No matter how indulgently we wanted to view this action, we could only characterise the reply as utterly insane.

The intelligent Communist, the serious Bolshevik, will say to the Social Democrat: 'You are aware of my enmity to the views expressed by the *Vorwärts*. I am devoting and shall devote all my energy to undermining the dangerous influence which this paper has among the workers. But I am doing that and shall do it by my speeches, by criticism and persuasion. But the fascists want to do away arbitrarily with the existence of the *Vorwärts*. I promise you that jointly with you I will defend your paper to the utmost of my ability, but I am waiting for you to say that at the first appeal you will likewise come to the defence of *Die Rote Fahne* [*The Red Flag*, the official German Communist Party newspaper] regardless of your attitude towards its views.' Is this not an irreproachable way of posing the question? Does not this method correspond with the fundamental interests of the whole of the proletariat?

The Bolshevik does not ask the Social Democrat to alter the opinion he has of Bolshevism and of the Bolshevik press. Moreover, he does not demand that the Social Democrat make a pledge for the duration of the agreement to keep silent on his opinion of Communism. Such a demand would be absolutely inexcusable. 'So long,' says the Communist 'as I have not convinced you and you have not convinced me, we shall criticize each other with full freedom, each using the arguments and expressions he deems necessary. But when the fascist wants to force a gag down our throats, we will repulse him together!' Can an intelligent Social Democratic worker counter this proposal with a refusal?

The polemic between Communist and Social Democratic newspapers, no matter how bitter it may be, cannot prevent the compositors of the papers from forming a fighting agreement to organise a joint defence of their presses from attacks of the fascist bands. The Social Democratic and Communist deputies in the Reichstag and the Landtags, the municipal counsellors, etc., are compelled to come to the physical defence of each other when the Nazis resort to loaded canes and chairs. Are more examples needed?

What is true in each particular case is also true as a general rule: the inevitable struggle in which Social Democracy and Communism are engaged for the leadership of the working class cannot and must not prevent them from closing their ranks when blows threaten the whole working class. Isn't this obvious?

Two Weights and Two Scales

The *Vorwärts* is indignant because the Communists accuse the Social Democrats (Ebert, Scheidemann, Noske, Hermann Müller, Grzesinsky) of paving the road for Hitler. The *Vorwärts* has a legitimate right to indignation. But this remark is too much: how can we, it cries out, make a united front with such slanderers? What have we here: sentimentalism? Prudish sensitiveness? No, that really smacks of hypocrisy. As a matter of fact, the leaders of the German Social Democracy cannot have forgotten that Wilhelm Liebknecht and August Bebel* often asserted that Social Democracy was ready, for the sake of definite objectives, to come to an agreement with the devil and his grandmother. The founders of Social Democracy certainly did not demand that during this occasion the devil should check his horns in the museum and that his grandmother should become converted to Lutheranism. Whence then comes this prudish sensitiveness among the Social Democratic politicians who, since 1914, have made united fronts with the Kaiser, Ludendorff, Gröner, Brüning, Hindenburg? Whence come these two weights and two scales: one for the bourgeois parties, the other for the Communists?

The leaders of the Centre [a moderate political party with a Catholic base] consider that every infidel who denies the dogmas of the Catholic Church, the only Saviour, is one of the damned and shortly destined for eternal torments. That did not prevent Hilferding, who has no particular reason for believing in the immaculate conception, from establishing a united front with the Catholics in the government and in parliament. Together with the Centre the Social Democrats set up the 'Iron Front' [against the Nazis]. However, not for a single instant did the Catholics cease their unbearable propaganda and their polemics in the churches. Why these demands on Hilferding's part with regard to

---

*   Comrades of Marx and founding leaders of the German Social Democratic Party. – Editors

the Communists? Either a complete cessation of mutual criticism, that is, of the struggle of tendencies within the working class, or a rejection of all joint action. 'All or nothing!' Social Democracy has never put such ultimatums to bourgeois society. Every Social Democratic worker should reflect upon these two weights and two measures.

Suppose at a meeting, even today, someone should ask [Social Democratic leader Otto] Wels how it happens that Social Democracy, which gave the republic its first Chancellor and its first president, has led the country to Hitler. Wels will surely reply that to a large extent it is the fault of Bolshevism. Surely the day hasn't passed that the *Vorwärts* has failed to repeat this explanation *ad nauseam*. Do you think that in the united front with the Communists it will forgo its right and its duty to tell the workers what it considers to be truth? The Communists certainly have no need of that. The united front against fascism is only one chapter in the book of the struggle of the proletariat. The chapters that went before cannot be effaced. The past cannot be forgotten. We must build on it. We preserve the memory of Ebert's alliance with Gröner and of Noske's role. We remember under what conditions Rosa Luxemburg and Karl Liebknecht died.* We Bolsheviks have taught the workers to forget nothing. We do not ask the devil to cut off his tail: that would hurt him and we would not profit by it. We accept the devil just as nature has created him. We have no need of the repentance of the Social Democratic leaders nor of their loyalty to Marxism; but we do need the will of Social Democracy to struggle against the enemy which actually threatens it with death. For our part, we are ready to carry out in the joint struggle all the promises which we have made. We promise to fight courageously and to carry the fight to a finish. That is quite enough for a fighting agreement.

Your Leaders Don't Want to Fight!

However, it still remains to be known why the Social Democratic leaders speak at all regarding polemics, non-aggression pacts, and

---

* Wilhelm Gröner and Gustav Noske were Social Democrats closely aligned with the German military – associated with the notorious paramilitary Freikorps of 1919 that murdered revolutionary socialists, including Karl Liebknecht and Rosa Luxemburg. – Editors

the disgusting manners of the Communists, instead of answering this simple question: In what way shall we fight the fascists? For the simple reason that the Social Democratic leaders do not want to fight. They cherished the hope that Hindenburg would save them from Hitler. Now they are waiting for some other miracle. They do not want to fight. They lost the habit of fighting long ago. The struggle frightens them.

Stampfer wrote regarding the actions of the fascist banditry at Eisleben: 'Faith in right and justice has not yet died in Germany' (*Vorwärts*, 14 February).*

It is impossible to read these words without being revolted. Instead of a call for a fighting united front, we get the consoling words: 'Faith in justice has not died.' Now, the bourgeoisie has its justice, and the proletariat its own, too. Armed injustice always comes out on top of disarmed justice. The whole history of humanity proves this. Whoever makes an appeal to this obvious phantom of justice is deceiving the workers. Whoever wants the victory of proletarian justice over fascist violence, must agitate for the struggle and set up the organs of the proletarian united front.

In the entire Social Democratic press it is impossible to find a single line indicating genuine preparation for the struggle. There is not a single thing, merely some general phrases, postponements to some indefinite future, nebulous consolations. 'Only let the Nazis start something, and then …' And the Nazis started something. They march forward step by step, they tranquilly take over one position after another. These petty bourgeois reactionary malefactors do not care for risks. Now, they do not need to risk anything at all: they are sure in advance that the enemy will retreat without a fight. And they are not mistaken in their calculations.

Of course, it often occurs that a combatant must retreat in order to get a good start for a leap forward. But the Social Democratic leaders are not inclined to make the leap forward. They do not want to leap. And all their dissertations are made in order to conceal this fact. Just a short time ago they kept asserting that so long as the Nazis do not quit the ground of legality, there is no room for a fight. Now we get a good look at what this legality was: a series of promissory notes on the *coup d'état*. Still, this

---

*   Refers to particularly violent repression of German workers and their families in Saxony and Silesia, involving Nazi stormtroopers. – Editors

coup d'état is possible only because the Social Democratic leaders lull the workers to sleep with phrases about the legality of the *coup d'état* and console them with hope of a new Reichstag yet more impotent than those that preceded it. The fascists can ask for nothing better.

Today Social Democracy has even ceased speaking of struggles in the indefinite future. On the subject of the destruction of the working-class organisations and press, already begun, the *Vorwärts* 'reminds' the government not to forget that 'in a developed capitalist country the conditions of production group the workers in factories'. These words indicate that the leadership of Social Democracy accepts in advance the destruction of the political, economic, and cultural organisations created by three generations of the proletariat. 'In spite of this' the workers will remain grouped by the industries themselves. Well then, what good are proletarian organisations if the question can be solved so simply?

The leaders of Social Democracy and the trade unions wash their hands, and relegate themselves to the sidelines while waiting. If the workers themselves, 'grouped together by industries', break the bonds of discipline and begin the struggle, the leaders, obviously, will intervene as they did in 1918, in the role of pacifiers and mediators, and will force themselves onto the workers' backs to re-establish the positions they have lost.

The leaders conceal from the eyes of the masses their refusal to fight and their dread of the struggle by means of hollow phrases about non-aggression pacts. Social Democratic workers, your leaders do not want to fight!

Then Is Our Proposal a Manoeuvre?

Here the Social Democrat will again interrupt us to say. 'Since you do not believe in our leaders' desire to fight against fascism, isn't your proposal for a united front an obvious maneouvre?' Even more, he will repeat the reflections printed in the *Vorwärts* to the effect that the workers need unity and not 'manoeuvres'.

This type of argument has quite a convincing sound. In actuality it is an empty phrase. Yes, we Communists are positive that the Social Democratic and trade union functionaries will continue to evade the struggle to the best of their ability. At the critical moment a large segment of the working-class bureaucracy will pass directly over to the fascists. The other segment, which succeeds in exporting its carefully hoarded financial resources to some other country, will emigrate at the opportune moment. All these actions have already begun, and their further development is inevitable. But we do not confuse this segment today the most influential in the reformist bureaucracy, with the Social Democratic Party or the entirety of the trade unions. The proletarian nucleus of the party will fight with sure blows, and it will carry behind it a good-sized section of the apparatus. Exactly where will the line of demarcation pass between the turncoats, traitors, and deserters, on one side, and those who want to fight, on the other? We can only find this out through experience. That is why, without possessing the slightest confidence in the Social Democratic bureaucracy, the Communists cannot abstain from addressing themselves to the whole party. Only in this manner will it be possible to separate those who want to fight from those who want to desert. If we are mistaken in our estimation of [Social Democratic leaders] Wels, Breitscheid, Hilferding, Crispien, and the rest, let them prove that we are liars by their actions. We will declare a mea culpa on the public squares. If all this is merely a 'manoeuvre' on our part, it is a correct and necessary manoeuvre which serves the interests of the cause.

You Social Democrats remain in your party because you have faith in its programme, in its tactics, and in its leadership. This is a fact with which we reckon. You regard our criticism as false. That is your privilege. You are by no means obliged to believe the Communists on faith, and no serious Communist will demand this of you. But on their side the Communists have the right to put no confidence in the functionaries of Social Democracy and not to consider the Social Democrats as Marxists, revolutionists, and genuine socialists. Otherwise, the Communists would have had no need to create a separate party and International. We must take the facts as they are. We must build the united front not in the clouds, but on the foundation which all the previous development has laid down. If you sincerely believe that your leadership will lead the workers to struggle against fascism, what Communist manoeuvre can you distrust? Then what is this manoeuvre of which the *Vorwärts* is continually speaking? Think it out carefully.

Is this not a manoeuvre on the part of your leaders who want to frighten you with the hollow word 'manoeuvre' and thus keep you away from the united front?

The Tasks and Methods of the United Front

The united front must have its organs. There is no need to imagine what these may be: the situation itself is dictating the nature of these organs. In many localities, the workers have already suggested the form of organisation of the united front, as a species of defence cartels basing themselves on all the local proletarian organisations and establishments. This is an initiative which must be grasped, deepened, consolidated, extended to cover the industrial centres with cartels, by linking them up with each other and by preparing a German workers' congress of defence.

The fact that the unemployed and the employed workers are becoming increasingly estranged from each other bears within itself a deadly danger not only for the collective bargaining agreements, but also for the trade unions, without even any need for a fascist crusade. The united front between Social Democrats and Communists means first of all a united front of the employed and unemployed workers. Without that, any serious struggle in Germany is quite unthinkable.

The RGO [Revolutionary Union Opposition] must enter into the Free Trade Unions as a Communist fraction. That is one of the principal conditions for the success of the united front. The Communists within the trade unions must enjoy the rights of workers' democracy and, in the first place, full freedom of criticism. On their part they must respect the statutes of the trade unions and their discipline.

Defence against fascism is not an isolated thing. Fascism is only a cudgel in the hands of finance capital. The aim of the crushing of proletarian democracy is to raise the rate of exploitation of labour power. There lies an immense field for the united front of the proletariat: the struggle for daily bread, extended and sharpened, leads directly under present conditions to the struggle for workers' control of production.

The factories, the mines, the large estates fulfil their social functions thanks only to the labour of the workers. Can it be that the latter have not the right to know whither the owner is directing the establishment, why he is reducing production and driving out the workers, how he is fixing prices, etc.? We will be answered: 'commercial secrets'. What are commercial secrets? A plot of the capitalists against the workers and the people as a whole. Producers and consumers, the workers in this two-fold capacity must conquer the right to control all the operations of their establishments, unmasking fraud and deceit in order to defend their interests and the interests of the people as a whole, facts and figures in hand. The struggle for workers' control of production can and should become the slogan of the united front.

With regard to organisation, the forms necessary for cooperation between Social Democratic workers and Communist workers will be found without difficulty: it is only necessary to pass over from words to deeds.

The Irreconcilable Character of the Social Democratic and the Communist Parties

Now, if a common defence against the attack of capital is possible, can we not go still farther and form a genuine bloc of the two parties on all the questions? Then the polemic between the two would take on an internal, pacific, and cordial character. Certain left Social Democrats, of the type of [Max] Seydewitz, as is known, even go so far as to dream of a complete union of Social Democracy and the Communist Party. But all this is a vain dream! What separates the Communists from Social Democracy are antagonisms on fundamental questions. The simplest way of translating the essence of their disagreements is this: Social Democracy considers itself the democratic doctor of capitalism, we are its revolutionary gravediggers.

The irreconcilable character of the two parties appears with particular clearness in the light of the recent evolution of Germany. [Social Democratic trade union leader Theodor] Leipart laments that in calling Hitler to power the bourgeois classes have disrupted the 'integration' of the workers into the state and he warns the bourgeoisie against the 'dangers' flowing from it (*Vorwärts*, 15 February 1933). Leipart thus makes himself the watchdog of the bourgeois state by desiring to preserve it from the proletarian revolution. Can we even dream of union with Leipart?

The *Vorwärts* prides itself every day on the fact that hundreds of thousands of Social Democrats died during the war 'for the ideal of a finer and freer Germany' ... It only forgets to explain why this finer Germany turned out to be the Germany of Hitler-Hugenberg.* In reality, the German workers, like the workers of the other belligerent countries, died as cannon fodder, as slaves of capital. To idealise this fact is to continue the treason of 4 August 1914.

The *Vorwärts* continues to appeal to Marx, to Engels, to Wilhelm Liebknecht, to Bebel, who from 1848 to 1871 spoke of the struggle for the unity of the German nation. Lying appeals! At that time, it was a question of completing the bourgeois revolution. Every proletarian revolutionist had to fight against the particularism and provincialism inherited from feudalism. Every proletarian revolutionist had to fight against this particularism and provincialism in the name of the creation of a national state. At the present time, such an objective is invested with a progressive character only in China, in Indochina, in India, in Indonesia, and other backward colonial and semi-colonial countries. For the advanced countries of Europe, the national frontiers are exactly the same reactionary chains as were the feudal frontiers at one time.

'The nation and democracy are twins', the *Vorwärts* says again. Quite true! But these twins have become aged, infirm, and have fallen into senility. The nation as an economic whole, and democracy as a form of the domination of the bourgeoisie, have been transformed into fetters upon the productive forces and civilisation. Let us recall Goethe once again: 'All that is born is doomed to perish.'

A few more millions may be sacrificed for the 'corridor', for Alsace-Lorraine, for Malmedy.† These disputed bits of land may be covered with three, five, ten tiers of corpses. All this may be called national defence. But humanity will not progress

---

* Alfred Hugenberg was a German banker who led the right-wing Nationalist Party and formed an alliance with Hitler's Nazis. – Editors

† The reference here is to former German territory lost after the German defeat in the First World War, which right-wing nationalists 'patriotically' vowed to get back again. – Editors

because of it; on the contrary, it will fall on all fours backward
into barbarism. The way out is not in the 'national liberation' of
Germany, but in the liberation of Europe from national barriers.
It is a problem which the bourgeoisie cannot resolve, any more
than the feudal lords in their time were able to put an end to
particularism. Hence the coalition with the bourgeoisie is doubly
reprehensible. A proletarian revolution is necessary. A federation
of the proletarian republics of Europe and the whole world
is necessary.

Social patriotism is the programme of the doctors of capitalism;
internationalism is the programme of the gravediggers of bourgeois
society. This antagonism is irreducible.

Democracy and Dictatorship

The Social Democrats consider the democratic constitution to be
above the class struggle. For us, the class struggle is above the
democratic constitution. Can it be that the experience undergone
by post-war Germany has passed without leaving a trace, just
as the experiences undergone during the war? The November
Revolution [of 1918] brought Social Democracy to power. Social
Democracy spurred the powerful movement of the masses along
the road of 'right' and the 'constitution'. The whole political life
which followed in Germany evolved on the bases and within the
framework of the Weimar Republic.

The results are at hand: bourgeois democracy transforms
itself legally, pacifically, into a fascist dictatorship. The secret
is simple enough: bourgeois democracy and fascist dictatorship
are the instruments of one and the same class, the exploiters. It is
absolutely impossible to prevent the replacement of one instrument
by the other by appealing to the Constitution, the Supreme Court
at Leipzig, new elections, etc. What is necessary is to mobilise the
revolutionary forces of the proletariat. Constitutional fetishism
brings the best aid to fascism. Today this is no longer a prognos-
tication, a theoretical affirmation, but the living reality. I ask you,
Social Democratic worker: if the Weimar democracy blazed the
trail for the fascist dictatorship, how can one expect it to blaze
the trail for socialism?

'But can't we Social Democratic workers win the majority in the democratic Reichstag?'

That you cannot. Capitalism has ceased to develop; it is putrefying. The number of industrial workers is no longer growing. An important section of the proletariat is being degraded in continual unemployment. By themselves, these social facts exclude the possibility of any stable and methodical development of a labour party in parliament as before the war. But even if, against all probability, the labour representation in parliament should grow rapidly, would the bourgeoisie wait for a peaceful expropriation? The governmental machinery is entirely in its hands! Even admitting that the bourgeoisie allows the moment to pass and permits the proletariat to gain a parliamentary representation of 51 per cent, wouldn't the Reichswehr [the German military], the police, the Stahlhelm [right-wing paramilitary groups], and the fascist storm troops disperse this parliament in the same way that the camarilla today disperses with a stroke of the pen all the parliaments which displease it?

'Then, down with the Reichstag and elections?'

No, that's not what I mean. We are Marxists and not anarchists. We are supporters of the utilisation of parliament: it is not an instrument for transforming society, but a means of rallying the workers. Nevertheless, in the development of the class struggle, a moment arrives when it is necessary to decide the question of who is to be master of the country: finance capital or the proletariat. Dissertations on the nation and on democracy in general constitute, under such conditions, the most impudent lying. Under our eyes, a small German minority is organising and arming, as it were, half of the nation to crush and strangle the other half. It is not a question today of secondary reforms, but of the life or death of bourgeois society. Never have such questions been decided by a vote. Whoever appeals today to the parliament or to the Supreme Court at Leipzig, is deceiving the workers and in practice is helping fascism.

There Is No Other Road

'What is to be done under such conditions?' my Social Democratic interlocutor will ask.

The proletarian revolution.

'And then?'

The dictatorship of the proletariat.

'As in Russia? The privations and the sacrifices? The complete stifling of freedom of opinion? No, not for me.'

It is precisely because you are not disposed to tread the road of the revolution and the dictatorship that we cannot form one single party together. But nevertheless allow me to tell you that your objection is not worthy of a conscious proletarian. Yes, the privations of the Russian workers are considerable. But in the first place, the Russian workers know in the name of what they are making these sacrifices. Even if they should undergo a defeat, humanity would have learned a great deal from their experience. But in the name of what did the German working class sacrifice itself in the years of the imperialist war? Or again, in the years of unemployment? To what do these sacrifices lead, what do they yield, what do they teach? Only those sacrifices are worthy of man which blaze the trail to a better future. That's the first objection I heard you make; the first, but not the only one.

The sufferings of the Russian workers are considerable because in Russia, as a consequence of specific historical factors, was born the first proletarian state, which is obliged to raise itself from extreme poverty by its own strength. Do not forget that Russia was the most backward country of Europe. The proletariat there constituted only a tiny part of the population. In that country, the dictatorship of the proletariat necessarily had to assume the harshest forms. Thence the consequences which flowed from it: the development of the bureaucracy which holds power, and the chain of errors committed by the political leadership which has fallen under the influence of this bureaucracy. If at the end of 1918, when power was completely in its hands, Social Democracy had entered boldly upon the road to socialism and had concluded an indissoluble alliance with Soviet Russia, the whole history of Europe would have taken another direction and humanity would have arrived at socialism in a much shorter space of time and with infinitely less sacrifice. It is not our fault that this did not happen.

Yes, the dictatorship in the Soviet Union at the present time has an extremely bureaucratic and distorted character. I have personally criticised more than once in the press the present Soviet regime which is a distortion of the workers' state. Thousands upon thousands of my comrades fill the prisons and the places of exile for having fought against the Stalinist bureaucracy. However, even when judging the negative sides of the present Soviet regime, it is necessary to preserve a correct historical perspective. If the German proletariat, much more numerous and more civilised than the Russian proletariat, were to take the power tomorrow, this would not only open up immense economic and cultural perspectives but would also lead immediately to a radical attenuation of the dictatorship in the Soviet Union.

It must not be thought that the dictatorship of the proletariat is necessarily connected with the methods of Red terror which we had to apply in Russia. We were the pioneers. Covered with crime, the Russian possessing classes did not believe that the new regime would last. The bourgeoisie of Europe and America supported the Russian counter-revolution. Under these conditions, one could hold on only at the cost of terrific exertion and the implacable punishment of our class enemies. The victory of the proletariat in Germany would have quite a different character. The German bourgeoisie, having lost the power, would no longer have any hope of retaking it. The alliance of Soviet Germany with Soviet Russia would multiply, not two-fold but ten-fold, the strength of the two countries. In all the rest of Europe, the position of the bourgeoisie is so compromised that it is not very likely that it would be able to get its armies to march against proletarian Germany. To be sure, the civil war would be inevitable: there are enough fascists for that. But the German proletariat, armed with state power and having the Soviet Union behind it, would soon bring about the atomisation of fascism by drawing to its side substantial sections of the petty bourgeoisie. The dictatorship of the proletariat in Germany would have incomparably more mild and more civilised forms than the dictatorship of the proletariat in Russia.

'In that case, why the dictatorship?'

To annihilate exploitation and parasitism; to crush the resistance of the exploiters; to end their inclination to think about a re-establishment of exploitation; to put all the power, all the means of production, all the resources of civilisation into the hands of the proletariat; and to permit it to utilise all these forces and means in the interest of the socialist transformation of society: there is no other road.

The German Proletariat Will Have the Revolution in German and Not in Russian

'Still, it often happens that our Communists approach us Social Democrats with this threat: just wait, as soon as we will get into power, we'll put you up against the wall.'

Only a handful of imbeciles, windbags, and braggarts, who are a safe bet to decamp at the moment of danger, can make such threats. A serious revolutionist, while acknowledging the inescapability of revolutionary violence and its creative function, understands at the same time that the application of violence in the socialist transformation of society has well-defined limits. The Communists cannot prepare themselves save by seeking mutual understanding and a rapprochement with the Social Democratic workers. The revolutionary unanimity of the overwhelming majority of the German proletariat will reduce to a minimum the repression which the revolutionary dictatorship will exercise. It is not a question of slavishly copying Soviet Russia, of making a virtue of each of its necessities. That is unworthy of Marxists. To profit by the experience of the October Revolution does not mean that it should be copied blindly. One must take into account differences among nations, in the social structure and above all in the relative importance and the cultural level of the proletariat. To assume that one can make the socialist revolution in a presumably constitutional, peaceful manner, with the acquiescence of the Supreme Court at Leipzig – that can be done only by incurable philistines. The German proletariat will be unable to walk around the revolution. But in its revolution, it will speak in German and not in Russian. I am convinced that it will speak much better than we did.

What Shall We Defend?

'Very good, but we Social Democrats propose nevertheless to come to power by democracy. You Communists consider that an absurd utopia. In that case, is the united front of defence possible? For it is necessary to have a clear idea of what there is to defend. If we defend one thing and you another, we will not end up with common actions. Do you Communists consent to defend the Weimar Constitution?'

The question is a fitting one and I will try to answer it candidly. The Weimar Constitution represents a whole system of institutions, of rights and of laws. Let us commence from the top. The republic has at its head a president. Do we Communists consent to defend Hindenburg against fascism? I think that the need for that doesn't make itself felt, Hindenburg having called the fascists to power. Then comes the government presided over by Hitler. This government does not need to be defended against fascism. In the third place comes the parliament. When these lines appear, the sort of parliament emerging from the elections of 5 March will probably have been determined. But even at this juncture one can say with certainty that if the composition of the Reichstag proves to be hostile to the government; if Hitler takes it into his head to liquidate the Reichstag and if Social Democracy shows a determination to fight for the latter, the Communists will help Social Democracy with all their strength.

We Communists cannot and do not want to establish the dictatorship of the proletariat against you or without you, Social Democratic workers. We want to come to this dictatorship together with you. And we regard the common defence against fascism as the first step in this sense. Obviously, in our eyes, the Reichstag is not a capital historical conquest which the proletariat must defend against the fascist vandals. There are more valuable things. Within the framework of bourgeois democracy and parallel to the incessant struggle against it, the elements of proletarian democracy have formed themselves in the course of many decades: political parties, labour press, trade unions, factory committees, clubs, cooperatives, sports societies, etc. The mission of fascism is not so much to complete the destruction of bourgeois democracy as to crush the first outlines of proletarian democracy. As for our mission, it consists in placing those elements of proletarian democracy, already created, at the foundation of the soviet system of the workers' state. To this end, it is necessary to break the husk of bourgeois democracy and free from it the kernel of workers' democracy. Therein lies the essence of the proletarian revolution. Fascism threatens the vital kernel of workers' democracy. This itself clearly dictates the programme of the united front. We are ready to defend your printing plants and our own, but also the democratic principle of freedom of the press; your meeting halls and ours, but also the democratic principle of the freedom of assembly and association. We are materialists and that is why we do not separate the soul from the body. So long as we do not yet have the strength to establish the soviet system, we place ourselves on the terrain of bourgeois democracy. But at the same time we do not entertain any illusions.

As to Freedom of the Press

'And what will you do with the Social Democratic press if you should succeed in seizing power? Will you prohibit our papers as the Russian Bolsheviks prohibited the Menshevik papers?'

You put the question badly. What do you mean by 'our' papers? In Russia the dictatorship of the proletariat proved possible only after the overwhelming majority of the worker-Mensheviks passed over to the side of the Bolsheviks, whereas the petty bourgeois debris of Menshevism undertook to help the bourgeoisie fight for the restoration of 'democracy', that is, of capitalism. However, even in Russia we did not at all inscribe upon our banner the prohibition of the Menshevik papers. We were led to do this by the incredibly harsh conditions of the struggle that had to be conducted to save and maintain the revolutionary dictatorship. In Soviet Germany, the situation will be, as I have already said, infinitely more favourable; and the regime of the press will necessarily feel the effects of it. I do not think that in this field the German proletariat needs to resort to repression.

To be sure, I do not want to say that the workers' state will tolerate even for a day the regime of '(bourgeois) freedom of the press', that is, the state of affairs in which only those who control the printing plants, the paper companies, the bookstores, and so on, that is, the capitalists, can publish papers and books. Bourgeois 'freedom of the press' signifies a monopoly for finance capital to impose capitalist prejudices upon the people by means of hundreds and thousands of papers charged with disseminating the virus of lies in the most perfect technical form. Proletarian freedom of the press will mean the nationalisation of the printing plants, the paper companies, and the bookstores in the interest of the workers. We do not separate the soul from the body. Freedom of the press without linotypes, without printing presses, and without paper is a miserable fiction. In the proletarian state the technical means of printing will be put at the disposal of groups of citizens in accordance with their real numerical importance. How is this to be done? Social Democracy will obtain printing facilities corresponding to the number of its supporters. I do not think that at that time this number will be very high: otherwise the very regime of the dictatorship of the proletariat would be impossible. Nevertheless, let us leave it to the future to settle this question. But the principle itself, of distributing the technical means of printing, not according to the thickness of the cheque book, but according to the number of supporters of a given programme, of a given current, of a given school, is, I hope, the most honest, the most democratic, the most authentically proletarian principle. Isn't that so?

'Maybe.'

Then shall we shake hands on it? 'I'd like to think it over a bit.'

I ask for nothing else, my dear friend: the aim of all my reflections is to have you meditate once more upon all the great problems of proletarian policy.

What is National Socialism?[*]
(June 1933)

Naive minds think that the office of kingship lodges in the king himself, in his ermine cloak and his crown, in his flesh and bones. As a matter of fact, the office of kingship is an interrelation between people. The king is king only because the interests and prejudices of millions of people are refracted through his person. When the flood of development sweeps away these interrelations, then the king appears to be only a washed-out man with a flabby lower lip. He who was once called Alfonso XIII could discourse upon this from fresh impressions [after being forced to abdicate in 1931 with the establishment of the Spanish Republic].

The leader by will of the people differs from the leader by will of God in that the former is compelled to clear the road for himself or, at any rate, to assist the conjuncture of events in discovering him. Nevertheless, the leader is always a relation between people, the individual supply to meet the collective

* From Trotsky Internet Archive (www.marxists.org/archive/trotsky/germany/1933/ 330610.htm), with revisions by the editors.

demand. The controversy over Hitler's personality becomes the sharper the more the secret of his success is sought in himself. In the meantime, another political figure would be difficult to find that is in the same measure the focus of anonymous historic forces. Not every exasperated petty bourgeois could have become Hitler, but a particle of Hitler is lodged in every exasperated petty bourgeois.

The rapid growth of German capitalism prior to the First World War by no means signified a simple destruction of the middle classes. Although it ruined some layers of the petty bourgeoisie it created others anew: around the factories, artisans and shopkeepers; within the factories, technicians and executives. But while preserving themselves and even growing numerically – the old and the new petty bourgeoisie compose a little less than one-half of the German nation – the middle classes have lost the last shadow of independence. They live on the periphery of large-scale industry and the banking system, and they live off the crumbs from the table of the monopolies and cartels, and off the spiritual alms of their theorists and professional politicians.

The defeat in 1918 raised a wall in the path of German imperialism. External dynamics changed to internal. The war passed over into revolution. Social Democracy, which aided the Hohenzollerns [Germany's monarchy] in bringing the war to its tragic conclusion, did not permit the proletariat to bring the revolution to its conclusion. The Weimar democracy spent 14 years finding interminable excuses for its own existence. The Communist Party called the workers to a new revolution but proved incapable of leading it. The German proletariat passed through the rise and collapse of war, revolution, parliamentarism, and pseudo-Bolshevism. At the time when the old parties of the bourgeoisie had drained themselves to the dregs, the dynamic power of the working class also found itself sapped.

The post-war chaos hit the artisans, the peddlers, and the civil employees no less cruelly than the workers. The economic crisis in agriculture was ruining the peasantry. The decay of the middle strata did not mean that they were made into proletarians, inasmuch as the proletariat itself was casting out a gigantic army of chronically unemployed. The pauperisation of the petty bourgeoisie, barely covered by ties and socks of artificial silk, eroded all official creeds and first of all the doctrine of democratic parliamentarism.

The multiplicity of parties, the icy fever of elections, the interminable changes of ministries aggravated the social crisis by creating a kaleidoscope of barren political combinations. In the atmosphere brought to white heat by war, defeat, reparations, inflation, occupation of the Ruhr, crisis, need, and despair, the petty bourgeoisie rose up against all the old parties that had bamboozled it. The sharp grievances of small proprietors never out of bankruptcy, of their university sons without posts and clients, of their daughters without dowries and suitors, demanded order and an iron hand.

The banner of National Socialism was raised by upstarts from the lower and middle commanding ranks of the old army. Decorated with medals for distinguished service, commissioned and non-commissioned officers could not believe that their heroism and sufferings for the Fatherland had not only come to naught, but also gave them no special claims to gratitude. Hence their hatred of the revolution and the proletariat. At the same time, they did not want to reconcile themselves to being sent by the bankers, industrialists, and ministers back to the modest posts of bookkeepers, engineers, postal clerks, and schoolteachers. Hence their 'socialism'. At the Yser and under Verdun they had learned to risk themselves and others, and to speak the language of command, which powerfully overawed the petty bourgeois behind the lines.* Thus these people became leaders.

At the start of his political career, Hitler stood out only because of his big temperament a voice much louder than others, and an intellectual mediocrity much more self-assured. He did not bring into the movement any ready-made programme, if one disregards the insulted soldier's thirst for vengeance. Hitler began with grievances and complaints about the Versailles terms, the high cost of living, the lack of respect for a meritorious non-commissioned officer, and the plots of bankers and journalists of the Mosaic persuasion. There were in the country plenty of ruined and drowning people with scars and fresh bruises. They all wanted to thump with their fists on the table. This Hitler could

---

* The river Yser and the city of Verdun in France were the scene of major battles in the First World War - resulting in well over a million deaths. - Editors

do better than others. True, he knew not how to cure the evil. But his harangues resounded, now like commands and now like prayers addressed to inexorable fate. Doomed classes, like those fatally ill, never tire of making variations on their plaints nor of listening to consolations. Hitler's speeches were all attuned to this pitch. Sentimental formlessness, absence of disciplined thought, ignorance along with gaudy erudition – all these minuses turned into pluses. They supplied him with the possibility of uniting all types of dissatisfaction in the beggar's bowl of National Socialism, and of leading the mass in the direction in which it pushed him. In the mind of the agitator was preserved, from among his early improvisations, whatever had met with approbation. His political thoughts were the fruits of oratorical acoustics. That is how the selection of slogans went on. That is how the programme was consolidated. That is how the 'leader' took shape out of the raw material.

Mussolini from the very beginning reacted more consciously to social materials than Hitler, to whom the police mysticism of a Metternich is much closer than the political algebra of Machiavelli.* Mussolini is mentally bolder and more cynical. It may be said that the Roman atheist only utilizes religion as he does the police and the courts, while his Berlin colleague really believes in the infallibility of the Church of Rome. During the time when the future Italian dictator considered Marx as 'our common immortal teacher', he defended not unskilfully the theory which sees in the life of contemporary society first of all the reciprocal action of two classes, the bourgeoisie and the proletariat. True, Mussolini wrote in 1914, there lie between them very numerous intermediate layers which seemingly form 'a joining web of the human collective'; but 'during periods of crisis, the intermediate classes gravitate, depending upon their interests and ideas, to one or the other of the basic classes'. A very important generalisation! Just as scientific medicine equips one with the possibility not only of curing the sick but of sending the healthy to meet their

---

* Prince Clemens von Metternich (1773–1859) was a reactionary Austrian statesman who, after the defeat of Napoleon, helped establish the Holy Alliance which ruthlessly suppressed liberal and revolutionary thought throughout Europe; Niccolò Machiavelli (1469–1527) was a philosopher of the Italian Renaissance whose cynical study of the use and abuse of power, *The Prince*, is considered to be an early classic of political science. – Editors

forefathers by the shortest route, so the scientific analysis of class relations, predestined by its creator for the mobilisation of the proletariat, enabled Mussolini, after he had jumped into the opposing camp, to mobilise the middle classes against the proletariat. Hitler accomplished the same feat in translating the methodology of fascism into the language of German mysticism. The bonfires which burn the impious literature of Marxism light up brilliantly the class nature of National Socialism. While the Nazis acted as a party and not as a state power, they did not quite find an approach to the working class. On the other side, the big bourgeoisie, even those who supported Hitler with money, did not consider his party theirs. The national 'renaissance' leaned wholly upon the middle classes, the most backward part of the nation, the heavy ballast of history. Political art consisted in fusing the petty bourgeoisie into oneness through its common hostility to the proletariat. What must be done in order to improve things? First of all, throttle those who are underneath. Impotent before big capital, the petty bourgeoisie hopes in the future to regain its social dignity through the ruin of the workers.

The Nazis call their overturn by the usurped title of revolution. As a matter of fact, in Germany as well as in Italy, fascism leaves the social system untouched. Taken by itself, Hitler's overturn has no right even to the name counter-revolution. But it cannot be viewed as an isolated event; it is the conclusion of a cycle of shocks which began in Germany in 1918. The November Revolution, which gave the power to the workers' and peasants' soviets, was proletarian in its fundamental tendencies. But the party that stood at the head of the proletariat returned the power to the bourgeoisie. In this sense Social Democracy opened the era of counter-revolution before the revolution could bring its work to completion. However, so long as the bourgeoisie depended upon Social Democracy, and consequently upon the workers, the regime retained elements of compromise. All the same, the international and the internal situation of German capitalism left no more room for concessions. As Social Democracy saved the bourgeoisie from the proletarian revolution, fascism came in its turn to liberate the bourgeoisie from Social Democracy. Hitler's coup is only the final link in the chain of counter-revolutionary shifts.

The petty bourgeois is hostile to the idea of development, for development goes immutably against him; progress has brought him nothing except irredeemable debts. National Socialism rejects not only Marxism but Darwinism. The Nazis curse materialism because the victories of technology over nature have signified the triumph of large capital over small. The leaders of the movement are liquidating 'intellectualism' because they themselves possess second- and third-rate intellects, and above all because their historic role does not permit them to pursue a single thought to its conclusion. The petty bourgeois needs a higher authority, which stands above matter and above history, and which is safeguarded from competition, inflation, crisis, and the auction block. To evolution, materialist thought, and rationalism – of the twentieth, nineteenth, and eighteenth centuries – is counterposed in his mind national idealism as the source of heroic inspiration. Hitler's nation is the mythological shadow of the petty bourgeoisie itself, a pathetic delirium of a thousand-year Reich.

In order to raise it above history, the nation is given the support of the race. History is viewed as the emanation of the race. The qualities of the race are construed without relation to changing social conditions. Rejecting 'economic thought' as base, National Socialism descends a stage lower: from economic materialism it appeals to zoologic materialism.

The theory of race, specially created, it seems, for some pretentious self-educated individual seeking a universal key to all the secrets of life, appears particularly melancholy in the light of the history of ideas. In order to create the religion of pure German blood, Hitler was obliged to borrow at second hand the ideas of racism from a Frenchman, Count Gobineau [a nineteenth-century pioneer of systematic racist theorising], a diplomat and a literary dilettante. Hitler found the political methodology ready-made in Italy, where Mussolini had borrowed largely from the Marxist theory of the class struggle. Marxism itself is the fruit of union among German philosophy, French history, and British economics. To investigate retrospectively the genealogy of ideas, even those most reactionary and muddleheaded, is to leave not a trace of racism standing.

The immense poverty of National Socialist philosophy did not, of course, hinder the academic sciences from entering Hitler's wake with all sails unfurled, once his victory was sufficiently plain. For the majority of the professorial rabble, the years of the Weimar regime were periods of riot and alarm. Historians, economists, jurists, and philosophers were lost in guesswork as to which of the contending criteria of truth was right, that is, which of the camps would turn out in the end the master of the situation. The fascist dictatorship eliminates the doubts of the Fausts and the vacillations of the Hamlets of the university rostrums. Coming out of the twilight of parliamentary relativity, knowledge once again enters into the kingdom of absolutes. Einstein has been obliged to pitch his tent outside the boundaries of Germany.

On the plane of politics, racism is a vapid and bombastic variety of chauvinism in alliance with phrenology. As the ruined nobility sought solace in the gentility of its blood, so the pauperised petty bourgeoisie befuddles itself with fairytales concerning the special superiorities of its race. Worthy of attention is the fact that the leaders of National Socialism are not native Germans but interlopers from Austria, like Hitler himself, from the former Baltic provinces of the Tsar's empire, like [Nazi racist propagandist Alfred] Rosenberg; and from colonial countries, like [Rudolf] Hess, who is Hitler's present alternate for the party leadership. A barbarous din of nationalisms on the frontiers of civilisation was required in order to instil into its 'leaders' those ideas which later found response in the hearts of the most barbarous classes in Germany.

Personality and class – liberalism and Marxism – are evil. The nation – is good. But at the threshold of private property this philosophy is turned inside out. Salvation lies only in personal private property. The idea of national property is the spawn of Bolshevism. Deifying the nation, the petty bourgeois does not want to give it anything. On the contrary, he expects the nation to endow him with property and to safeguard him from the worker and the process-server. Unfortunately, the Third Reich will bestow nothing upon the petty bourgeois except new taxes.

In the sphere of modern economy, international in its ties and anonymous in its methods, the principle of race seems unearthed from a medieval graveyard. The Nazis set out with concessions beforehand; the purity of race, which must be certified in the kingdom of the spirit by a passport must be demonstrated in the sphere of economy chiefly by efficiency. Under contemporary conditions this means competitive capacity. Through the back door, racism returns to economic liberalism, freed from political liberties.

Nationalism in economy comes down in practice to impotent though savage outbursts of anti-Semitism. The Nazis abstract the usurious or banking capital from the modern economic system because it is of the spirit of evil; and, as is well known, it is precisely in this sphere that the Jewish bourgeoisie occupies an important position. Bowing down before capitalism as a whole, the petty bourgeois declares war against the evil spirit of gain in the guise of the Polish Jew in a long-skirted caftan and usually without a cent in his pocket. The pogrom becomes the supreme evidence of racial superiority.

The program with which National Socialism came to power reminds one very much – alas – of a Jewish department store in an obscure province. What won't you find here – cheap in price and in quality still lower! Recollections of the 'happy' days of free competition, and hazy evocations of the stability of class society; hopes for the regeneration of the colonial empire, and dreams of a shut-in economy; phrases about a return from Roman law back to the Germanic, and pleas for an American moratorium; an envious hostility to inequality in the person of a proprietor in an automobile, and animal fear of equality in the person of a worker in a cap and without a collar; the frenzy of nationalism, and the fear of world creditors … all the refuse of international political thought has gone to fill up the spiritual treasury of the new Germanic Messianism.

Fascism has opened up the depths of society for politics. Today, not only in peasant homes but also in city skyscrapers, there lives alongside of the twentieth century the tenth or the thirteenth. A hundred million people use electricity and still believe in the magic power of signs and exorcisms. The Pope of Rome broadcasts over the radio about the miraculous transformation of water into wine. Movie stars go to mediums. Aviators who pilot miraculous mechanisms created by man's genius wear amulets on their sweaters. What inexhaustible reserves they possess of darkness, ignorance, and savagery! Despair has raised them to their feet, fascism has given them a banner. Everything that should have been eliminated from the national organism in the form of cultural excrement in the course of the normal development of society has now come gushing out from the throat; capitalist society is puking up the undigested barbarism. Such is the physiology of National Socialism.

German fascism, like Italian fascism, raised itself to power on the backs of the petty bourgeoisie, which it turned into a battering ram against the organisations of the working class and the institutions of democracy. But fascism in power is least of all the rule of the petty bourgeoisie. On the contrary, it is the most ruthless dictatorship of monopoly capital. Mussolini is right: the middle classes are incapable of independent policies. During periods of great crisis they are called upon to reduce to absurdity the policies of one of the two basic classes. Fascism succeeded in putting them at the service of capital. Such slogans as state control of trusts and the elimination of unearned income were thrown overboard immediately upon the assumption of power. Instead, the particularism of German 'lands' leaning upon the peculiarities of the petty bourgeoisie gave way to capitalist-police centralism. Every success of the internal and foreign policies of National Socialism will inevitably mean the further crushing of small capital by large.

The programme of petty bourgeois illusions is not discarded; it is simply torn away from reality, and dissolved in ritualistic acts. The unification of all classes reduces itself to semi-symbolic compulsory labour and to the confiscation of the labour holiday of May Day for the 'benefit of the people'. The preservation of the Gothic script as opposed to the Latin is a symbolic revenge for the yoke of the world market. The dependence upon the international bankers, Jews among their number, is not eased an iota, wherefore it is forbidden to slaughter animals according to the Talmudic ritual. If the road to hell is paved with good intentions, then the avenues of the Third Reich are paved with symbols.

Reducing the programme of petty bourgeois illusions to a naked bureaucratic masquerade, National Socialism raises itself over the nation as the worst form of imperialism. Absolutely vain are hopes that Hitler's government will fail today or tomorrow, a victim of its internal inconsistency. The Nazis required the programme in order to assume power; but power serves Hitler not at all for the purpose of fuming the programme. His tasks are assigned him by monopoly capital. The compulsory concentration of all forces and resources of the people in the interests of imperialism – the true historic mission of the fascist dictatorship – means preparation for war; and this task, in its turn, brooks no internal resistance and leads to a further mechanical concentration of power. Fascism cannot be reformed or retired from service. It can only be overthrown. The political orbit of the regime leans upon the alternative, war or revolution.

Postscript

The first anniversary of the Nazi dictatorship is approaching. All the tendencies of the regime have had time to take on a clear and distinct character. The 'socialist' revolution pictured by the petty bourgeois masses as a necessary supplement to the national revolution is officially liquidated and condemned. The brotherhood of classes found its culmination in the fact that on a day especially appointed by the government the haves renounced the hors d'oeuvre and dessert in favour of the have-nots. The struggle against unemployment is reduced to the cutting of semi-starvation doles in two. The rest is the task of uniformed statistics. 'Planned' autarky is simply a new stage of economic disintegration.

The more impotent the police regime of the Nazi is in the field of national economy, the more it is forced to transfer its efforts to the field of foreign policy. This corresponds fully to the inner dynamics of German capitalism, aggressive through and through. The sudden turn of the Nazi leaders to peaceful declarations could deceive only utter simpletons. What other method remains at Hitler's disposal to transfer the responsibility for internal distresses to external enemies and to accumulate under the press of the dictatorship the explosive force of nationalism? This part of the programme, outlined openly even prior to the Nazis' assumption of power, is now being fulfilled with iron logic before the eyes of the world. The date of the new European catastrophe will be determined by the time necessary for the arming of Germany. It is not a question of months, but neither is it a question of decades. It will be but a few years before Europe is again plunged into a war, unless Hitler is forestalled in time by the inner forces of Germany.

2 November 1933

The Lessons of Spain: The Last Warning*
(December 1937)

Menshevism and Bolshevism in Spain

All general staffs are studying closely the military operations in Ethiopia, in Spain, and in the Far East in preparation for the great future war. The battles of the Spanish proletariat, heat lightning flashes of the coming world revolution, should be no less attentively studied by the revolutionary staffs. Under this condition and this condition alone will the coming events not take us unawares.

Three ideologies fought – with unequal forces – in the so-called republican camp, namely, Menshevism, Bolshevism, and anarchism. As regards the bourgeois republican parties, they were without either independent ideas or independent political significance and were able to maintain themselves only by climbing on the backs of the reformists and Anarchists. Moreover, it is no exaggeration to say that the leaders of Spanish anarcho-syndicalism did everything to repudiate their doctrine and virtually reduce its significance to zero. Actually two doctrines in the so-called republican camp fought – Menshevism and Bolshevism.

According to the Socialists and Stalinists, that is, the Mensheviks of the first and second instances, the Spanish revolution was called upon to solve only its 'democratic' tasks, for which a united front with the 'democratic' bourgeoisie was indispensable. From this point of view, any and all attempts of the proletariat to go beyond the limits of bourgeois democracy are not only premature but also fatal. Furthermore, on the agenda stands not the revolution but the struggle against insurgent Franco.

Fascism, however, is not feudal but bourgeois reaction. A successful fight against bourgeois reaction can be waged only with the forces and methods of the proletariat revolution. Menshevism, itself a branch of bourgeois thought, does not have and cannot have any inkling of these facts.

The Bolshevik point of view, clearly expressed only by the young section of the Fourth International, takes the theory of permanent revolution as its starting point, namely, that even

* From Trotsky Internet Archive (www.marxists.org/archive/trotsky/1937/xx/spain01. htm), with revisions by the editors.

purely democratic problems, like the liquidation of semi-feudal landownership, cannot be solved without the conquest of power by the proletariat; but this in turn places the socialist revolution on the agenda. Moreover, during the very first stages of the revolution, the Spanish workers themselves posed in practice not merely democratic problems but also purely socialist ones. The demand not to transgress the bounds of bourgeois democracy signifies in practice not a defence of the democratic revolution but a repudiation of it. Only through an overturn in agrarian relations could the peasantry, the great mass of the population, have been transformed into a powerful bulwark against fascism. But the landowners are intimately bound up with the commercial, industrial, and banking bourgeoisie, and the bourgeois intelligentsia that depends on them. The party of the proletariat was thus faced with a choice between going with the peasant masses or with the liberal bourgeoisie. There could be only one reason to include the peasantry and the liberal bourgeoisie in the same coalition at the same time: to help the bourgeoisie deceive the peasantry and thus isolate the workers. The agrarian revolution could have been accomplished only against the bourgeoisie, and therefore only through the masses of the dictatorship of the proletariat. There is no third, intermediate regime.

From the standpoint of theory, the most astonishing thing about Stalin's Spanish policy is the utter disregard for the ABC of Leninism. After a delay of several decades – and what decades! – the Comintern has fully rehabilitated the doctrine of Menshevism. More than that, the Comintern has contrived to render this doctrine more 'consistent' and by that token more absurd. In tsarist Russia, on the threshold of 1905, the formula of 'purely democratic revolution' had behind it, in any case, immeasurably more arguments than in 1937 in Spain. It is hardly astonishing that in modern Spain 'the liberal labour policy' of Menshevism has been converted into the reactionary anti-labour policy of Stalinism. At the same time the doctrine of the Mensheviks, this caricature of Marxism, has been converted into a caricature of itself.

'Theory' of the Popular Front

It would be naive, however, to think that the politics of the Comintern in Spain stem from a theoretical 'mistake'. Stalinism is not guided by Marxist theory, or for that matter any theory at all, but by the empirical interests of the Soviet bureaucracy. In their intimate circles, the Soviet cynics mock Dimitrov's 'philosophy' of the Popular Front. But they have at their disposal for deceiving the masses large cadres of propagators of this holy formula, sincere ones and cheats, simpletons and charlatans. Louis Fischer [a well-known US left liberal journalist], with his ignorance and smugness, with his provincial rationalism and congenital deafness to revolution, is the most repulsive representative of this unattractive brotherhood. 'The union of progressive forces!' 'The Triumph of the idea of the Popular Front!' 'The assault of the Trotskyists on the unity of the anti-fascist ranks!' ... Who will believe that the *Communist Manifesto* was written 90 years ago?

The theoreticians of the Popular Front do not essentially go beyond the first rule of arithmetic, that is, addition: 'Communists' plus Socialists plus Anarchists plus liberals add up to a total which is greater than their respective isolated numbers. Such is all their wisdom. However, arithmetic alone does not suffice here. One needs as well at least mechanics. The law of the parallelogram of forces applies to politics as well. In such a parallelogram, we know that the resultant is shorter, the more component forces diverge from each other. When political allies tend to pull in opposite directions, the resultant may prove equal to zero.

A bloc of divergent political groups of the working class is sometimes completely indispensable for the solution of common practical problems. In certain historical circumstances, such a bloc is capable of attracting the oppressed petty bourgeois masses whose interests are close to the interests of the proletariat. The joint force of such a bloc can prove far stronger than the sum of the forces of each of its component parts. On the contrary, the political alliance between the proletariat and the bourgeoisie, whose interests on basic questions in the present epoch diverge at an angle of 180 degrees, as a general rule is capable only of paralysing the revolutionary force of the proletariat.

Civil war, in which the force of naked coercion is hardly effective, demands of its participants the spirit of supreme self-abnegation. The workers and peasants can assure victory only if they wage a struggle for their own emancipation. Under these conditions, to subordinate the proletariat to the leadership of the bourgeoisie means beforehand to assure defeat in the civil war.

These simple truths are least of all the products of pure theoretical analysis. On the contrary, they represent the unassailable deduction from the entire experience of history, beginning at least with 1848. The modern history of bourgeois society is filled with all sorts of Popular Fronts, i.e. the most diverse political combinations for the deception of the toilers. The Spanish experience is only a new and tragic link in this chain of crimes and betrayals.

Alliance with the Bourgeoisie's Shadow

Politically most striking is the fact that the Spanish Popular Front lacked in reality even a parallelogram of forces. The bourgeoisie's place was occupied by its shadow. Through the medium of the Stalinists, Socialists, and Anarchists, the Spanish bourgeoisie subordinated the proletariat to itself without even bothering to participate in the Popular Front. The overwhelming majority of the exploiters of all political shades openly went over to the camp of Franco. Without any theory of 'permanent revolution,' the Spanish bourgeoisie understood from the outset that the revolutionary mass movement, no matter how it starts, is directed against private ownership of land and the means of production, and that it is utterly impossible to cope with this movement by democratic measures.

That is why only insignificant debris from the possessing classes remained in the republican camp: Messrs Azaña, Companys, and the like* – political attorneys of the bourgeoisie but not the bourgeoisie itself. Having staked everything on a military dictatorship, the possessing classes were able, at the same time, to make use of the political representatives of yesterday in order to paralyse, disorganise, and afterward strangle the socialist movement of the masses in 'republican' territory.

Without in the slightest degree representing the Spanish bourgeoisie, the left republicans still less represented the workers and peasants. They represented no one but themselves. Thanks, however, to their allies – the Socialists, Stalinists, and Anarchists –

---

* Manuel Azaña was President of the Spanish Republic and a leader of the liberal Republican Party; Luis Companys, an advocate of Catalonian nationalism, was a part of Spain's popular front as a leader of the Esquerra Party, serving as president of the province of Catalonia. – Editors

these political phantoms played the decisive role in the revolution. How? Very simply. By incarnating the principles of the 'democratic revolution', that is, the inviolability of private property.

The Stalinists in the Popular Front

The reasons of the rise of the Spanish Popular Front and its inner mechanics are perfectly clear. The task of the retired leaders of the left bourgeoisie consisted in checking the revolution of the masses and the regaining for themselves the lost confidence of the exploiters: 'Why do you need Franco if we, the republicans, can do the same thing?' The interests of Azaña and Companys fully coincided at this central point with the interests of Stalin, who needed to gain the confidence of the French and British bourgeoisie by proving to them in action his ability to preserve 'order' against 'anarchy'. Stalin needed Azaña and Companys as a cover before the workers: Stalin himself, of course, is for socialism, but one must take care not to repel the republican bourgeoisie! Azaña and Companys needed Stalin as an experienced executioner, with the authority of a revolutionist. Without him, so insignificant a crew never could nor would have dared to attack the workers.

The classic reformists of the Second International, long ago derailed by the course of the class struggle, began to feel a new tide of confidence, thanks to the support of Moscow. This support, incidentally, was not given to all reformists but only to those most reactionary. Caballero represented that face of the Socialist Party that was turned toward the workers' aristocracy. Negrin and Prieto always looked towards the bourgeoisie.* Negrin won over Caballero with the help of Moscow. The left Socialists and Anarchists, the captives of the Popular Front, tried, it is true, to save whatever could be saved of democracy. But inasmuch as they did not dare to mobilise the masses against the gendarmes of the Popular Front, their efforts at the end were reduced to plaints and wails. The Stalinists were thus in alliance with the extreme right, avowedly bourgeois wing of the Socialist Party. They directed their repressions against the left – the POUM, the Anarchists, the

---

*   Largo Caballero was a leader of the left wing of the Spanish Socialist Party and for a time served as prime minster, later replaced by Juan Negrin who, with Indalacio Prieto, led the reformist wing of the Socialist Party. – Editors

'left' Socialists – in other words, against the centrist groupings who reflected, even in a most remote degree, the pressure of the revolutionary masses.

This political fact, very significant in itself, provides at the same time the measure of the degeneration of the Comintern in the last few years. I once defined Stalinism as bureaucratic centrism, and events brought a series of corroborations of the correctness of this definition. But it is obviously obsolete today. The interests of the Bonapartist bureaucracy can no longer be reconciled with centrist hesitation and vacillation. In search of reconciliation with the bourgeoisie, the Stalinist clique is capable of entering into alliances only with the most conservative groupings among the international labour aristocracy. This has acted to fix definitively the counter-revolutionary character of Stalinism on the international arena.

Counter-Revolutionary Superiorities of Stalinism

This brings us right up to the solution of the enigma of how and why the Communist Party of Spain, so insignificant numerically and with a leadership so poor in calibre, proved capable of gathering into its hands all reins of power, in the face of the incomparably more powerful organisations of the Socialists and Anarchists. The usual explanation that the Stalinists simply bartered Soviet weapons for power is far too superficial. In return for munitions, Moscow received Spanish gold. According to the laws of the capitalist market, this covers everything. How then did Stalin contrive to get power in the bargain?

The customary answer is that the Soviet government, having raised its authority in the eyes of the masses by furnishing military supplies, demanded as a condition of its 'collaboration' drastic measures against revolutionists and thus removed dangerous opponents from its path. All this is quite indisputable but it is only one aspect of the matter, and the least important at that.

Despite the 'authority' created by Soviet shipments, the Spanish Communist Party remained a small minority and met with ever-growing hatred on the part of the workers. On the other hand, it was not enough for Moscow to set conditions; Valencia had to accede to them. This is the heart of the matter. Not only

Zamora, Companys, and Negrin, but also Caballero, during his incumbency as premier, were all more or less ready to accede to the demands of Moscow. Why? Because these gentlemen themselves wished to keep the revolution within bourgeois limits. They were deathly afraid of every revolutionary onslaught of the workers. Stalin with his munitions and with his counterrevolutionary ultimatum was a saviour for all these groups. He guaranteed them, so they hoped, military victory over Franco, and at the same time, he freed them from all responsibility for the course of the revolution. They hastened to put their Socialist and Anarchist masks into the closet in the hope of making use of them again after Moscow re-established bourgeois democracy for them. As the finishing touch to their comfort, these gentlemen could henceforth, justify their betrayal to the workers by the necessity of a military agreement with Stalin. Stalin on his part justifies his counter-revolutionary politics by the necessity of maintaining an alliance with the republican bourgeoisie.

Only from this broader point of view can we get a clear picture of the angelic toleration which such champions of justice and freedom as Azaña, Negrin, Companys, Caballero, Garcia Oliver,* and others showed towards the crimes of the GPU [the Soviet Union's secret police, who were operating in Spain]. If they had no other choice, as they affirm, it was not at all because they had no means of paying for airplanes and tanks other than with the heads of the revolutionists and the rights of the workers, but because their own 'purely democratic', that is, anti-socialist, programme could be realised by no other measures save terror. When the workers and peasants enter on the path of their revolution – when they seize factories and estates, drive out old owners, conquer power in the provinces – then the bourgeois counter-revolution – democratic, Stalinist, or fascist alike – has no other means of checking this movement except through bloody coercion, supplemented by lies and deceit. The superiority of the Stalinist clique on this road consisted in its ability to apply instantly measures that were beyond the capacity of Azaña, Companys, Negrin, and their left allies.

---

* José Garcia Oliver was in the right wing of the anarchist movement, served as minister of justice in the Republican government, and collaborated with the Stalinists in repressing revolutionaries. – Editors

Stalin Confirms in His Own Way the Correctness of the Theory of Permanent Revolution

Two irreconcilable programmes thus confronted each other on the territory of republican Spain. On the one hand, the programme of saving at any cost private property from the proletariat, and saving as far as possible democracy from Franco; on the other hand, the programme of abolishing private property through the conquest of power by the proletariat. The first programme expressed the interest of capitalism through the medium of the labour aristocracy, the top petty bourgeois circles, and especially the Soviet bureaucracy. The second programme translated into the language of Marxism the tendencies of the revolutionary mass movement, not fully conscious but powerful. Unfortunately for the revolution, between the handful of Bolsheviks and the revolutionary proletariat stood counter-revolutionary wall of the Popular Front.

The policy of the Popular Front was, in its turn, not at all determined by the blackmail of Stalin as supplier of arms. There was, of course, no lack of blackmail. But the reason for the success of this blackmail was inherent in the inner conditions of the revolution itself. For six years, its social setting was the growing onslaught of the masses against the regime of semi-feudal and bourgeois property. The need of defending this property by the most extreme measures threw the bourgeoisie into Franco's arms. The republican government had promised the bourgeoisie to defend property by 'democratic' measures, but revealed, especially in July 1936, its complete bankruptcy. When the situation on the property front became even more threatening than on the military front, the democrats of all colours, including the Anarchists, bowed before Stalin; and he found no other methods, in his own arsenal than the methods of Franco.

The hounding of 'Trotskyists', POUMists, revolutionary Anarchists and left Socialists; the filthy slander; the false documents; the tortures in Stalinist prisons; the murders from ambush – without all this the bourgeois regime under the republican flag could not have lasted even two months. The GPU proved to be the master of the situation only because it defended the interests of the bourgeoisie against the proletariat more consistently than the others, that is, with the greatest baseness and bloodthirstiness.

In the struggle against the socialist revolution, the 'democratic' Kerensky at first sought support in the military dictatorship of Kornilov and later tried to enter Petrograd in the baggage train of the monarchist general Krasnov. On the other hand, the Bolsheviks were compelled, in order to carry the democratic revolution through to the end, to overthrow the government of 'democratic' charlatans and babblers. In the process they put an end thereby to every kind of attempt at military (or 'fascist') dictatorship.

The Spanish Revolution once again demonstrates that it is impossible to defend democracy against the revolutionary masses otherwise than through the methods of fascist reaction. And conversely, it is impossible to conduct a genuine struggle against fascism otherwise than through the methods of the proletarian revolution. Stalin waged war against 'Trotskyism' (proletarian revolution), destroying democracy by the Bonapartist measures of the GPU. This refutes once again and once and for all the old Menshevik theory, adopted by the Comintern, in accordance with which the democratic and socialist revolutions are transformed into two independent historic chapters, separated from each other in point of time. The work of the Moscow executioners confirms in its own way the correctness of the theory of permanent revolution.

Role of the Anarchists

The Anarchists had no independent position of any kind in the Spanish Revolution. All they did was waver between Bolshevism and Menshevism. More precisely, the Anarchist workers instinctively yearned to enter the Bolshevik road (19 July 1936, and May Days of 1937) while their leaders, on the contrary, with all their might drove the masses into the camp of the Popular Front, that is, of the bourgeois regime.

The Anarchists revealed a fatal lack of understanding of the laws of the revolution and its tasks by seeking to limit themselves to their own trade unions, that is, to organisations permeated with the routine of peaceful times, and by ignoring what went on outside the framework of the trade unions, among the masses, among the political parties, and in the government apparatus. Had the Anarchists been revolutionists, they would first of all have called for the creation of soviets, which unite the representatives of all the toilers of city and country, including the most oppressed strata, who never joined the trade unions. The revolutionary workers would have naturally occupied the dominant position in these soviets. The Stalinists would have remained an insignificant minority. The proletariat would have convinced itself of its own invincible strength. The apparatus of the bourgeois state would have hung suspended in the air. One strong blow would have sufficed to pulverise this apparatus. The socialist revolution would have received a powerful impetus. The French proletariat would not for long permitted Leon Blum to blockade the proletariat revolution beyond the Pyrenees. Neither could the Moscow bureaucracy have permitted itself such a luxury. The most difficult questions would have been solved as they arose.

Instead of this, the anarcho-syndicalists, seeking to hide from 'politics' in the trade unions, turned out to be, to the great surprise of the whole world and themselves, a fifth wheel in the cart of bourgeois democracy. But not for long; a fifth wheel is superfluous. After Garcia Oliver and his cohorts helped Stalin and his henchmen to take power away from the workers, the anarchists themselves were driven out of the government of the Popular Front. Even then they found nothing better to do than jump on the victor's bandwagon and assure him of their devotion. The fear of the petty bourgeois before the big bourgeois, of the petty bureaucrat before the big bureaucrat, they covered up with lachrymose speeches about the sanctity of the united front (between a victim and the executioners) and about the inadmissibility of every kind of dictatorship, including their own. 'After all, we could have taken power in July 1936 …' 'After all, we could have taken power in May 1937 …' The Anarchists begged Stalin-Negrin to recognise and reward their treachery to the revolution. A revolting picture!

In and of itself, this self-justification that 'we did not seize power not because we were unable but because we did not wish to, because we were against every kind of dictatorship', and the like, contains an irrevocable condemnation of anarchism as an utterly anti-revolutionary doctrine. To renounce the conquest of power is voluntarily to leave the power with those who wield it, the exploiters. The essence of every revolution consisted and consists in putting a new class in power, thus enabling it to realise its own programme in life. It is impossible to wage war and to reject victory. It is impossible to lead the masses towards insurrection without preparing for the conquest of power.

No one could have prevented the Anarchists after the conquest of power from establishing the sort of regime they deem necessary, assuming, of course, that their programme is realisable. But the Anarchist leaders themselves lost faith in it. They hid from power not because they are against 'every kind of dictatorship' – in actuality, grumbling and whining, they supported and still support the dictatorship of Stalin-Negrin – but because they completely lost their principles and courage, if they ever had any. They were afraid of everything: 'isolation', 'involvement', 'fascism'. They were afraid of France and England. More than anything these phrasemongers feared the revolutionary masses.

The renunciation of the conquest of power inevitably throws every workers' organisation into the swamp of reformism and turns it into a toy of the bourgeoisie; it cannot be otherwise in view of the class structure of society. In opposing the goal, the conquest of power, the Anarchists could not in the end fail to oppose the means, the revolution. The leaders of the CNT [National Confederation of Labour] and the FAI [Iberian Anarchist Federation] not only helped the bourgeoisie hold on to the shadow of power in July 1936; they also helped it to re-establish bit by bit what it had lost at one stroke. In May 1937, they sabotaged the uprising of the workers and thereby saved the dictatorship of the bourgeoisie. Thus anarchism, which wished merely to be anti-political, proved in reality to be anti-revolutionary and in the more critical moments – counter-revolutionary.

The Anarchist theoreticians, who after the great test of 1931–37 continue to repeat the old reactionary nonsense about Kronstadt, and who affirm that 'Stalinism is the inevitable result of Marxism and Bolshevism', simply demonstrate by this they are forever dead for the revolution.

You say that Marxism is in itself depraved and Stalinism is its legitimate progeny? But why are we revolutionary Marxists engaged in mortal combat with Stalinism throughout the world? Why does the Stalinist gang see in Trotskyism its chief enemy? Why does every approach to our views or our methods of action (Durruti, Andrés Nin, Landau, and others*) compel the Stalinist

---

* Kurt Landau was an Austrian and former Trotskyist who supported the POUM, and Andrés Nin was a former Trotskyist and a leader of the POUM – both were kidnapped and murdered by the GPU. Buenaventura Durruti was a revolutionary anarchist leader who died under mysterious circumstances during the defence of Madrid. – Editors

gangsters to resort to bloody reprisals. Why, on the other hand, did the leaders of Spanish anarchism serve, during the time of the Moscow and Madrid crimes of the GPU, as ministers under Caballero-Negrin, that is as servants of the bourgeoisie and Stalin? Why even now, under the pretext of fighting fascism, do the Anarchists remain voluntary captives of Stalin-Negrin, the executioners of the revolution, who have demonstrated their incapacity to fight fascism?

By hiding behind Kronstadt and Makhno, the attorneys of anarchism will deceive nobody. In the Kronstadt episode and the struggle with Makhno, we defended the proletarian revolution from the peasant counter-revolution.* The Spanish Anarchists defended and continue to defend bourgeois counter-revolution from the proletariat revolution. No sophistry will delete from the annals of history the fact that anarchism and Stalinism in the Spanish Revolution were on one side of the barricades while the working masses with the revolutionary Marxists were on the other. Such is the truth which will forever remain in the consciousness of the proletariat!

Role of the POUM

The record of the POUM is not much better. In the point of theory, it tried, to be sure, to base itself on the formula of permanent revolution (that is why the Stalinists called the POUMists 'Trotskyists'). But the revolution is not satisfied with theoretical avowals. Instead of mobilising the masses against the reformist leaders, including the Anarchists, the POUM tried to convince these gentlemen of the superiorities of socialism over capitalism. This tuning fork gave the pitch to all the articles and speeches of the POUM leaders. In order not to quarrel with the Anarchist leaders, they did not form their own nuclei inside the CNT, and in general did not conduct any kind of work there. To avoid

---

* This refers to an anarchist-supported uprising in 1921 in the early Soviet Republic, and to the peasant guerrilla forces led by anarchist Nestor Makhno during the Russian Civil War of 1918–21 – sometimes allied with the Bolsheviks, sometimes fighting against them. Both were repressed by the Red Army which Trotsky commanded, actions denounced by anarchists down through the 1930s and beyond. For balanced accounts of both, see Paul Avrich, *Kronstadt 1921* (New York: W. W. Norton, 1974) and *The Russian Anarchists* (New York: W. W. Norton, 1978). – Editors

sharp conflicts, they did not carry on revolutionary work in the republican army. They built instead 'their own' trade unions and 'their own' militia, which guarded 'their own' institutions or occupied 'their own' section of the front.

By isolating the revolutionary vanguard from the class, the POUM rendered the vanguard impotent and left the class without leadership. Politically the POUM remained throughout far closer to the Popular Front, for whose left wing it provided the cover, than to Bolshevism. That the POUM nevertheless fell victim to bloody and base repressions was due to the failure of the Popular Front to fulfil its mission, namely to stifle the socialist revolution – except by cutting off, piece by piece, its own left flank.

Contrary to its own intentions, the POUM proved to be, in the final analysis, the chief obstacle on the road to the creation of a revolutionary party. The platonic or diplomatic partisans of the Fourth International like [Henricus] Sneevliet, the leader of the Dutch Revolutionary Socialist Workers Party, who demonstratively supported the POUM in its halfway measures, its indecisiveness and evasiveness, in short, in its centrism, took upon themselves the greatest responsibility. Revolution abhors centrism. Revolution exposes and annihilates centrism. In passing, the revolution discredits the friends and attorneys of centrism. That is one of the most important lessons of the Spanish Revolution.

The Problem of Arming

The Socialists and Anarchists who seek to justify their capitulation to Stalin by the necessity of paying for Moscow's weapons with principles and conscience simply lie unskilfully. Of course, many of them would have preferred to disentangle themselves without murders and frame-ups. But every goal demands corresponding means. Beginning with April 1931, that is, long before the military intervention of Moscow, the Socialists and Anarchists did everything in their power to check the proletariat revolution. Stalin taught them how to carry this work to its conclusion. They became Stalin's criminal accomplices only because they were his political co-thinkers.

Had the Anarchist leaders in the least resembled revolutionists, they would have answered the first piece of blackmail from

Moscow not only by continuing the socialist offensive but also by exposing Stalin's counter-revolutionary conditions before the world's working class. They would have thus forced the Moscow bureaucracy to choose openly between the socialist revolution and the Franco dictatorship. The Thermidorian bureaucracy fears and hates revolution. But it also fears being strangled in a fascist ring. Besides, it depends on the workers. All indications are that Moscow would have been forced to supply arms, and possibly at more reasonable prices.

But the world does not revolve around Stalinist Moscow. During a year and a half of civil war, the Spanish war industry could and should have been strengthened and developed by converting a number of civilian plants to war production. This work was not carried out only because Stalin and his Spanish allies equally feared the initiative of the workers' organisations. A strong war industry would have become a powerful instrument in the hands of the workers. The leaders of the Popular Front preferred to depend on Moscow.

It is precisely on this question that the perfidious role of the Popular Front was very strikingly revealed. It thrust upon the workers' organisations the responsibility for the treacherous deals of the bourgeoisie of Stalin. Insofar as the Anarchists remained a minority, they could not, of course, immediately hinder the ruling bloc from assuming whatever obligations they pleased toward Moscow and the masters of Moscow: London and Paris. But without ceasing to be the best fighters on the front, they could have and should have openly dissociated themselves from the betrayals and betrayers; they could and should have explained the real situation to the masses, mobilised them against the bourgeois government, and augmented their own forces from day to day in order in the end to conquer power and with it the Moscow arms.

And what if Moscow, in the absence of a Popular Front, should have refused to give arms altogether? And what, we answer to this, if the Soviet Union did not exist altogether? Revolutions have been victorious up to this time not at all thanks to high and mighty foreign patrons who supplied them with arms. As a rule, counter-revolution enjoyed foreign patronage. Must we recall the experiences of the intervention of French, English, American, Japanese, and other armies against the Soviets? The proletariat of Russia conquered domestic reaction and foreign interventionists without military support from the outside. Revolutions succeed, in the first place, with the help of a bold social programme, which gives the masses the possibility of seizing weapons that are on the territory and disorganising the army of the enemy. The Red Army seized French, English, and American military supplies and drove the foreign expeditionary corps into the sea. Has this really been forgotten?

If at the head of the armed workers and peasants, that is, at the head of so-called republican Spain, were revolutionists and not cowardly agents of the bourgeoisie, the problem of arming would never have been paramount. The army of Franco, including the colonial Riffians [Berber tribes from the colony of Spanish Morocco] and the soldiers of Mussolini, was not at all immune to revolutionary contagion. Surrounded by the conflagration of the socialist uprising, the soldiers of fascism would have proved to be an insignificant quantity. Arms and military 'geniuses' were not lacking in Madrid and Barcelona; what was lacking was a revolutionary party!

Conditions for Victory

The conditions for victory of the masses in the civil war against the army exploiters are very simple in their essence.

1. The fighters of a revolutionary army must be clearly aware of the fact that they are fighting for their full social liberation and not for the re-establishment of the old ('democratic') forms of exploitation.
2. The workers and peasants in the rear of the revolutionary army as well as in the rear of the enemy must know and understand the same thing.
3. The propaganda on their own front as well as on the enemy front and in both rears must be completely permeated with the spirit of social revolution. The slogan 'First victory, then reforms', is the slogan of all oppressors and exploiters from the biblical kings down to Stalin.
4. Politics are determined by those classes and strata that participate in the struggle. The revolutionary masses must have a state apparatus that directly and immediately

expresses their will. Only the soviets of workers', soldiers', and peasants' deputies can act as such an apparatus.

5. The revolutionary army must not only proclaim but also immediately realise in life the more pressing measures of social revolution in the provinces won by them: the expropriation of provisions, manufactured articles, and other stores on hand and the transfer of these to the needy; the re-division of shelter and housing in the interests of the toilers and especially of the families of the fighters; the expropriation of the land and agricultural inventory in the interests of the peasants; the establishment of workers' control and soviet power in the place of the former bureaucracy.

6. Enemies of the socialist revolution, that is, exploiting elements and their agents, even if masquerading as 'democrats', 'republicans', 'Socialists', and 'Anarchists', must be mercilessly driven out of the army.

7. At the head of each military unit must be placed commissars possessing irreproachable authority as revolutionists and soldiers.

8. In every military unit there must be a firmly welded nucleus of the most self-sacrificing fighters, recommended by the workers' organisations. The members of this nucleus have but one privilege: to be first under fire.

9. The commanding corps necessarily includes at first many alien and unreliable elements among the personnel. Their testing, retesting, and sifting must be carried through on the basis of combat experience, recommendations of commissars, and testimonials of rank-and-file fighters. Coincident with this must proceed an intense training of commanders drawn from the ranks of revolutionary workers.

10. The strategy of civil war must combine the rules of military art with the tasks of the social revolution. Not only in propaganda but also in military operations it is necessary to take into account the social composition of the various military units of the enemy (bourgeois volunteers, mobilised peasants or, as in Franco's case, colonial slaves); and in choosing lines of operation, it is necessary to rigorously take into consideration the social structure of the corresponding territories (industrial regions, peasant regions, revolutionary

or reactionary, regions of oppressed nationalities, etc.). In brief, revolutionary policy dominates strategy.

11. Both the revolutionary government and the executive committee of the workers and peasants must know how to win the complete confidence of the army and of the toiling population.

12. Foreign policy must have as its main objective the awakening of the revolutionary consciousness of the workers, the exploited peasants, and oppressed nationalities of the whole world.

Stalin Guaranteed the Conditions of Defeat

The conditions for victory, as we see, are perfectly plain. In their aggregate they bear the name of the socialist revolution. Not a single one of these conditions existed in Spain. The basic reason is – the absence of a revolutionary party. Stalin tried, it is true, to transfer to the soil of Spain, the outward practices of Bolshevism: the Politburo, commissars, cells, the GPU, etc. But he emptied these forms of their social content. He renounced the Bolshevik programme and with it the soviets as the necessary form for the revolutionary initiative of the masses. He placed the technique of Bolshevism at the service of bourgeois property. In his bureaucratic narrow-mindedness, he imagined that 'commissars' by themselves could guarantee victory. But the commissars of private property proved capable only of guaranteeing defeat.

The Spanish proletariat displayed first-rate military qualities. In its specific gravity in the country's economic life, in its political and cultural level, the Spanish proletariat stood on the first day of the revolution not below but above the Russian proletariat at the beginning of 1917. On the road to victory, its own organisations stood as the chief obstacles. The commanding clique of Stalinists, in accordance with their counter-revolutionary function, consisted of hirelings, careerists, declassed elements, and in general, all types of social refuse. The representatives of other labour organisations – incurable reformists, Anarchists phrasemongers, helpless centrists of the POUM – grumbled, groaned, wavered, manoeuvred, but in the end adapted themselves to the Stalinists. As a result of their joint activity, the camp of social revolution – workers and peasants

– proved to be subordinated to the bourgeoisie, or more correctly, to its shadow. It was bled white and its character destroyed.

There was no lack of heroism on the part of the masses or courage on the part of individual revolutionists. But the masses were left to their own resources while the revolutionists remained disunited, without a programme, without a plan of action. The 'republican' military commanders were more concerned with crushing the social revolution than with scoring military victories. The soldiers lost confidence in their commanders, the masses in the government; the peasants stepped aside; the workers became exhausted; defeat followed defeat; demoralisation grew apace. All this was not difficult to foresee from the beginning of the civil war. By setting itself the task of rescuing the capitalist regime, the Popular Front doomed itself to military defeat. By turning Bolshevism on its head, Stalin succeeded completely in fulfilling the role of gravedigger of the revolution.

It ought to be added that the Spanish experience once again demonstrates that Stalin failed completely to understand either the October Revolution or the Russian civil war. His slow moving provincial mind lagged hopelessly behind the tempestuous march of events in 1917–21. In those of his speeches and articles in 1917 where he expressed his own ideas, his later Thermidorian 'doctrine' is fully implanted. In this sense, Stalin in Spain in 1937 is the continuator of Stalin of the March 1917 conference of the Bolsheviks. But in 1917 he merely feared the revolutionary workers; in 1937 he strangled them. The opportunist had become the executioner.

'Civil War in the Rear'

But, after all, victory over the governments of Caballero and Negrin would have necessitated a civil war in the rear of the republican army! – the democratic philistine exclaims with horror. As if apart from this, in republican Spain no civil war has ever existed, and at that the basest and most perfidious one – the war of the proprietors and exploiters against the workers and peasants. This uninterrupted war finds expression in the arrests and murders of revolutionists, the crushing of the mass movement, the disarming of the workers, the arming of the bourgeois police, the abandoning of workers' detachments without arms and without help on the front, and finally, the artificial restriction of the development of war industry.

Each of these acts as a cruel blow to the front, direct military treason, dictated by the class interests of the bourgeoisie. But 'democratic' philistines – including Stalinists, Socialists, and Anarchists – regard the civil war of the bourgeoisie against the proletariat, even in areas most closely adjoining the front, as a natural and inescapable war, having as its tasks the safeguarding of the 'unity of the Popular Front'. On the other hand, the civil war of the proletariat against the 'republican' counter-revolution is, in the eyes of the same philistines, a criminal, 'fascist', Trotskyist war, disrupting ... 'the unity of the anti-fascist forces'. Scores of Norman Thomases, Major Atlees, Otto Bauers, Zyromskys, Malrauxes, and such petty pedlars of lies as Duranty and Louis Fischer spread this slavish wisdom throughout our planet.*
Meanwhile the government of the Popular Front moves from Madrid to Valencia, from Valencia to Barcelona.

If, as the facts attest, only the socialist revolution is capable of crushing fascism, then on the other hand a successful uprising of the proletariat is conceivable only when the ruling classes are caught in the vice of the greatest difficulties. However, the democratic philistines invoke precisely these difficulties as proof of the impressibility of the proletarian uprising. Were the proletariat to wait for the democratic philistines to tell them the hour of their liberation, they would remain slaves forever. To teach workers to recognise reactionary philistines under all their masks and to despise them regardless of the mask is the first and paramount duty of a revolutionist!

The Outcome

The dictatorship of the Stalinists over the republican camp is not long-lived in its essence. Should the defeats stemming from the politics of the Popular Front once more impel the Spanish

*   In addition to those already identified in previous footnotes, reference is made here to French novelist André Malraux, French Socialist Jean Zyromsky (who would soon join the Communist Party), and pro-Stalin *New York Times* correspondent Walter Duranty. All those cited were supporters of the Popular Front and hostile to revolutionary challenges to it in Spain.

proletariat to a revolutionary assault, this time successfully, the Stalinist clique will be swept away with an iron broom. But should Stalin – as is unfortunately the likelihood – succeed in bringing the work of gravedigger of the revolution to its conclusion, he will not even in this case earn thanks. The Spanish bourgeoisie needed him as executioner, but it has no need for him at all as patron or tutor. London and Paris, on the one hand, and Berlin and Rome, on the other, are in its eyes considerably more solvent firms than Moscow. It is possible that Stalin himself wants to cover his traces in Spain before the final catastrophe; he thus hopes to unload the responsibility for the defeat on his closest allies. After this Litvinov will solicit Franco for the re-establishment of diplomatic relations. All this we have seen more than once.

Even a complete military victory of the so-called republican army over General Franco, however, would not signify the triumph of 'democracy'. The workers and peasants have twice placed bourgeois republicans and their left agents in power: in April 1931 and in February 1936. Both times the heroes of the Popular Front surrendered the victory of the people to the most reactionary and the most serious representatives of the bourgeoisie. A third victory, gained by the generals of the Popular Front, would signify their inevitable agreement with the fascist bourgeoisie on the backs of the workers and peasants. Such a regime will be nothing but a different form of military dictatorship, perhaps without a monarchy and without the open domination of the Catholic Church.

Finally, it is possible that the partial victories of the republicans will be utilised by the 'disinterested' Anglo-French intermediaries in order to reconcile the fighting camps. It is not difficult to understand that in the event of such a variant the final remnants of the 'democracy' will be stifled in the fraternal embrace of the generals Miaja (communist!) and Franco (fascist!). Let me repeat once again: victory will go either to the socialist revolution or to fascism.

It is not excluded, by the way, that the tragedy might at the last moment make way for farce. When the heroes of the Popular Front have to flee their last capital, they might, before embarking on steamers and airplanes, perhaps proclaim a series of 'socialist' reforms in order to leave a 'good memory' with the people. But nothing will avail. The workers of the world will remember with hatred and contempt the parties that ruined the heroic revolution.

The tragic experience of Spain is a terrible – perhaps final – warning before still greater events, a warning addressed to all the advanced workers of the world. 'Revolutions', Marx said, 'are the locomotives of history.' They move faster than the thought of semi-revolutionary or quarter-revolutionary parties. Whoever lags behind falls under the wheels of the locomotive, and consequently – and this is the chief danger – the locomotive itself is also not infrequently wrecked.

It is necessary to think out the problem of the revolution to the end, to its ultimate concrete conclusions. It is necessary to adjust policy to the basic laws of the revolution, that is, to the movement of the embattled classes and not the prejudices or fears of the superficial petty bourgeois groups who call themselves 'Popular' Fronts and every other kind of front. During revolution the line of least resistance is the line of greatest disaster. To fear 'isolation' from the bourgeoisie is to incur isolation from the masses. Adaptation to the conservative prejudices of the labour aristocracy is betrayal of the workers and the revolution. An excess 'caution' is the most baneful lack of caution. This is the chief lesson of the destruction of the most honest political organisation in Spain, namely, the centrist POUM. The parties and groups of the London Bureau* obviously either do not wish to draw the necessary conclusions from the last warning of history or are unable to do so. By this token they doom themselves.

By way of compensation, a new generation of revolutionists is now being educated by the lessons of the defeats. This generation has verified in action the ignominious reputation of the Second International. It has plumbed the depths of the Third International's downfall. It has learned how to judge the Anarchists not by their words but by their deeds. It is a great inestimable school, paid for with the blood of countless fighters! The revolutionary cadres are now gathering only under the banner of the Fourth International. Born amid the roar of defeats, the Fourth International will lead the toilers to victory.

---

* The London Bureau of Revolutionary Socialist Parties was a loose association of left socialist parties – not affiliated either to the reformist Socialist International or the Stalin-dominated Communist International – including the Independent Labour Party in Britain, the POUM in Spain, the Socialist Workers Party (SAP) of Germany, and the Workers and Peasants Socialist Party (PSOP) of France. Trotsky criticised them as 'centrists', because he perceived them as wavering between reformism and revolutionary socialism. – Editors

4

IMPERIALISM AND
GLOBAL REVOLUTION

One of the distinguishing characteristics of Trotsky's political orientation is a thoroughgoing revolutionary internationalism. Like other revolutionary Marxists, in 1905 he was explaining: 'Binding all countries together with its mode of production and its commerce, capitalism has converted the world into a single economic and political organism.' Through its imperialist development and global financial and political manipulations, however, 'the bourgeoisie has managed to postpone the denouement [of crisis and collapse], but thereby has prepared a radical liquidation of its rule on a world-wide scale'. This had implications, he insisted, for the 1905 revolutionary upsurge in Russia:

> This immediately gives the events now unfolding an international character, and opens up a wide horizon. The political emancipation of Russia led by the working class will raise that class to a height as yet unknown in history, will transfer to it colossal power and resources, and will make it the initiator of the liquidation of world capitalism, for which history has created all the objective conditions.[1]

In order to survive, he explained as he developed the early version of his theory of permanent revolution, if the workers were able to win political power in Russia, they could not survive unless the newly-established workers' state threw all of its power 'into the scales of the class struggle of the entire capitalist world', sending forth 'to its comrades the world over the old rallying cry, which will this time be a call for the last attack: *workers of all countries*, unite!'[2]

With the 1919 founding of the Third International, a 'Manifesto of the Communist International to the Proletariat of the Entire World' was adopted by the International's first congress. This was written by Trotsky, who gave emphasis to anti-colonial uprisings 'in Madagascar, Annam [Vietnam], and other countries', going on to mention Algeria, Bengal, Persia, and Armenia. Appealing to the 'colonial slaves of Africa and Asia', he linked their future to the worldwide socialist revolution which – he and his comrades expected – would soon spread from Soviet Russia throughout Europe. The Manifesto concluded:

> Workers of the world: in struggle against imperialist barbarism, against monarchy, against the privileged classes, against the bourgeois state and bourgeois property, and against all forms and kinds of social and national oppression – unite!
>
> Under the banner of workers' councils and the revolutionary struggle for power and the dictatorship of the proletariat, under the banner of the Third International – workers of the world, unite![3]

Trotsky returned to these themes in a manifesto written for the Communist International's 1920 second congress. Reviewing the horrific impact of the First World War, he noted: 'Workers and peasants of Europe, America, Asia, Africa and Australia! You have suffered 10 million dead, 20 million wounded and crippled. Today you at least know what you have gained at this price!' He emphasised: 'It is necessary to destroy imperialism in order to give mankind an opportunity to live.' Commenting that 'the Communist International is the party of the revolutionary education of the world proletariat', he added that 'it does not possess any panaceas or magic formulas but bases itself on the past and present international experience of the working class'.[4]

In his 1928 critique of the draft programme, advanced by Nikolai Bukharin and Josef Stalin for the Communist International's Sixth Congress, he took special aim at their argument that socialism could actually be built in a single country regardless of the fortunes of the world revolution. 'Revolutionary and historical dialectic has been displaced by a skinflint reactionary utopia of self sufficient socialism, built on low technology, developing with "the speed of a tortoise" within national boundaries, connected with the external world only by its fear of [imperialist military] intervention.' Soon there would be a break between Bukharin and Stalin – the former wanting to maintain the 'tortoise' pace and the latter pushing through rapid industrialisation and a brutal forced land-collectivisation – but both missed, in Trotsky's opinion, the need to face the global economic challenge of capitalism:

> The capitalist world shows us by its export and import figures that it has other instruments of persuasion than those of military intervention. To the extent that productivity of labor and the productivity of a social system as a whole are not measured on the market by the correlation of prices, it is not so much military intervention as the intervention of cheaper capitalist commodities that constitutes perhaps the greatest immediate menace to Soviet economy.[5]

In his 1930 polemic and explication *The Permanent Revolution*, Trotsky repeated the thought from 1919 that 'insofar as capitalism has created a world market, a world division of labour, and world reproductive forces, it has also prepared world economy as a whole for socialist transformation'. But he also emphasised that 'the completion of socialist revolution within national limits is unthinkable … The socialist revolution begins on the national arena, it unfolds on the international arena, and it is completed on the world arena. Thus the socialist revolution becomes a permanent revolution in a newer and broader sense of the word; it attains completion only in the final victory of the new society on our entire planet.' Returning to his critique of Stalin's 'Socialism in One Country' theory, he emphasised: 'The world division of labour, the dependence of Soviet industry upon foreign technology, the dependence of productive forces of the advanced countries of Europe upon Asiatic raw materials, etc., etc., make the construction of an independent socialist society in any single country in the world impossible.'[6]

In the previous two selections of Trotsky's writings in this volume, we can see his attention focused on what might be called two different sectors of the world revolution – the Soviet workers' state, suffering from bureaucratic degeneration, and then advanced capitalist countries that by the 1930s seemed to him ripe for socialist revolution. Here we can see his attention focused on a third sector of the world revolution – the less capitalistically-developed, colonial and semi-colonial regions of Asia, Africa and Latin America.

The readings in this section reflect not simply a revolutionary-internationalist continuity in Trotsky's orientation, but a further application of the Communist International's breakthrough embrace of the labouring and oppressed masses beyond the

European working class that had been the focal point of the earlier Socialist (Second) International – evident, for example, in the first reading, 'Closer to the Proletarians of the Coloured Races'. Sent in 1933 to the International Secretariat of the International Left Opposition (a network of dissident Communist groups in various countries that were in agreement with the orientation Trotsky had fought for in the Soviet Union and the Communist International), it suggested that the most oppressed sectors of the global working class – those subjected to racist and colonial oppression – were likely to be the most consistently revolutionary and militant elements in the worldwide struggle against capitalist oppression. He focuses on African labourers both on their native continent and in the African diaspora – but at the conclusion also points to Chinese and Indian workers.

The next two selections – 'The Chinese Revolution' and 'An Open Letter to the Workers of India' – highlight the central importance Trotsky attributes to these groups and their struggles.

The first is an introduction to the 1938 work *The Tragedy of the Chinese Revolution*, an account of inspiring revolutionary struggles and devastating defeats in 1925–27, by eyewitness journalist Harold Isaacs (at the time a revolutionary socialist). Connecting Chinese realities and struggles to a broader range of realities and struggles throughout Asia, Africa, and Latin America (while insisting on the dynamics of what elsewhere he defined as uneven and combined development), Trotsky highlights the value of the theory of permanent revolution in shedding light on the realities and suggesting a forward path for the struggles of the oppressed labourers of China. Following the more 'moderate' Stalinist line of working closely with the forces of the pro-capitalist nationalistic general Chiang Kai-shek had resulted in disastrously bloody defeats for the Communist-led workers' movement. The key is that national liberation struggles must be interlinked with the struggle to advance the interests of the workers and peasants beyond the limits that the native capitalists want to go. Trotsky is insistent that to do this, the workers' movement must maintain its own political independence and revolutionary programme.[7]

The same is true of his 1939 letter to Indian workers, which includes an uncompromising critique of the radical pacifism of Mohandas Gandhi. (Here Trotsky mistakenly predicts that Gandhi would end up supporting the British imperialist war effort, as he did during the First World War, once the impending Second World War broke out). Trotsky emphasised that those suffering from colonialism 'must always seek out their main enemy at home, cast in the role of their own immediate oppressors and exploiters', which in India 'above all is the British bourgeoisie'. If the Indian business classes (with whom Gandhi was aligned) proved willing to take even 'tiny steps' in the direction of the national liberation struggle, the workers should support such steps – while maintaining their own political independence and preparing to push the revolutionary struggle further than India's upper classes would want to go.[8]

The next two selections – 'Mexico and British Imperialism' and 'Nationalised Industry and Workers' Management' – focus on Latin American realities that also have implications for developments on other continents victimised by imperialist exploitation. Mexico had achieved its independence from Spain through successful anti-colonial struggles in the early nineteenth century, but over the following century largely fallen under the economic domination of European and US capitalism. The revitalisation of revolutionary struggles beginning in 1910 had begun to advance the interests of the common people, only to become compromised and corrupted – but in the radical ferment of the 1930s, a new insurgent spirit had enabled radical nationalist Lázaro Cárdenas to establish a presidency that initiated far-reaching reforms and stood up to the imperialists, taking possession of Mexican oil that was being exploited by foreign companies. In full support of this measure, Trotsky called for international working-class solidarity around the revolutionary anti-imperialist policy and for defence of the Cárdenas regime in the face of a rising crescendo of international capitalist hostility.[9] The item on nationalised industry and workers' self-management was first published in 1946, after Trotsky's death, by the US Trotskyist journal *Fourth International*, whose editors provided this explanation:

> In 1938, when the Cárdenas government of Mexico expropriated the oil industry from the Anglo-American imperialists, such newspapers as the *NY Daily News* ascribed the act to the influence of Leon Trotsky then in exile in Mexico. This, of course, was untrue.
>
> Trotsky had made an agreement, which he scrupulously observed, that in return for asylum he would not intervene in Mexican politics. He was

forced consequently to limit himself to stating his position in general on the expropriation. He supported the act, explaining his views in an article dated June 5, 1938, published in the *Socialist Appeal* ... of June 25, 1938. It was not known that Trotsky had written more fully on another aspect of the expropriation: the placing by the Mexican government of the oil industry under the management of the workers.

In April 1946, Joseph Hansen, former Secretary of Leon Trotsky, visited Natalia Trotsky. He also called on friends of Trotsky. Among them was one who had made a study of the expropriation. This friend told about talking with Trotsky for a whole afternoon on the uniqueness of workers' management of an expropriated industry in a capitalist country.

Trotsky promised to consider the subject more fully. Some three days later, Trotsky's French secretary called on the telephone that Trotsky had written a short article. This remarkable article had never been printed anywhere ...[10]

The final reading in this section deals with an aspect of the African diaspora – in particular, the situation and struggles of African-Americans in the United States. It contains excerpts from two discussions; the first taking place in 1933, the second in 1939. In the first, the participants include Trotsky, US follower Arne Swabeck, and one of Trotsky's secretaries, Pierre Frank. In the second, the two primary discussants are Trotsky and the outstanding Afro-Caribbean intellectual C. L. R. James, then a Trotskyist engaged in political activity in the United States (in the interview identified by the name 'Johnson'). This is the first of three transcribed discussions held at that time.[11]

Up until the founding of the Communist International, US socialists of all persuasions (mostly white but also black) did not see African-Americans as an oppressed national minority, seeing the question only in class terms. For some, influenced by racism, they tended not to take African-Americans seriously as part of the working class, while the more anti-racist socialists believed that black and white workers should simply join together to struggle for socialism, after which 'the race question' would be positively resolved. The Russian Communists, more alert to the complexities of race, ethnicity, and nationality, insisted on a more complex analysis. Once Stalin became predominant by the early 1930s, a more rigid understanding was imposed on US Communists – insisting that African-Americans were part of a Southern 'Black-Belt nation' that should be granted independence in the wake of a US socialist revolution. During the popular front period beginning in the mid-1930s, US Communists switched to a position of supporting racial integration and mobilizing black and white support for the New Deal policies of Franklin D. Roosevelt. The discussions presented here show Trotsky engaged in searching explorations with his comrades, attempting to develop more consistently revolutionary analyses and policies consistent with the revolutionary perspectives of the early Communist International. These would find reflection in future anti-racist efforts in the US.[12]

Notes

1. Here Trotsky is quoting from an article he wrote in the revolutionary paper *Nachalo* [The Beginning], 17 October 1905 – reproduced in his 1906 pamphlet 'Results and Prospects', in Leon Trotsky, *The Permanent Revolution and Results and Prospects* (London: Socialist Resistance, 2007), 87.
2. Ibid., 94.
3. 'Manifesto of the Communist International to the Proletariat of the Entire World (Trotsky)', *The Founding of the Communist International, Proceedings and Documents of the First Congress: March 1919*, ed. John Riddell (New York: Pathfinder Press, 1987), 227, 231–2.
4. Leon Trotsky, 'Manifesto of the Second World Congress', in *The First Five Years of the Communist International*, vol. 1, ed. John G. Wright (New York: Monad/Pathfinder, 1972), 107, 114, 130, 131.
5. Leon Trotsky, *The Third International After Lenin* (New York: Pathfinder Press, 1970), 45–6, 49.
6. Trotsky, *The Permanent Revolution and Results and Prospects*, 253–4, 255.
7. See Harold R. Isaacs, *The Tragedy of the Chinese Revolution* (Chicago: Haymarket Books, 2010); Gregor Benton, *China's Urban Revolutionaries: Explorations in the History of Chinese Trotskyism, 1921–1952* (Atlantic Highlands, NJ: Humanities Press, 1996); Leon Trotsky, *Leon Trotsky on China*, ed. Les Evans and Russell Block (New York: Monad/Pathfinder, 1976).
8. A rich collection of Marxist-influenced writings on India is provided by the Marxist Internet Archive –www.marxists.org/subject/india/index.htm; also see Bhikhu Parekh, *Gandhi: A Very Short Introduction* (Oxford: Oxford University Press, 2001); Kunal Chattopadhyay, 'Mohandas Gandhi', in *International Encyclopedia of Revolution and Protest*, ed. Immanuel Ness et al., vol. III (Malden, MA/Oxford: Wiley-Blackwell, 2009), 1324–32; Sumit Sarkar, *Modern India: 1885–1947* (Basingstoke: Palgrave Macmillan, 1989); and on post-Gandhi India, Achin Vanaik, *The Painful Transition: Bourgeois Democracy in India* (London: Verso, 1990). It is worth noting that in 1942, when Gandhi initiated a militantly anti-colonial 'Quit India' struggle, Trotskyists and others on the non-Stalinist Left did critically participate,

in contrast to the Communist Party of India (which was influenced by the war-time alliance between Britain and the USSR).

9. See Adolfo Gilly, *The Mexican Revolution: A People's History* (New York: The New Press, 2006), and Dan La Botz, 'Viva La Revolución!' Part 1', *Against the Current*, no. 147, July–August 2010 (www.solidarity-us.org/current/node/2938) and 'Viva La Revolución! Part 2', *Against the Current*, no. 148, September–October 2010 (www.solidarity-us.org/current/node/3032).

10. *Fourth International*, vol. 7, no. 8, August 1946, 238.

11. See George Breitman, ed., *Leon Trotsky on Black Nationalism and Self-Determination* (New York: Pathfinder Press, 1978) for full transcripts and other material.

12. A considerable amount of material on matters discussed here can be found in: Robert L. Allen, *The Reluctant Reformers: Racism and Social Reform Movements in the United States* (Washington, DC: Howard University Press, 1983); Scott McLemee and Paul Le Blanc, eds, *C. L. R. James and Revolutionary Marxism: Selected Writings of C. L. R. James 1939–1949* (Atlantic Highlands, NJ: Humanities Press, 1994; Scott McLemee, ed., *C. L. R. James on the 'Negro Question'* (Jackson, MS: University of Mississippi Press, 1996); Anthony Marcus, ed., *Malcolm X and the Third American Revolution: The Writings of George Breitman* (Amherst, NY: Humanity Books, 2005); George Breitman, *The Last Year of Malcolm X: The Evolution of a Revolutionary* (New York: Merit Publishers, 1967).

Closer to the Proletarians of the Coloured Races*
(1932)

To the International Secretariat:

(Copy to the National Committee of the American League)

I have received a copy of the letter dated 26 April 1932, sent by an organisation of Negro comrades from Johannesburg. This letter, it seems to me, is of great symptomatic significance. The Left Opposition (Bolshevik-Leninists) can and must become the banner for the most oppressed sections of the world proletariat, and consequently, first and foremost, for the Negro workers. Upon what do I base this proposition?

The Left Opposition represents at present the most consistent and most revolutionary tendency in the world. Its sharply critical attitude to any and all varieties of bureaucratic haughtiness in the labour movement makes it possible for it to pay particular

* From Trotsky Internet Archive (www.marxists.org/archive/trotsky/1932/06/black01. htm).

attention to the voice of the most oppressed sections of the working class and the toilers as a whole.

The Left Opposition is the target for the blows not only of the Stalinist apparatus but also of all the bourgeois governments of the world. This fact, which, despite all the slanders, is entering gradually into the consciousness of the masses, is bound increasingly to attract towards the Left Opposition the warm sympathies of the most oppressed sections of the international working class. From this point of view, the communication addressed to us by the South African comrades seems to me not at all accidental, but profoundly symptomatic.

In their letter, to which 24 signatures are appended (with the notation 'and others'), the South African comrades expressed particular interest in the questions of the Chinese Revolution. This interest, it ought to be acknowledged, is wholly justified. The working masses of the oppressed peoples who have to carry on the struggle for elementary national rights and for human dignity, are precisely those who incur the greatest risk of suffering the penalties for the muddled teachings of the Stalinist bureaucracy on the subject of the 'democratic dictatorship'. Under this false banner, the policy à la Kuomintang, that is, the vile deception and the unpunished crushing of the toiling masses by their own 'national' bourgeoisie, may still do the greatest harm to the liberating cause of the toilers. The programme of the permanent revolution based on the incontestable historic experience of a number of countries can and must assume primary significance for the liberation movement of the Negro proletariat.

The Johannesburg comrades may not as yet have had the opportunity to acquaint themselves more closely with the views of the Left Opposition on all the most important questions. But this cannot be an obstacle in our getting together with them as closely as possible at this very moment, and helping them fraternally to come into the orbit of our programme and our tactics.

When ten intellectuals, whether in Paris, Berlin, or New York, who have already been members of various organisations, address themselves to us with a request to be taken into our midst, I would offer the following advice: Put them through a series of tests on all the programmatic questions; wet them in the rain, dry them in the sun, and then after a new and careful examination accept maybe one or two.

The case is radically altered when ten workers connected with the masses turn to us. The difference in our attitude to a petty bourgeois group and to the proletarian group does not require any explanation. But if a proletarian group functions in an area where there are workers of different races, and in spite of this remains composed solely of workers of a privileged nationality, then I am inclined to view them with suspicion. Are we not dealing perhaps with the labour aristocracy? Isn't the group infected with slave-holding prejudices, active or passive?

It is an entirely different matter when we are approached by a group of Negro workers. Here I am prepared to take it for granted in advance that we shall achieve agreement with them, even if such an agreement is not actual as yet. Because the Negro workers, by virtue of their whole position, do not and cannot strive to degrade anybody, oppress anybody, or deprive anybody of his rights. They do not seek privileges and cannot rise to the top except on the road of the international revolution.

We can and we must find a way to the consciousness of the Negro workers, the Chinese workers, the Indian workers, and all the oppressed in the human ocean of the coloured races to whom belongs the decisive word in the development of mankind.

L. Trotsky
Prinkipo, 13 June 1932

The Chinese Revolution*
(1938)

First of all, the mere fact that the author of this book belongs to the school of historical materialism would be entirely insufficient in our eyes to win approval for his work. In present-day conditions the Marxist label would predispose us to mistrust rather than to acceptance. In close connection with the degeneration of the Soviet state, Marxism has in the past 15 years passed through an unprecedented period of decline and debasement. From an instrument of analysis and criticism, it has been turned into an instrument of cheap apologetics. Instead of analysing facts,

---

* From Trotsky Internet Archive (www.marxists.org/archive/trotsky/1938/xx/china.htm), with revisions by the editors.

it occupies itself with selecting sophisms in the interests of exalted clients.

In the Chinese Revolution of 1925–27 the Communist International played a very great role, depicted in this book quite comprehensively. We would, however, seek in vain in the library of the Communist International for a single book which attempts in any way to give a rounded picture of the Chinese Revolution. Instead, we find scores of 'conjunctural' works' which docilely reflect each zigzag in the politics of the Communist International, or, more correctly, of Soviet diplomacy in China, and subordinating to each zigzag facts as well as general treatment. In contrast to this literature, which cannot arouse anything but mental revulsion, Isaacs' book represents a scientific work from beginning to end. It is based on a conscientious study of a vast number of original sources and supplementary material. Isaacs spent more than three years on this work. It should be added that he had previously passed about five years in China as a journalist and observer of Chinese life.

The author of this book approaches the revolution as a revolutionist, and he sees no reason for concealing it. In the eyes of a philistine a revolutionary point of view is virtually equivalent to an absence of scientific objectivity. We think just the opposite: only a revolutionist – provided, of course, that he is equipped with the scientific method – is capable of laying bare the objective dynamics of the revolution. Apprehending thought in general is not contemplative, but active. The element of will is indispensable for penetrating the secrets of nature and society. Just as a surgeon, on whose scalpel a human life depends, distinguishes with extreme care between the various tissues of an organism, so a revolutionist, if he has a serious attitude toward his task, is obliged with strict conscientiousness to analyse the structure of society, its functions and reflexes.

To understand the present war between Japan and China one must take the Second Chinese Revolution as a point of departure. In both cases we meet not only identical social forces, but frequently the same personalities. Suffice it to say that the person of Chiang Kai-shek occupies the central place in this book. As these lines are being written it is still difficult to forecast when and in what manner the Sino-Japanese war will end. But the outcome of the present conflict in the Far East will in any case have a provisional character. The world war which is approaching with irresistible force will review the Chinese problem together with all other problems of colonial domination. For it is in this that the real task of the second world war will consist: to divide the planet anew in accord with the new relationship of imperialist forces. The principal arena of struggle will, of course, not be that Lilliputian bath tub, the Mediterranean, nor even the Atlantic Ocean, but the basin of the Pacific. The most important object of struggle will be China, embracing about one-fourth of the human race. The fate of the Soviet Union – the other big stake in the coming war – will also to a certain degree be decided in the Far East. Preparing for this clash of Titans, Tokyo is attempting today to assure itself of the broadest possible drill-ground on the continent of Asia. Great Britain and the United States are likewise losing no time. It can, however, be predicted with certainty – and this is in essence acknowledged by the present makers of destiny – that the world war will not produce the final decision: it will be followed by a new series of revolutions which will review not only the decisions of the war but all those property conditions which give rise to war.

History is No Pacifist

This prospect, it must be confessed, is very far from being an idyll, but Clio, the muse of history, was never a member of a Ladies' Peace Society. The older generation which passed through the war of 1914–18 did not discharge a single one of its tasks. It leaves to the new generation as heritage the burden of wars and revolutions. These most important and tragic events in human history have often marched side by side. They will definitely form the background of the coming decades. It remains only to hope that the new generation, which cannot arbitrarily cut loose from the conditions it has inherited, has learned at least to understand better the laws of its epoch. For acquainting itself with the Chinese Revolution of 1925–27 it will not find today a better guide than this book.

Despite the unquestionable greatness of the Anglo Saxon genius, it is impossible not to see that the laws of revolutions are least understood precisely in the Anglo Saxon countries. The explanation for this lies, on the one hand, in the fact that the very appearance of revolution in these countries relates to a long-distant past, and evokes in official 'sociologists' a condescending smile, as would childish pranks. On the other hand, pragmatism, so characteristic of Anglo Saxon thinking, is least of all useful for understanding revolutionary crises.

The English Revolution of the seventeenth century, like the French Revolution of the eighteenth, had the task of 'rationalising' the structure of society, that is, cleansing it of feudal stalactites and stalagmites, and subjecting it to the laws of free competition, which in that epoch seemed to be the laws of 'common sense'. In doing this, the Puritan revolution draped itself in biblical dress, thereby revealing a purely infantile incapacity to understand its own significance. The French Revolution, which had considerable influence on progressive thought in the United States, was guided by formulas of pure rationalism. Common sense, which is still afraid of itself and resorts to the mask of biblical prophets, or secularised common sense, which looks upon society as the product of a rational 'contract', remain to this day the fundamental forms of Anglo Saxon thinking in the domains of philosophy and sociology.

Yet the real society of history has not been constructed, following Rousseau, upon a rational 'contract', nor, as according to Bentham, upon the principle of the 'greatest good,' but has unfolded 'irrationally', on the basis of contradictions and antagonisms. For revolution to become inevitable, class contradictions have to be strained to the breaking point. It is precisely this historically inescapable necessity for conflict, which depends neither on good nor ill will but on the objective inter-relationship of classes, that makes revolution, together with war, the most dramatic expression of the 'irrational' foundation of the historic process.

'Irrational' does not, however, mean arbitrary. On the contrary, in the molecular preparation of revolution, in its explosion, in its ascent and decline, there is lodged a profound inner lawfulness which can be apprehended and, in the main, foreseen. Revolutions, as has been said more than once, have a logic of their own. But this is not the logic of Aristotle, and even less the pragmatic demi-logic of 'common sense'. It is the higher function of thought: the logic of development and its contradictions, that is, the dialectic.

The obstinacy of Anglo Saxon pragmatism and its hostility to dialectical thinking thus have their material causes. Just as a poet cannot attain to the dialectic through books without his own personal experiences, so a well-to-do society, unused to convulsions and habituated to uninterrupted 'progress', is incapable of understanding the dialectic of its own development. However, it is only too obvious that this privilege of the Anglo Saxon world has receded into the past. History is preparing to give Great Britain as well as the United States serious lessons in the dialectic.

Character of Chinese Revolution

The author of this book tries to deduce the character of the Chinese Revolution not from *a priori* definitions and not from historical analogies, but from the living structure of Chinese society and from the dynamics of its inner forces. In this lies the chief methodological value of the book. The reader will carry away not only a better-knit picture of the march of events but – what is more important – will learn to understand their social mainsprings. Only on this basis is it possible correctly to appraise political programs and the slogans of struggling parties – which, even if neither independent nor in the final analysis the decisive factors in the process, are nevertheless its most manifest signs.

In its immediate aims the uncompleted Chinese Revolution is 'bourgeois'. This term, however, which is used as a mere echo of the bourgeois revolutions of the past, actually helps us very little. Lest the historical analogy turn into a trap for the mind, it is necessary to check it in the light of a concrete sociological analysis. What are the classes which are struggling in China? What are the interrelationships of these classes? How, and in what direction, are these relations being transformed? What are the objective tasks of the Chinese Revolution, that is, those tasks dictated by the course of development? On the shoulders of which classes rests the solution of these tasks? With what methods can they be solved? Isaacs' book gives the answers to precisely these questions.

Colonial and semi-colonial – and therefore backward – countries, which embrace by far the greater part of mankind, differ extraordinarily from one another in their degree of backwardness, representing an historical ladder reaching from nomadry, and even cannibalism, up to the most modern industrial culture. The combination of extremes in one degree or another characterises all of the backward countries. However, the hierarchy of backwardness, if one may employ such an expression, is determined by the specific weight of the elements of barbarism and culture in the life of each colonial country. Equatorial Africa lags far behind Algeria, Paraguay behind Mexico, Abyssinia behind India or China. With their common economic dependence upon the imperialist metropolis, their political dependence bears in some instances the character of open colonial slavery (India, Equatorial Africa), while in others it is concealed by the fiction of State independence (China, Latin America).

In agrarian relations backwardness finds its most organic and cruel expression. Not one of these countries has carried its democratic revolution through to any real extent. Half-way agrarian reforms are absorbed by semi-serf relations, and these are inescapably reproduced in the soil of poverty and oppression. Agrarian barbarism always goes hand-in-hand with the absence of roads, with the isolation of provinces, with 'medieval' particularism, and absence of national consciousness. The purging of social relations of the remnants of ancient and the encrustations of modern feudalism is the most important task in all these countries.

The achievement of the agrarian revolution is unthinkable, however, with the preservation of dependence upon foreign imperialism, which with one hand implants capitalist relations while supporting and re-creating with the other all the forms of slavery and serfdom. The struggle for the democratisation of social relations and the creation of a national state thus uninterruptedly passes into an open uprising against foreign domination.

Historical backwardness does not imply a simple reproduction of the development of advanced countries, England or France, with a delay of one, two, or three centuries. It engenders an entirely new 'combined' social formation in which the latest conquests of capitalist technique and structure root themselves into relations of feudal or pre-feudal barbarism, transforming and subjecting them and creating peculiar relations of classes.

Bourgeoisie Hostile to People

Not a single one of the tasks of the 'bourgeois' revolution can be solved in these backward countries under the leadership of the 'national' bourgeoisie, because the latter emerges at once with foreign support as a class alien or hostile to the people. Every stage in its development binds it only the more closely to the foreign finance capital of which it is essentially the agency. The petty bourgeoisie of the colonies, that of handicrafts and trade, is the first to fall victim in the unequal struggle with foreign capital, declining into economic insignificance, becoming declassed and pauperised. It cannot even conceive of playing an independent political role. The peasantry, the largest numerically and the most atomised, backward, and oppressed class, is capable of local uprisings and partisan warfare, but requires the leadership of a more advanced and centralised class in order for this struggle to be elevated to an all-national level. The task of such leadership falls in the nature of things upon the colonial proletariat, which, from its very first steps, stands opposed not only to the foreign but also to its own national bourgeoisie.

Out of the conglomeration of provinces and tribes, bound together by geographical proximity and the bureaucratic apparatus, capitalist development has transformed China into the semblance of an economic entity. The revolutionary movement of the masses translated this growing unity for the first time into the language of national consciousness. In the strikes, agrarian uprisings, and military expeditions of 1925–27 a new China was born. While the generals, tied to their own and the foreign bourgeoisie, could only tear the country to pieces, the Chinese workers became the standard-bearers of an irresistible urge to national unity. This movement provides an incontestable analogy with the struggle of the French Third Estate against particularism, or with the later struggle of the Germans and Italians for national unification. But in contrast to the first-born countries of capitalism, where the problem of achieving national unity fell to the petty bourgeoisie, in part under the leadership of the bourgeoisie and even of the landlords (Prussia!), in China it was the proletariat that emerged as the primary motive force and potential leader of this movement. But precisely thereby, the proletariat confronted the bourgeoisie with the danger that the leadership of the unified fatherland would not remain in the latter's hands. Patriotism has been throughout all history inseparably bound up with power and property. In the face of danger the ruling classes have never stopped short of dismembering their own country so long as they were able in this way to preserve power over one part of it. It is not at all surprising, therefore, if the Chinese bourgeoisie, represented by Chiang Kai-shek, turned its weapons in 1927 against the proletariat, the standard-bearer of national unity. The exposition and explanation of this turn, which occupies the central place in Isaacs' book, provides the key to the understanding of the fundamental problems of the Chinese Revolution as well as of the present Sino-Japanese war.

The so-called 'national' bourgeoisie tolerates all forms of national degradation so long as it can hope to maintain its own privileged existence. But at the moment when foreign capital sets out to assume undivided domination of the entire wealth of the country, the colonial bourgeoisie is forced to remind itself of its 'national' obligations. Under pressure of the masses it may even find itself plunged into a war. But this will be a war waged against one of the imperialist powers, the one least amenable to negotiations, with the hope of passing into the service of some other, more magnanimous power. Chiang Kai-shek struggles against the Japanese violators only within the limits indicated to him by his British or American patrons. Only that class which has nothing to lose but its chains can conduct to the very end the war against imperialism for national emancipation.

Grandiose Historical Test

The above developed views regarding the special character of the 'bourgeois' revolutions in historically belated countries are by no means the product of theoretical analysis alone. Before the second Chinese Revolution (1925–27) they had already been submitted to a grandiose historical test. The experience of the three Russian Revolutions (1905, February and October 1917) bears no less significance for the twentieth century than the French Revolution bore for the nineteenth. To understand the destinies of modern China the reader must have before his eyes the struggle of conceptions in the Russian revolutionary movement, because these conceptions exerted, and still exert, a direct and, moreover, powerful influence upon the politics of the Chinese proletariat and an indirect influence upon the politics of the Chinese bourgeoisie. It was precisely because of its historical backwardness that Tsarist Russia turned out to be the only European country where Marxism as a doctrine and Social Democracy as a party attained powerful development before the bourgeois revolution. It was in Russia, quite naturally, that the problem of the correlation between the struggle for democracy and the struggle for socialism, or between the bourgeois revolution and the socialist, was submitted to theoretical analysis. The first to pose this problem in the early eighties of the last century was the founder of Russian Social Democracy, Plekhanov. In the struggle against so-called Populism (Narodnikism), a variety of socialist Utopianism, Plekhanov established that Russia had no reason whatever to expect a privileged path of development, that like the 'profane' nations, it would have to pass through the stage of capitalism and that along this path it would acquire the regime of bourgeois democracy indispensable for the further struggle of the proletariat for socialism. Plekhanov not only separated the bourgeois revolution as a task distinct from the socialist revolution – which he postponed to the indefinite future – but he depicted entirely different combinations of forces. The bourgeois revolution was to be achieved by the proletariat in alliance with the liberal bourgeoisie, and thus clear the path for capitalist progress; after a number of decades and on a higher level of capitalist development, the proletariat would carry out the socialist revolution in direct struggle against the bourgeoisie.

Lenin – not immediately, to be sure – reviewed this doctrine. At the beginning of the present century, with much greater force and consistency than Plekhanov, he posed the agrarian problem as the central problem of the bourgeois revolution in Russia. With this he came to the conclusion that the liberal bourgeoisie was hostile to the expropriation of the landlords' estates, and precisely for this reason would seek a compromise with the monarchy on the basis of a constitution on the Prussian pattern. To Plekhanov's idea of an alliance between the proletariat and the liberal bourgeoisie, Lenin opposed the idea of an alliance between the proletariat and the peasantry. The aim of the revolutionary collaboration of these two classes he proclaimed to be the establishment of the 'bourgeois-democratic dictatorship of the proletariat and the peasantry' as the only means of cleansing the Tsarist empire of its feudal-police refuse, of creating a free farmers' system, and of clearing the road for the development of capitalism along American lines. Lenin's formula represented a gigantic step forward in that, in contrast to Plekhanov's it correctly indicated the central task of the revolution, namely, the democratic overturn of agrarian relations, and equally correctly sketched out the only realistic combination of class forces capable of solving this task. But up to 1917 the thought of Lenin himself remained bound to the traditional concept of the 'bourgeois' revolution. Like Plekhanov, Lenin proceeded from the premise that only after the 'completion of the bourgeois democratic revolution' would the tasks of the socialist revolution come on the order of the day. Lenin, however, contrary to the legend later manufactured by the epigones, considered that after the completion of the democratic overturn, the peasantry, as peasantry, could not remain the ally of the proletariat. Lenin based his socialist hopes on the agricultural labourers and the semi-proletarianised peasants who sell their labour power.

An Internal Contradiction

The weak point in Lenin's conception was the internally contradictory idea of the 'bourgeois-democratic dictatorship of the proletariat and the peasantry'. A political bloc of two classes whose interests only partially coincide excludes a dictatorship. Lenin himself emphasised the fundamental limitation of the 'dictatorship of the proletariat and the peasantry' when he openly called it bourgeois. By this he meant to say that for the sake of maintaining the alliance with the peasantry the proletariat would, in the coming revolution, have to forgo the direct posing of the socialist tasks. But this would signify, to be precise, that the proletariat would have to give up the dictatorship. In that event, in whose hands would the revolutionary power be concentrated? In the hands of the peasantry? But it is least capable of such a role.

Lenin left these questions unanswered up to his famous Theses of 4 April 1917. Only here did he break for the first time with the traditional understanding of the 'bourgeois' revolution and with the formula of the 'bourgeois democratic dictatorship of the proletariat and the peasantry'. He declared the struggle for the dictatorship of the proletariat to be the sole means of carrying out the agrarian revolution to the end and of securing the freedom of the oppressed nationalities. The regime of the proletarian dictatorship, by its very nature, however, could not limit itself to the framework of bourgeois property. The rule of the proletariat automatically placed on the agenda the socialist revolution, which in this case was not separated from the democratic revolution by any historical period, but was uninterruptedly connected with it, or, to put it more accurately, was an organic outgrowth of it. At what tempo the socialist transformation of society would occur and what limits it would attain in the nearest future would depend not only upon internal but upon external conditions as well. The Russian Revolution was only a link in the international revolution. Such was, in broad outline, the essence of the conception of the permanent (uninterrupted) revolution. It was precisely this conception that guaranteed the victory of the proletariat in October.

But such is the bitter irony of history: the experience of the Russian Revolution not only did not help the Chinese proletariat but, on the contrary, it became in its reactionary, distorted form, one of the chief obstacles in its path. The Comintern of the epigones began by canonising for all countries of the Orient the formula of the 'democratic dictatorship of the proletariat and peasantry' which Lenin, influenced by historical experience, had acknowledged to be without value. As always in history, a formula that had outlived itself served to cover a political content which was the direct opposite of that which the formula had served in its day. The mass plebeian, revolutionary alliance of the workers and peasants, sealed through the freely elected Soviets as the direct organs of action, the Comintern replaced by a bureaucratic bloc of party centres. The right to represent the peasantry in this bloc was unexpectedly given to the Kuomintang, that is, a thoroughly bourgeois party vitally interested in the preservation of capitalist property, not only in the means of production but in land. The alliance of the proletariat and the peasantry was broadened into a 'bloc of four classes'; workers, peasants, urban petty bourgeoisie, and the so-called 'national' bourgeoisie. In other words, the Comintern picked up a formula discarded by Lenin only in order to open the road to the politics of Plekhanov and, moreover, in a masked and therefore more harmful form.

To justify the political subordination of the proletariat to the bourgeoisie, the theoreticians of the Comintern (Stalin, Bukharin) adduced the fact of imperialist oppression which supposedly impelled 'all the progressive forces in the country' to an alliance. But this was precisely in its day the argument of the Russian Mensheviks, with the difference that in their case the place of imperialism was occupied by Tsarism. In reality, the subjection of the Chinese Communist Party to the Kuomintang signified its break with the mass movement and a direct betrayal of its historical interests. In this way the catastrophe of the second Chinese Revolution was prepared under the direct leadership of Moscow.

Significance of Russian Marxism

To many political philistines who in politics are inclined to substitute 'common sense' guesses for scientific analysis, the controversy among the Russian Marxists over the nature of the revolution and the dynamics of its class forces seemed to be sheer scholasticism. Historical experience revealed, however, the profoundly vital significance of the 'doctrinaire formulas' of Russian Marxism. Those who have not understood this up to today can learn a great deal from Isaacs' book. The politics of the Communist International in China showed convincingly what the Russian Revolution would have been converted into if the Mensheviks and the Social Revolutionaries had not been thrust aside in time by the Bolsheviks. In China the conception of the permanent revolution was confirmed once more, this time not in the form of a victory, but of a catastrophe.

It would, of course, be impermissible to identify Russia and China. With all their important common traits, the differences are all too obvious. But it is not hard to convince oneself that these differences do not weaken but, on the contrary, strengthen the fundamental conclusions of Bolshevism. In one sense Tsarist Russia was also a colonial country, and this found its expression in the predominant role of foreign capital. But the

Russian bourgeoisie enjoyed the benefits of an immeasurably greater independence from foreign imperialism than the Chinese bourgeoisie. Russia itself was an imperialist country. With all its meagreness, Russian liberalism had far more serious traditions and more of a basis of support than the Chinese. To the left of the liberals stood powerful petty bourgeois parties, revolutionary or semi-revolutionary in relation to Tsarism. The party of the Social Revolutionaries managed to find considerable support among the peasantry, chiefly from its upper layers. The Social Democratic (Menshevik) Party led behind it broad circles of the urban petty bourgeoisie and labour aristocracy. It was precisely these three parties – the Liberals, the Social Revolutionaries, and the Mensheviks – who for a long time prepared, and in 1917 definitely formed, a coalition which was not yet then called the People's Front but which had all of its traits. In contrast to this the Bolsheviks, from the eve of the revolution in 1905, took up an irreconcilable position in relation to the liberal bourgeoisie. Only this policy, which achieved its highest expression in the 'defeatism' of 1914–17, enabled the Bolshevik Party to conquer power.

The differences between China and Russia, the incomparably greater dependence of the Chinese bourgeoisie on foreign capital, the absence of independent revolutionary traditions among the petty bourgeoisie, the mass gravitation of the workers and peasants to the banner of the Comintern – demanded a still more irreconcilable policy – if such were possible, than that pursued in Russia. Yet the Chinese section of the Comintern, at Moscow's command, renounced Marxism, accepted the reactionary scholastic 'principles of Sun Yat-Sen', and entered the ranks of the Kuomintang, submitting to its discipline. In other words, it went much further along the road of submission to the bourgeoisie than the Russian Mensheviks or Social Revolutionaries ever did. The same fatal policy is now being repeated in the conditions of the war with Japan.

New Methods of Bureaucracy

How could the bureaucracy emerging from the Bolshevik Revolution apply in China, as throughout the world, methods fundamentally opposed to those of Bolshevism? It would be far too superficial to answer this question with a reference to the incapacity or ignorance of this or that individual. The gist of the matter lies in this: together with the new conditions of existence the bureaucracy acquired new methods of thinking. The Bolshevik Party led the masses. The bureaucracy began to order them about. The Bolsheviks won the possibility of leadership by correctly expressing the interests of the masses. The bureaucracy was compelled to resort to command in order to secure its own interests against those of the masses. The method of command was naturally extended to the Communist International as well. The Moscow leaders began quite seriously to imagine that they could compel the Chinese bourgeoisie to move to the left of its interests and the Chinese workers and peasants to the right of theirs, along the diagonals drawn in the Kremlin. Yet it is the very essence of revolution that the exploited as well as the exploiters invest their interests with the most extreme expression. If hostile classes would move along diagonals, there would be no need for a civil war. Armed by the authority of the October Revolution and the Communist International, not to mention inexhaustible financial resources, the bureaucracy transformed the young Chinese Communist Party from a motive force into a brake at the most important moment of the revolution. In contrast to Germany and Austria, where the bureaucracy could shift part of the responsibility for defeat to Social Democracy, there was no Social Democracy in China. The Comintern had the monopoly in ruining the Chinese Revolution.

The present domination of the Kuomintang over a considerable section of Chinese territory would have been impossible without the powerful national revolutionary movement of the masses in 1925–27. The massacre of this movement on the one hand concentrated power in the hands of Chiang Kai-shek, and on the other doomed Chiang Kai-shek to half-measures in the struggle against imperialism. The understanding of the course of the Chinese Revolution has in this way the most direct significance for an understanding of the course of the Sino-Japanese war. This historical work acquires thereby the most actual political significance.

War and revolution will be interlaced in the nearest future history of China. Japan's aim, to enslave forever, or at least for a long time to come, a gigantic country by dominating its strategic centres, is characterised not only by greediness but by wooden-headedness. Japan has arrived much too late. Torn by internal contradictions, the empire of the Mikado cannot reproduce the history of Britain's ascent. On the other hand, China has advanced far beyond the India of the seventeenth and eighteenth centuries. Old colonial countries are nowadays waging with ever greater success a struggle for their national independence. In these historic conditions, even if the present war in the Far East were to end with Japan's victory, and even if the victor himself could escape an internal catastrophe during the next few years – and neither the former nor the latter is in the least assured – Japan's domination over China would be measured by a very brief period, perhaps only the few years required to give a new impulse to the economic life of China and to mobilise its labouring masses once more.

The big Japanese trusts and concerns are already following in the wake of the army to divide the still unsecured booty. The Tokyo government is seeking to regulate the appetites of the financial cliques that would tear North China to pieces. If Japan were to succeed in maintaining its conquered positions for an interval of some ten years, this would mean, above all, the intensive indus-trialisation of north China in the military interests of Japanese imperialism. New railways, mines, power stations, mining and metallurgical enterprises, and cotton plantations would rapidly spring up. The polarisation of the Chinese nation would receive a feverish impulse. New hundreds of thousands and millions of Chinese proletarians would be mobilised in the briefest possible space of time. On the other hand, the Chinese bourgeoisie would fall into an ever greater dependence on Japanese capital. Even less than in the past would it be capable of standing at the head of a national war, no less a national revolution. Face to face with the foreign violator would stand the numerically larger, socially strengthened, politically matured Chinese proletariat, called to lead the Chinese village. Hatred of the foreign enslaver is a mighty revolutionary cement. The new national revolution will, one must think, be placed on the agenda still in the lifetime of the present generation. To solve the tasks imposed upon it, the vanguard of the Chinese proletariat must thoroughly assimilate the lessons of the Chinese Revolution. Isaacs' book can serve it in this sense as an irreplaceable aid. It remains to be hoped that the book will be translated into Chinese as well as other foreign languages.

Coyoacán, D. F., 1938

An Open Letter to the Workers of India*
(1939)

Dear Friends:

Titanic and terrible events are approaching with implacable force. Mankind lives in expectation of war which will, of course, also draw into its maelstrom the colonial countries and which is of vital significance for their destiny. Agents of the British government depict the matter as though the war will be waged for principles of 'democracy' which must be saved from fascism. All classes and peoples must rally around the 'peaceful' 'democratic' governments so as to repel the fascist aggressors. Then 'democracy' will be saved and peace stabilised forever. This gospel rests on a deliberate lie. If the British government were really concerned with the flowering of democracy then a very simple opportunity to demonstrate this exists: let the government give complete freedom to India. The right of national independence is one of the elementary democratic rights. But actually, the London government is ready to hand over all the democracies in the world in return for one tenth of its colonies.

If the Indian people do not wish to remain as slaves for all eternity, then they must expose and reject those false preachers who assert that the sole enemy of the people is fascism. Hitler and Mussolini are, beyond doubt, the bitterest enemies of the toilers and oppressed. They are gory executioners, deserving of the greatest hatred from the toilers and oppressed of the world. But they are, before everything, the enemies of the German and Italian peoples on whose backs they sit. The oppressed classes and peoples – as Marx, Engels, Lenin, and Liebknecht have taught us – must always seek out their main enemy at home, cast in the role of their own immediate oppressors and exploiters. In India that enemy above all is the British bourgeoisie. The overthrow

* From Trotsky Internet Archive (www.marxists.org/archive/trotsky/1939/07/india.htm), with revisions by the editors.

of British imperialism would deliver a terrible blow at all the oppressors, including the fascist dictators. In the long run the imperialists are distinguished from one another in form – not in essence. German imperialism, deprived of colonies, puts on the fearful mask of fascism with its sabre teeth protruding. British imperialism, gorged, because it possesses immense colonies, hides its sabre teeth behind a mask of democracy. But this democracy exists only for the metropolitan centre, for the 45,000,000 souls – or more correctly, for the ruling bourgeoisie – in the metropolitan centre. India is deprived not only of democracy but of the most elementary right of national independence. Imperialist democracy is thus the democracy of slave owners fed by the lifeblood of the colonies. But India seeks her own democracy, and not to serve as fertiliser for the slave owners.

Those who desire to end fascism, reaction and all forms of oppression must overthrow imperialism. There is no other road. This task cannot, however, be accomplished by peaceful methods, by negotiations and pledges. Never before in history have slave owners voluntarily freed their slaves. Only a bold, resolute struggle of the Indian people for their economic and national emancipation can free India.

The Indian bourgeoisie is incapable of leading a revolutionary struggle. They are closely bound up with and dependent upon British capitalism. They tremble for their own property. They stand in fear of the masses. They seek compromises with British imperialism no matter what the price and lull the Indian masses with hopes of reforms from above. The leader and prophet of this bourgeoisie is Gandhi. A fake leader and a false prophet! Gandhi and his compeers have developed a theory that India's position will constantly improve, that her liberties will continually be enlarged and that India will gradually become a Dominion on the road of peaceful reforms. Later on, perhaps even achieve full independence. This entire perspective is false to the core. The imperialist classes were able to make concessions to colonial peoples as well as to their own workers, only so long as capitalism marched uphill, so long as the exploiters could firmly bank on the further growth of profits. Nowadays there cannot even be talk of this. World imperialism is in decline. The condition of all imperialist nations daily becomes more difficult while the contradictions between them become more and more aggravated.

Monstrous armaments devour an ever greater share of national incomes. The imperialists can no longer make serious concessions either to their own toiling masses or to the colonies. On the contrary, they are compelled to resort to an ever more bestial exploitation. It is precisely in this that capitalism's death agony is expressed. To retain their colonies, markets and concessions, from Germany, Italy and Japan, the London government stands ready to mow down millions of people. Is it possible, without losing one's senses, to pin any hopes that this greedy and savage financial oligarchy will voluntarily free India?

True enough, a government of the so-called Labour Party may replace the Tory government. But this will alter nothing. The Labour Party – as witness its entire past and present programme – is in no way distinguished from the Tories on the colonial question. The Labour Party in reality expresses not the interests of the working class, but only the interests of the British labour bureaucracy and labour aristocracy. It is to this stratum that the bourgeoisie can toss juicy morsels, due to the fact that they themselves ruthlessly exploit the colonies, above all India. The British labour bureaucracy – in the Labour Party as well as in the trade unions – is directly interested in the exploitation of colonies. It has not the slightest desire to think of the emancipation of India. All these gentlemen – Major Atlee, Sir Walter Citrine & Co.[*] – are ready at any moment to brand the revolutionary movement of the Indian people as 'betrayal', as aid to Hitler and Mussolini and to resort to military measures for its suppression.

In no way superior is the policy of the present-day Communist International. To be sure, 20 years ago the Third, or Communist, International was founded as a genuine revolutionary organisation. One of its most important tasks was the liberation of the colonial peoples. Only recollections today remain of this program, however. The leaders of the Communist International have long since become the mere tools of the Moscow bureaucracy which has stifled the Soviet working masses and which has become transformed into a new aristocracy. In the ranks of the Communist Parties of various countries – including India – there are no

---

[*]   Clement Atlee and Walter Citrine were leading figures in the British Labour Party, whose socialist credentials were compromised – Trotsky suggests – by their reformist acceptance of capitalism and of Britain's royalty and empire. – Editors

doubt many honest workers, students, etc.: but they do not fix the politics of the Comintern. The deciding word belongs to the Kremlin which is guided not by the interests of the oppressed, but by those of the USSR's new aristocracy.

Stalin and his clique, for the sake of an alliance with the imperialist governments, have completely renounced the revolutionary programme for the emancipation of the colonies. This was openly avowed at the last Congress of Stalin's party in Moscow in March of the current year by [Dmitri] Manuilski, one of the leaders of the Comintern, who declared: 'The Communists advance to the forefront the struggle for the realisation of the right of self-determination of nationalities enslaved by fascist governments. They demand free self-determination for Austria ... the Sudeten regions ... Korea, Formosa, Abyssinia ... .' And what about India, Indo-China, Algeria and other colonies of England and France? The Comintern representative answers this question as follows, 'The Communists demand of the imperialist governments of the so called bourgeois democratic states the immediate [sic] drastic [!] improvement in the living standards of the toiling masses in the colonies and the granting of broad democratic rights and liberties to the colonies' (Pravda, issue no. 70, 12 March 1939.) In other words, as regards the colonies of England and France the Comintern has completely gone over to Gandhi's position and the position of the colonialist bourgeoisie in general. The Comintern has completely renounced revolutionary struggle for India's independence. It 'demands' (on its hands and knees) the 'granting' of 'democratic liberties' to India by British imperialism. The words 'immediate drastic improvement in the living standards of the toiling masses in the colonies' have an especially false and cynical ring. Modern capitalism – declining, gangrenous, disintegrating – is more and more compelled to worsen the position of workers in the metropolitan centre itself. How then can it improve the position of the toilers in the colonies from whom it is compelled to squeeze out all the juices of life so as to maintain its own state of equilibrium? The improvement of the conditions of the toiling masses in the colonies is possible only on the road to the complete overthrow of imperialism.

But the Communist International has travelled even further on this road of betrayal. Communists, according to Manuilski, 'subordinate the realisation of this right of secession ... in the interests of defeating fascism'. In other words, in the event of war between England and France over colonies, the Indian people must support their present slave owners, the British imperialists. That is to say, must shed their blood not for their own emancipation, but for the preservation of the rule of 'the City' over India. And these cheaply to be bought scoundrels dare to quote Marx and Lenin! As a matter of fact, their teacher and leader is none other than Stalin, the head of a new bureaucratic aristocracy, the butcher of the Bolshevik Party, the strangler of workers and peasants.

*   *   *

The Stalinists cover up their policy of servitude to British, French, and US imperialism with the formula of 'People's Front'. What a mockery of the people! 'People's Front' is only a new name for that old policy, the gist of which lies in class collaboration, in a coalition between the proletariat and the bourgeoisie. In every such coalition, the leadership invariably turns out to be in the hands of the right wing, that is, in the hands of the propertied class. The Indian bourgeoisie, as has already been stated, wants a peaceful horse trade and not a struggle. Coalition with the bourgeoisie leads to the proletariat's abnegating the revolutionary struggle against imperialism. The policy of coalition implies marking time on one spot, temporising, cherishing false hopes, engaging in hollow manoeuvres and intrigues. As a result of this policy disillusionment inevitably sets in among the working masses, while the peasants turn their backs on the proletariat, and fall into apathy. The German Revolution, the Austrian Revolution, the Chinese Revolution and the Spanish Revolution have all perished as a result of the policy of coalition.* The self-same danger also menaces the Indian Revolution where the Stalinists, under the guise of 'People's Front', are putting across a policy of subordinating the proletariat to the bourgeoisie. This signifies, in action, a rejection of the revolutionary agrarian program, a rejection of arming the workers, a rejection of the struggle for power, a rejection of revolution.

---

*   The experience of the Chinese Revolution of 1925–27 is of the most direct significance for India. I heartily recommend to the Indian revolutionists Harold Isaacs' excellent book, *The Tragedy of the Chinese Revolution*. – Trotsky

In the event that the Indian bourgeoisie finds itself compelled to take even the tiniest step on the road of struggle against the arbitrary rule of Great Britain, the proletariat will naturally support such a step. But they will support it with *their own* methods: mass meetings, bold slogans, strikes, demonstrations, and more decisive combat actions, depending on the relationship of forces and the circumstances. Precisely to do this must the proletariat have its hands free. Complete independence from the bourgeoisie is indispensable to the proletariat, above all in order to exert influence on the peasantry, the predominant mass of India's population. Only the proletariat is capable of advancing a bold, revolutionary agrarian programme, of rousing and rallying tens of millions of peasants and leading them in struggle against the native oppressors and British imperialism. The alliance of workers and poor peasants is the only honest, reliable alliance that can assure the final victory of the Indian Revolution.

* * *

All peace-time questions will preserve their full force in time of war, except that they will be invested with a far sharper expression. First of all, exploitation of the colonies will become greatly intensified. The metropolitan centres will not only pump from the colonies foodstuffs and raw materials, but they will also mobilise vast numbers of colonial slaves who are to die on the battlefields for their masters. Meanwhile, the colonial bourgeoisie will have its snout deep in the trough of war orders and will naturally renounce opposition in the name of patriotism and profits. Gandhi is already preparing the ground for such a policy. These gentlemen will keep drumming: 'We must wait patiently till the war ends – and then London will reward us for the assistance we have given.' As a matter of fact, the imperialists will redouble and triple their exploitation of the toilers both at home and especially in the colonies so as to rehabilitate the country after the havoc and devastation of the war. In these circumstances there cannot even be talk of new social reforms in the metropolitan centres or of grants of liberties to the colonies. Double chains of slavery – that will be the inevitable consequence of the war if the masses of India follow the politics of Gandhi, the Stalinists, and their friends.

The war, however, may bring to India as well as to the other colonies not a redoubled slavery but, on the contrary, complete liberty: the proviso for this is a correct revolutionary policy. The Indian people must divorce their fate from the very outset from that of British imperialism. The oppressors and the oppressed stand on opposite sides of the trenches. No aid whatsoever to the slave owners! On the contrary, those immense difficulties which the war will bring in its wake must be utilised so as to deal a mortal blow to all the ruling classes. That is how the oppressed classes and peoples in all countries should act, irrespective of whether Messrs. Imperialists don democratic or fascist masks.

To realise such a policy a *revolutionary party*, basing itself on the vanguard of the proletariat, is necessary. Such a party does not yet exist in India. The Fourth International offers this party its programme, its experience, its collaboration. The basic conditions for this party are: complete independence from imperialist democracy, complete independence from the Second and Third Internationals and complete independence from the national Indian bourgeoisie.

In a number of colonial and semi-colonial countries sections of the Fourth International already exist and are making successful progress. First place among them is unquestionably held by our section in French Indo-China which is conducting an irreconcilable struggle against French imperialism and 'People's Front' mystifications. 'The Stalinist leaders', it is stated in the newspaper of the Saigon workers (*The Struggle – La Lutte*) of 7 April 1939, 'have taken yet another step on the road of betrayal. Throwing off their masks as revolutionists, they have become champions of imperialism and openly speak out against emancipation of the oppressed colonial peoples.' Owing to their bold revolutionary politics, the Saigon proletarians, members of the Fourth International, scored a brilliant victory over the bloc of the ruling party and the Stalinists at the elections to the colonial council held in April of this year.

The very same policy ought to be pursued by the advanced workers of British India. We must cast away false hopes and repel false friends. We must pin hope only upon ourselves, our own revolutionary forces. The struggle for national independence, for an independent Indian republic is indissolubly linked up with the agrarian revolution, with the nationalisation of banks and trusts, with a number of other economic measures aiming to raise the living standard of the country and to make the toiling masses the masters of their own destiny. Only the proletariat in an alliance with the peasantry is capable of executing these tasks. In its initial stage the revolutionary party will no doubt comprise a tiny minority. In contrast to other parties, however, it will render a cleat accounting of the situation and fearlessly march towards its great goal. It is indispensable in all the industrial centres and cities to establish workers groups, standing under the banner of the Fourth International. Only those intellectuals who have completely come over to the side of the proletariat must be allowed into these groups. Alien to sectarian self-immersion, the revolutionary worker-Marxists must actively participate in the work of the trade unions, educational societies, the Congress Socialist Party and, in general, all mass organisations. Everywhere they remain as the extreme left wing, everywhere they set the example of courage in action, everywhere, in a patient and comradely manner, they explain their programme to the workers, peasants, and revolutionary intellectuals. Impending events will come to the aid of the Indian Bolshevik-Leninists, revealing to the masses the correctness of their path. The party will grow swiftly and become tempered in the fire. Allow me to express my firm hope that the revolutionary struggle for the emancipation of India will unfold under the banner of the Fourth International.

With warmest comradely greetings,
Leon Trotsky,
Coyoacán, Mexico
25 July 1939

Mexico and British Imperialism*
(1938)

The international campaign which imperialist circles are waging over the expropriation of Mexican oil enterprises by the Mexican government has been distinguished by all the features of imperialism's propagandistic bacchanalias – combining impudence,

* From Trotsky Internet Archive (www.marxists.org/archive/trotsky/1938/06/mexico02.htm), with revisions by the editors.

deceitfulness, speculation in ignorance, with cocksureness in its own impunity. The signal for this campaign was given by the British government when it declared a boycott of Mexican oil. Boycott, as is known, always involves self-boycott, and is therefore accompanied by great sacrifices on the part of the boycotter. Great Britain was until recently the largest consumer of Mexican oil; naturally not out of sympathy for the Mexican people, but out of consideration for her own advantage.

Britain and Cedillo[*]

Heaviest consumer of oil in Great Britain itself is the state, with its gigantic navy and rapidly growing air force. A boycott of Mexican oil by the British government signifies, therefore, a simultaneous boycott not only of British industry but also of national defence. Mr Chamberlain's government has shown with unusual frankness that the profits of Britain's capitalist robbers loom above state interests themselves. Oppressed classes and oppressed peoples must thoroughly learn this fundamental conclusion.

Both chronologically and logically the uprising of General Cedillo grew out of Chamberlain's policy. The Monroe Doctrine prevents the British admiralty from applying a military-naval blockade of the Mexican coast. They must act through internal agents, who, it is true, do not openly fly the British flag, yet serve the same interests as Chamberlain – the interests of a clique of oil magnates. In the *White Book* issued by British diplomacy just a few days ago we may be sure that the negotiations of its agents with General Cedillo are not included. Imperialist diplomacy carries on its major business under cover of secrecy.

Ignorance and Deceit

In order to compromise the expropriation in the eyes of bourgeois public opinion, they represent it as a 'Communist' measure. Historical ignorance combines here with conscious deceit. Semi-colonial Mexico is fighting for its national independence, political and economic. This is the basic meaning of the Mexican

---

[*]   In 1938 General Saturnino Cedillo, Governor of San Luis Potosí, led an ill-fated rebellion against the Cárdenas government. – Editors

revolution at *this* stage. The oil magnates are not rank-and-file capitalists, not ordinary bourgeoisie. Having seized the richest natural resources of a foreign country, standing on their billions and supported by the military and diplomatic forces of their metropolis, they strive to establish in the subjugated country a regime of imperialistic feudalism, subordinating to themselves legislation, jurisprudence, and administration. Under these conditions expropriation is the only effective means of safeguarding national independence and the elementary conditions of democracy.

What direction the further economic development of Mexico may take depends decisively upon factors of an international character. But this is a question of the future. The Mexican revolution is now carrying out the same work as, for instance, the United States of America accomplished in three-quarters of a century, beginning with the Revolutionary War for independence and finishing with the Civil War for the abolition of slavery and for national unification. The British government not only did everything at the end of the eighteenth century to retain the United States under the status of a colony, but later, in the years of the Civil War, supported the slaveholders of the South against the abolitionists of the North, striving for the sake of its imperialist interests to thrust the young republic into a state of economic backwardness and national disunity.

Britain and Slavery

To the Chamberlains of that time, too, the expropriation of the slaveholders seemed a diabolical 'Bolshevik' measure. In reality the historic task of the Northerners consisted in clearing the arena for the independent democratic development of bourgeois society. Precisely this task is being solved at this stage by the government of Mexico. General Cárdenas stands among those statesmen of his country who have been fulfilling work comparable to that of Washington, Jefferson, Abraham Lincoln, and General Grant. And, of course, it is not accidental that the British government, in this case, too, finds itself on the other side of the historic trench.

The world press, in particular the French, preposterous as it may seem, continues to drag my name into the question of the expropriation of the oil industry. If I have already refuted this nonsense once it is not at all because I fear 'responsibility', as was insinuated by one talkative agent of the GPU. On the contrary, I would consider it an honour to carry even a part of the responsibility for this courageous and progressive measure of the Mexican government. But I do not have the least basis for it. I first learned of the decree of expropriation from the newspapers. But, naturally, this is not the question.

Two Aims Pursued

Two aims are pursued in interjecting my name. First, the organisers of the campaign wish to impart to the expropriation a 'Bolshevik' coloration. Second, they are attempting to strike a blow at the national self-respect of Mexico. The imperialists are endeavouring to represent the affair as if Mexico's statesmen were incapable of determining their own road. A wretched and ignoble hereditary slaveholders' psychology! Precisely because Mexico today still belongs to those backward nations which are only now impelled to fight for their independence, greater audacity of thought is engendered among its statesmen than is granted to the conservative dregs of a great past. We have witnessed similar phenomena in history more than once!

The French weekly *Marianne*, a notorious organ of the French People's Front, even asserts that on the oil question the government of General Cárdenas acted not only as one with Trotsky but also ... in the interests of Hitler. It is a question, you see, of depriving the great-hearted 'democracies' of oil in case of war and, contrariwise, of supplying Germany and other fascist nations. This is not one whit more clever than the Moscow trials. Humanity learns, not without amazement, that Great Britain is being deprived of Mexican oil because of the ill-will of General Cárdenas and not because of Chamberlain's self-boycott. But then the 'democracies' possess a simple way of paralysing this 'fascist' plot: let them buy Mexican oil, once more Mexican oil, and again Mexican oil! To every honest and sensible person it is now beyond all doubt that if Mexico should find itself forced to sell liquid gold to fascist countries, the responsibility for this act would fall fully and completely upon the governments of the imperialist 'democracies'.

Prompting from Moscow

Behind the back of *Marianne* and its ilk stand the Moscow prompters. At first glance this seems preposterous, since other prompters of the same school use diametrically opposed librettos. But the whole secret consists in the fact that the friends of the GPU adapt their views to geographic gradations of latitude and longitude. If some of them promise support to Mexico, others picture General Cárdenas as an ally of Hitler. From the latter point of view, Cedillo's oil rebellion should be viewed, it would seem, as a struggle in the interests of world democracy.

Let us, however, leave the clowns and intriguers to their own fate. We do not have them in mind, but the class-conscious workers of the entire world. Without succumbing to illusions and without fear of slander, the advanced workers will completely support the Mexican people in their struggle against the imperialists. The expropriation of oil is neither socialism nor communism. But it is a highly progressive measure of national self-defence. Marx did not, of course, consider Abraham Lincoln a communist; this did not, however, prevent Marx from entertaining the deepest sympathy for the struggle that Lincoln headed. The First International sent the Civil War president a message of greeting, and Lincoln in his answer greatly appreciated this moral support.

Workers, Support Mexico

The international proletariat has no reason to identify its programme with the programme of the Mexican government. Revolutionists have no need of changing colour, adapting themselves, and rendering flattery in the manner of the GPU school of courtiers, who in a moment of danger will sell out and betray the weaker side. Without giving up its own identity, every honest working-class organisation of the entire world, and first of all in Great Britain, is duty-bound to take an irreconcilable position against the imperialist robbers, their diplomacy, their press, and their fascist hirelings. The cause of Mexico, like the cause of Spain, like the cause of China, is the cause of the international working class. The struggle over Mexican oil is only one of the advance-line skirmishes of future battles between the oppressors and the oppressed.

Nationalised Industry and Workers' Management*
(1938)

In the industrially backward countries foreign capital plays a decisive role. Hence the relative weakness of the *national* bourgeoisie in relation to the *national* proletariat. This creates special conditions of state power. The government veers between foreign and domestic capital, between the weak national bourgeoisie and the relatively powerful proletariat. This gives the government a Bonapartist character of a distinctive character. It raises itself, so to speak, above classes. Actually, it can govern either by making itself the instrument of foreign capitalism and holding the proletariat in the chains of a police dictatorship, or by manoeuvring with the proletariat and even going so far as to make concessions to it, thus gaining the possibility of a certain freedom from the foreign capitalists. The present policy [of the Mexican government] is in the second stage; its greatest conquests are the expropriations of the railways and the oil industries.

These measures are entirely within the domain of state capitalism. However, in a semi-colonial country, state capitalism finds itself under the heavy pressure of private foreign capital and of its governments, and cannot maintain itself without the active support of the workers. That is why it tries, without letting the real power escape from its hands, to place on the workers' organisations a considerable part of the responsibility for the march of production in the nationalised branches of industry.

What should be the policy of the workers' party in this case? It would of course be a disastrous error, an outright deception, to assert that the road to socialism passes, not through the proletarian revolution, but through nationalisation by the bourgeois state of various branches of industry and their transfer into the hands of the workers' organisations. But it is not a question of that. The bourgeois government has itself carried through the nationalisation and has been compelled to ask participation of the workers in the management of the nationalised industry. One can of course evade the question by citing the fact that unless the proletariat takes possession of the power, participation by the trade unions

*   From Trotsky Internet Archive (www.marxists.org/archive/trotsky/1938/xx/mexico03. htm), with revisions by the editors.

in the management of the enterprises of state capitalism cannot give socialist results. However, such a negative policy from the revolutionary wing would not be understood by the masses and would strengthen the opportunist positions. For Marxists it is not a question of building socialism with the hands of the bourgeoisie, but of utilising the situations that present themselves within state capitalism and advancing the revolutionary movement of the workers.

Participation in bourgeois parliaments can no longer give important positive results; under certain conditions it even leads to the demoralisation of the worker deputies. But this is not an argument for revolutionists in favour of anti-parliamentarism.

It would be inexact to identify the policy of workers' participation in the management of nationalised industry with the participation of socialists in a bourgeois government (which we called *ministerialism*). All the members of the government are bound together by ties of solidarity. A party represented in the government is answerable for the entire policy of the government as a whole. Participation in the management of a certain branch of industry allows full opportunity for political opposition. In case the workers' representatives are in a minority in the management, they have every opportunity to declare and publish their proposals, which were rejected by the majority, to bring them to the knowledge of the workers, etc.

The participation of the trade unions in the management of nationalised industry may be compared to the participation of socialists in the *municipal governments*, where the socialists sometimes win a majority and are compelled to direct an important municipal economy, while the bourgeoisie still has domination in the state and bourgeois property laws continue. Reformists in the municipality adapt themselves passively to the bourgeois regime. Revolutionists in this field do all they can in the interests of the workers and at the same time teach the workers at every step that municipality policy is powerless without conquest of state power.

The difference, to be sure, is that in the field of municipal government the workers win certain positions by means of democratic elections, whereas in the domain of nationalised industry the government itself invites them to take certain posts. But this difference has a purely formal character. In both cases the bourgeoisie is compelled to yield to the workers certain spheres of activity. The workers utilise these in *their own* interests.

It would be light-minded to close one's eye to the dangers that flow from a situation where the trade unions play a leading role in nationalised industry. The basis of the danger is the connection of the top trade union leaders with the apparatus of state capitalism, the transformation of mandated representatives of the proletariat into hostages of the bourgeois state. But however great this danger may be, it constitutes only a part of a general danger – more exactly, of a general sickness. That is to say, the bourgeois degeneration of the trade union apparatuses in the imperialist epoch, not only in the old metropolitan centres, but also in the colonial countries. The trade union leaders are, in an overwhelming majority of cases, *political* agents of the bourgeoisie and of its state. In nationalised industry they can become and already are becoming direct *administrative* agents. Against this there is no other course than the struggle for the independence of the workers' movement in general, and in particular through the formation within the trade unions of firm revolutionary nuclei, which, while at the same time maintaining the unity of the trade union movement, are capable of struggling for a class policy and for a revolutionary composition of the leading bodies.

A danger of another sort lies in the fact that the banks and other capitalist enterprises, upon which a given branch of nationalised industry depends in the economic sense, may and will use special methods of sabotage to put obstacles in the way of the workers' management, to discredit it and push it to disaster. The reformist leaders will try to ward off this danger by servile adaptation to the demands of their capitalist providers, in particular the banks. The revolutionary leaders, on the contrary, will draw the conclusion, from the sabotage by the banks, that it is necessary to expropriate the banks and to establish a *single national bank*, which would be the accounting house of the whole economy. Of course this question must be indissolubly linked to the question of the *conquest of power by the working class*.

The various capitalist enterprises, national and foreign, will inevitably enter into a conspiracy with the state institutions to put obstacles in the way of the workers' management of nationalised industry. On the other hand, the workers' organisations that are in the management of the various branches of nationalised industry must join together to exchange their experiences, must give each other economic support, must act with their joint forces on the government on the conditions of credit, etc. Of course such a central bureau of the workers' management of nationalised branches of industry must be in closest contact with the trade unions.

To sum up, one can say that this new field of work includes within it both the greatest opportunities and the greatest dangers. The dangers consist in the fact that, through the intermediary of controlled trade unions, state capitalism can hold the workers in check, exploit them cruelly, and paralyse their resistance. The revolutionary possibilities consist of the fact that, basing themselves upon their positions in the exceptionally important branches of industry, the workers can lead the attack against all the forces of capital and against the bourgeois state. Which of these possibilities will win out? And in what period of time? It is naturally impossible to predict. That depends entirely on the struggle of the different tendencies within the working class, on the experience of the workers themselves, on the world situation. In any case, to use this new form of activity in the interests of the working class, and not of the labour aristocracy and bureaucracy, only one condition is needed: the existence of a revolutionary Marxist party that carefully studies every form of working class activity, criticizes every deviation, educates and organises the workers, wins influence in the trade unions, and assures a revolutionary workers' representation in nationalised industry.

On Black Nationalism*
(1933, 1939)

I. The Negro Question in America

Swabeck: We have in this question within the American League no noticeable differences of an important character, nor have we yet formulated a programme. I present therefore only the views which we have developed in general.

---

* From Trotsky Internet Archive (www.marxists.org/archive/trotsky/works/1940/negro1. htm), with revisions by the editors.

How must we view the position of the American Negro: As a national minority or as a racial minority? This is of the greatest importance for our programme.

The Stalinists maintain as their main slogan the one of 'self-determination for the Negroes' and demand in connection therewith a separate state and state rights for the Negroes in the black belt. The practical application of the latter demand has revealed much opportunism. On the other hand, I acknowledge that in the practical work amongst the Negroes, despite the numerous mistakes, the [Communist] party can also record some achievements. For example, in the Southern textile strikes, where to a large extent the colour lines were broken down.

[Albert] Weisbord [leader of a small organisation called the Communist League of Struggle], I understand, is in agreement with the slogan of 'self-determination' and separate state rights. He maintains that is the application of the theory of the permanent revolution for America.

We proceed from the actual situation: There are approximately 13 million Negroes in America; the majority are in the Southern states (black belt). In the Northern states the Negroes are concentrated in the industrial communities as industrial workers, in the South they are mainly farmers and sharecroppers.

Trotsky: Do they rent from the state or from private owners?

Swabeck: From private owners, from white farmers and plantation owners; some Negroes own the land they till.

The Negro population of the North are kept on a lower level – economically, socially, and culturally; in the South under oppressive Jim Crow conditions. They are barred from many important trade unions. During and since the war the migration from the South has increased; perhaps about 4–5 million Negroes now live in the North. The Northern Negro population is overwhelmingly proletarian, but also in the South the proletarianisation is progressing.

Today none of the Southern states have a Negro majority. This lends emphasis to the heavy migration, to the North. We put the question thus: Are the Negroes, in a political sense, a national minority or a racial minority? The Negroes have become fully assimilated, Americanised, and their life in America has overbalanced the traditions of the past, modified and changed them. We cannot consider the Negroes a national minority in the sense of having their own separate language. They have no special national customs, or special national culture or religion; nor have they any special national minority interests. It is impossible to speak of them as a national minority in this sense. It is therefore our opinion that the American Negroes are a racial minority whose position and interests are subordinated to the class relations of the country and depending upon them.

To us the Negroes represent an important factor in the class struggle, almost a decisive factor. They are an important section of the proletariat. There is also a Negro petty bourgeoisie in America but not as powerful or as influential or playing the role of the petty bourgeoisie and bourgeoisie among the nationally oppressed people (colonial).

The Stalinist slogan 'self-determination' is in the main based upon an estimate of the American Negroes as a national minority, to be won over as allies. To us the question occurs: Do we want to win the Negroes as allies on such a basis and who do we want to win, the Negro proletariat or the Negro petty bourgeoisie? To us it appears that we will with this slogan win mainly the petty bourgeoisie and we cannot have much interest in winning them as allies on such a basis. We recognise that the poor farmers and sharecroppers are the closest allies of the proletariat but it is our opinion that they can be won as such mainly on the basis of the class struggle. Compromise on this principled question would put the petty bourgeois allies ahead of the proletariat and the poor farmers as well. We recognise the existence of definite stages of development which require specific slogans. But the Stalinist slogan appears to us to lead directly to the 'democratic dictatorship of the proletariat and peasantry'. The unity of the workers, black and white, we must prepare proceeding from a class basis, but in that it is necessary to also recognise the racial issues and in addition to the class slogans also advance the racial slogans. It is our opinion that in this respect the main slogan should be 'social, political and economic equality for the Negroes', as well as the slogans which flow therefrom. This slogan is naturally quite different from the Stalinist slogan of 'self-determination' for a national minority. The [Communist] party leaders maintain that the Negro workers and farmers can be won only on the basis of this slogan. To begin with it was advanced for the Negroes throughout the country, but today only for the Southern states. It is our opinion that we can win the Negro workers only on a class basis advancing also the racial slogans for the necessary intermediary stages of development. In this manner we believe also the poor Negro farmers can best be won as direct allies.

In the main the problem of slogans in regard to the Negro question is the problem of a practical programme.

Trotsky: The point of view of the American comrades appears to me not fully convincing. 'Self-determination' is a democratic demand. Our American comrades advance as against this democratic demand, the liberal demand. This liberal demand is, moreover, complicated. I understand what 'political equality' means. But what is the meaning of economical and social equality within capitalist society? Does that mean a demand to public opinion that all enjoy the equal protection of the laws? But that is political equality. The slogan 'political, economic, and social equality' sounds equivocal and while it is not clear to me it nevertheless suggests itself easy of misinterpretation.

The Negroes are a race and not a nation: Nations grow out of the racial material under definite conditions. The Negroes in Africa are not yet a nation but they are in the process of building a nation. The American Negroes are on a higher cultural level. But while they are there under the pressure of the Americans they become interested in the development of the Negroes in Africa. The American Negro will develop leaders for Africa, that one can say with certainty and that in turn will influence the development of political consciousness in America.

We do, of course, not obligate the Negroes to become a nation; if they are, then that is a question of their consciousness, that is, what they desire and what they strive for. We say: If the Negroes want that then we must fight against imperialism to the last drop of blood, so that they gain the right, wherever and how they please, to separate a piece of land for themselves. The fact that they are today not a majority in any state does not matter. It is not a question of the authority of the states but of the Negroes. That in the overwhelming Negro territory also whites have existed and will remain henceforth is not the question and we do not need today to break our heads over a possibility that sometime the whites will be suppressed by the Negroes. In any case the suppression of the Negroes pushes them toward a political and national unity.

That the slogan 'self-determination' will rather win the petty bourgeois instead of the workers – that argument holds good also for the slogan of equality. It is clear that the special Negro elements who appear more in the public eye (businessmen, intellectuals, lawyers, etc.) are more active and react more actively against the inequality. It is possible to say that the liberal demand just as well as the democratic one in the first instance will attract the petty bourgeois and only later the workers.

If the situation was such that in America common actions existed between the white and the coloured workers, that the class fraternisation had already become a fact, then perhaps the arguments of our comrades would have a basis – I do not say that they would be correct – then perhaps we would separate the coloured workers from the white if we commence with the slogan 'self-determination'.

But today the white workers in relation to the Negroes are the oppressors, scoundrels, who persecute the black and the yellow, hold them in contempt and lynch them. When the Negro workers today unite with their own petty bourgeois that is because they are not yet sufficiently developed to defend their elementary rights. To the workers in the Southern states the liberal demand for 'social, political, and economic equality' would undoubtedly mean progress, but the demand for 'self-determination' a greater progress. However, with the slogan 'social, political, and economic equality' they can much easier be misled ('according to the law you have this equality').

When we are so far that the Negroes say we want autonomy, they then take a position hostile toward American imperialism. At that stage already the workers will be much more determined than the petty bourgeoisie. The workers will then see that the petty bourgeoisie is incapable of struggle and gets nowhere, but they will also recognise simultaneously that the white Communist workers fight for their demands and that will push them, the Negro proletarians, toward Communism.

Weisbord is correct in a certain sense that the 'self-determination' of the Negroes belongs to the question of the permanent revolution in America. The Negroes will through their awakening, through their demand for autonomy, and through the democratic mobilisation of their forces, be pushed on toward the class basis. The petty bourgeoisie will take up the demand for 'social, political, and economic equality' and for 'self-determination' but prove absolutely incapable in the struggle; the Negro proletariat will march over the petty bourgeoisie in the direction toward the proletarian revolution. That is perhaps for them the most important road. I can therefore see no reason why we should not advance the demand for 'self-determination'.

I am not sure if the Negroes do not also in the Southern states speak their own Negro language. Now that they are being lynched just because of being Negroes they naturally fear to speak their Negro language; but when they are set free their Negro language will again become alive. I will advise the American comrades to study this question very seriously, including the language in the Southern states. Because of all these reasons I would in this question rather lean toward the standpoint of the [Communist] party; of course, with the observation: I have never studied this question and in my remarks I proceed from the general considerations. I base myself only upon the arguments brought forward by the American comrades. I find them insufficient and consider them a certain concession to the point of view of American chauvinism, which seems to me to be dangerous.

What can we lose in this question when we go ahead with our demands, and what have the Negroes today to lose? We do not compel them to separate from the States, but they have the full right to self-determination when they so desire and we will support and defend them with all the means at our disposal in the conquestion [conquest] of this right, the same as we defend all oppressed peoples.

Swabeck: I admit that you have advanced powerful arguments but I am not yet entirely convinced. The existence of a special Negro language in the Southern states is possible; but in general all American Negroes speak English. They are fully assimilated. Their religion is the American Baptist and the language in their churches is likewise English.

Economic equality we do not at all understand in the sense of the law. In the North (as of course also in the Southern states) the wages for Negroes are always lower than for white workers and mostly their hours are longer, that is so to say accepted as a natural basis. In addition, the Negroes are allotted the most disagreeable work. It is because of these conditions that we demand economic equality for the Negro workers.

We do not contest the right of the Negroes to self-determination. That is not the issue of our disagreement with the Stalinists. But we contest the correctness of the slogan of 'self-determination' as a means to win the Negro masses. The impulse of the Negro population is first of all in the direction toward equality in a social, political, and economic sense. At present the party advances the slogan for 'self-determination' only for the Southern states. Of course, one can hardly expect that the Negroes from the Northern industries should want to return to the South and there are no indications of such a desire. On the contrary. Their unformulated demand is for 'social, political, and economic equality' based upon the conditions under which they live. That is also the case in the South. It is because of this that we believe this to be the important racial slogan. We do not look upon the Negroes as being under national oppression in the same sense as the oppressed colonial peoples. It is our opinion that the slogan of the Stalinists tends to lead the Negroes away from the class basis and more in the direction of the racial basis. That is the main reason for our being opposed to it. We are of the belief that the racial slogan in the sense as presented by us leads directly toward the class basis.

Frank: Are there special Negro movements in America?

Swabeck: Yes, several. First we had the Garvey movement based upon the aim of migration to Africa. It had a large following but busted up as a swindle. Now there is not much left of it. Its slogan was the creation of a Negro republic in Africa. Other Negro movements in the main rest upon a foundation of social and political equality demands as, for example, the League [National Association] for Advancement of Colored People. This is a large racial movement.

Trotsky: I believe that also the demand for 'social, political, and economic equality' should remain and I do not speak *against* this demand. It is progressive to the extent that it is not realised. The explanation of Comrade Swabeck in regard to the question of economic equality is very important. But that alone does not yet decide the question of the Negro fate as such, the question of the 'nation', etc. According to the arguments of the American comrades one could say for example that also Belgium has no right as a 'nation'. The Belgians are Catholics and a large section of them speak French. What if France would annex them with such an argument? Also the Swiss people, through their historical connection, feel themselves, despite different languages and religion, as one nation. An abstract criterion is not decisive in this question, but much more decisive is the historical consciousness, their feelings and their impulses. But that also is not determined accidentally but rather by the general conditions. The question of religion has absolutely nothing to do with this question of the nation. The Baptism of the Negro is something entirely different from the Baptism of Rockefeller: These are two different religions.

The political argument rejecting the demand for 'self-determination' is doctrinarism. That we heard always in Russia in regard to the question of 'self-determination'. The Russian experiences have shown to us that the groups who live on a peasant basis retain peculiarities, their customs, their language, etc., and given the opportunity they develop again.

The Negroes are not yet awakened and they are not yet united with the white workers. Ninety-nine point nine per cent of the American workers are chauvinists. In relation to the Negroes they are hangmen and they are so also toward the Chinese. It is necessary to teach the American beasts. It is necessary to make them understand that the American state is not their state and that they do not have to be the guardians of this state. Those American workers who say: 'The Negroes should separate when they so desire and we will defend them against our American police' – those are revolutionists, I have confidence in them.

The argument that the slogan for 'self-determination' leads away from the class basis is an adaptation to the ideology of the white workers. The Negro can be developed to a class standpoint only when the white worker is educated. On the whole the question of the colonial people is in the first instance a question of the development of the metropolitan worker.

The American worker is indescribably reactionary. It is shown today that he is not even yet won for the idea of social insurance. Because of this the American Communists are obligated to advance reform demands.

When today the Negroes do not demand self-determination that is naturally for the same reason that the white workers do not yet advance the slogan of the proletarian dictatorship. The Negro has not yet got it into his head that he dares to carve out for himself a piece of the great and mighty States. But the white worker must meet the Negroes half-way and say to them: 'When you want to separate you will have our support.' Also the Czech workers came only through the disillusion with their own state to Communism.

I believe that by the unheard-of political and theoretical backwardness and the unheard-of economic advance the awakening of the working class will proceed quite rapidly. The old ideological covering will burst, all questions will emerge at once, and since the country is so economically mature the adaptation of the political and theoretical to the economic level will be achieved very rapidly. It is then possible that the Negroes will become the most advanced section. We have already a similar example in Russia. The Russians were the European Negroes. It is very possible that the Negroes also through the self-determination will proceed to the proletarian dictatorship in a couple of gigantic strides, ahead of the great bloc of white workers. They will then furnish the vanguard. I am absolutely sure that they will in any case fight better than the white workers. That, however, can happen only provided the Communist Party carries on an uncompromising merciless struggle not against the supposed national prepossessions of the Negroes but against the colossal prejudices of the white workers and gives it no concession whatever.

Swabeck: It is then your opinion that the slogan for 'self-determination' will be a means to set the Negroes into motion against American imperialism?

Trotsky: Naturally, thereby that the Negroes can carve out their own state out of mighty America and with the support of the white workers their self-consciousness develops enormously.

The reformists and the revisionists have written much on the subject that capitalism is carrying on the work of civilisation in Africa and if the peoples of Africa are left to themselves they will be the more exploited by businessmen, etc., much more than now where they at least have a certain measure of lawful protection. To a certain extent this argument can be correct. But in this case it is also first of all a question of the European workers: without their liberation the real colonial liberation is also not possible. When the white worker performs the role of the oppressor he cannot liberate himself, much less the colonial peoples. The self-determination of the colonial peoples can, in certain periods, lead to different results; in the final instance, however, it will lead to the struggle against imperialism and to the liberation of the colonial peoples.

Austrian Social Democracy (particularly Renner) also put before the [First World] War the question of the national minorities abstractly. They argued likewise that the slogan for 'self-determination' would only lead the workers away from the class standpoint and that such minority states could not live independently. Was this way of putting the question correct or false? It was abstract. The Austrian Social Democrats said that the national minorities were not nations. What do we see today? The separate pieces [of the old Austro-Hungarian empire, beaded by the Hapsburgs] exist, rather bad, but they exist. The Bolsheviks fought in Russia always for the self-determination of the national minorities including the right of complete separation. And yet, by achieving self-determination these groups remained with the Soviet Union. If Austrian Social Democracy had before accepted a correct policy in this question, they would have said to the national minority groups: 'You have the full right to self-determination, we have no interest whatever to keep you in the hands of the Hapsburg monarchy' – it would then have been possible after the revolution to create a great Danube federation. The dialectic of the developments shows that where the tight centralism existed the state went to pieces and where the complete self-determination was proposed a real state emerged and remained united.

The Negro question is of enormous importance for America. The League must undertake a serious discussion of this question, perhaps in an internal bulletin.

II. Self-Determination for the American Negroes

Trotsky: Comrade Johnson proposes that we discuss the Negro question in three parts, the first to be devoted to the programmatic question of self-determination for the Negroes.

[Statistical material was introduced which was not included in the report.]

Johnson: The basic proposals for the Negro question have already been distributed and here it is only necessary to deal with the question of self-determination. No one denies the Negroes' right to self-determination. It is a question of whether we should advocate it. In Africa and in the West Indies we advocate self-determination because a large majority of the people want it. In Africa the great masses of the people look upon self-determination as a restoration of their independence. In the West Indies, where we have a population similar in origin to the Negroes in America, there, has been developing a national sentiment. The Negroes are a majority. Already we hear ideas, among the more advanced, of a West Indian nation, and it is highly probable that, even let us suppose that the Negroes were offered full and free rights as citizens of the British Empire, they would probably oppose it and wish to be absolutely free and independent ... It is progressive. It is a step in the right direction. We weaken the enemy. It puts the workers in a position to make great progress toward socialism.

In America the situation is different. The Negro desperately wants to be an American citizen. He says, 'I have been here from the beginning; I did all the work here in the early days. Jews, Poles, Italians, Swedes and others come here and have all the privileges. You say that some of the Germans are spies. I will never spy. I have nobody for whom to spy. And yet you exclude me from the army and from the rights of citizenship.'

In Poland and Catalonia there is a tradition of language, literature and history to add to the economic and political oppression and to help weld the population in its progressive demand for self-determination. In America it is not so. Let us look at certain historic events in the development of the Negro America. [Marcus] Garvey raised the slogan 'Back to Africa' [through the United Negro Improvement Association in the 1920s], but the

Negroes who followed him did not believe for the most part that they were really going back to Africa. We know that those in the West Indies who were following him had not the slightest intention of going back to Africa, but they were glad to follow a militant leadership. And there is the case of a black woman who was pushed by a white woman in a street car and said to her. 'You wait until Marcus gets into power and all you people will be treated in the way you deserve.' Obviously she was not thinking of poor Africa.

There was, however, this concentration on the Negroes' problems simply because the white workers in 1919 were not developed. There was no political organisation of any power calling upon the blacks and the whites to unite. The Negroes were just back from the war – militant and having no offer of assistance; they naturally concentrated on their own particular affairs.

In addition, however, we should note that in Chicago, where a race riot took place, the riot was deliberately provoked by the employers. Some time before it actually broke out, the black and white meatpackers had struck and had paraded through the Negro quarter in Chicago with the black population cheering the Whites in the same way that they cheered the blacks. For the capitalists this was a very dangerous thing and they set themselves to creating race friction. At one stage, motor cars, with white people in them, sped through the Negro quarter shooting at all whom they saw. The capitalist press played up the differences and thus set the stage and initiated the riots that took place for dividing the population and driving the Negro back upon himself.

During the period of the crisis there was a rebirth of these nationalist movements. There was a movement toward the 49th state and the movement concentrated around Liberia was developing. These movements assumed fairly large proportions up to at least 1934.

Then in 1936 came the organization of the CIO [Congress of Industrial Organizations]. [CIO president] John L. Lewis appointed a special Negro department. The New Deal made gestures to the Negroes. Blacks and whites fought together in various struggles. These nationalist movements have tended to disappear as the Negro saw the opportunity to fight with the organised workers and to gain something.

The danger of our advocating and injecting a policy of self-determination is that it is the surest way to divide and confuse the workers in the South. The white workers have centuries of prejudice to overcome, but at the present time many of them are working with the Negroes in the Southern sharecroppers' union and with the rise of the struggle there is every possibility that they will be able to overcome their age-long prejudices. But for us to propose that the Negro have this black state for himself is asking too much from the white workers, especially when the Negro himself is not making the same demand. The slogans of 'abolition of debts', 'confiscation of large properties', etc., are quite sufficient to lead them both to fight together and on the basis of economic struggle to make a united fight for the abolition of social discrimination.

I therefore propose concretely: (1) That we are for the right of self-determination. (2) If some demand should arise among the Negroes for the right of self-determination we should support it. (3) We do not go out of our way to raise this slogan and place an unnecessary barrier between ourselves and socialism. (4) An investigation should be made into these movements; the one led by Garvey, the movement for the 49th state, the movement centring around Liberia. Find out what groups of the population supported them and on this basis come to some opinion as to how far there is any demand among the Negroes for self-determination.

Trotsky: I do not quite understand whether Comrade Johnson proposes to eliminate the slogan of self-determination for the Negroes from our programme,[*] or is it that we do not say that we are ready to do everything possible for the self-determination of the Negroes if they want it themselves. It is a question for the party as a whole, if we eliminate it or not. We are ready to help them if they want it. As a party we can remain absolutely neutral on this. We cannot say it will be reactionary. It is not reactionary.

---

[*] In the internal bulletin of the Socialist Workers Party of the US, Johnson had written: 'The Negro must be won for socialism. There is no other way out for him in America or elsewhere. But he must be won on the basis of his own experiences and his own activity. There is no other way for him to learn, nor for that matter, for any other group of toilers! If he wanted self-determination, then however reactionary it might be in every other respect, it would be the business of the revolutionary party to raise that slogan. If after the revolution he insisted on carrying out that slogan and forming his own Negro state, the revolutionary party would have to stand by its promises and patiently trust to economic development and education to achieve an integration. But the Negro, fortunately for socialism, does not want self-determination.' – Editors

We cannot tell them to set up a state because that will weaken imperialism and so will be good for us, the white workers. That would be against internationalism itself. We cannot say to them, 'Stay here, even at the price of economic progress.' We can say, 'It is for you to decide. If you wish to take a part of the country, it is all right, but we do not wish to make the decision for you.'

I believe that the differences between the West Indies, Catalonia, Poland, and the situation of the Negroes in the States are not so decisive. Rosa Luxemburg was against self-determination for Poland. She felt that it was reactionary and fantastic, as fantastic as demanding the right to fly. It shows that she did not possess the necessary historic imagination in this case. The landlords and representatives of the Polish ruling class were also opposed to self-determination for their own reasons.

Comrade Johnson used three verbs: 'support', 'advocate', and 'inject' the idea of self-determination. I do not propose for the party to advocate, I do not propose to inject, but only to proclaim our obligation to support the struggle for self-determination if the Negroes themselves want it. It is not a question of our Negro comrades. It is a question of 13 or 14 million Negroes. The majority of them are very backward. They are not very clear as to what they wish now and we must give them a credit for the future. They will decide then.

What you said about the Garvey movement is interesting – but it proves that we must be cautious and broad and not base ourselves upon the status quo. The black woman who said to the white woman, 'Wait until Marcus is in power. We will know how to treat you then', was simply expressing her desire for her own state. The American Negroes gathered under the banner of the 'Back to Africa' movement because it seemed a possible fulfilment of their wish for their own home. They did not want actually to go to Africa. It was the expression of a mystic desire for a home in which they would be free of the domination of the whites, in which they themselves could control their own fate. That also was a wish for self-determination. It was once expressed by some in a religious form and now it takes the form of a dream of an independent state. Here in the United States the whites are so powerful, so cruel and rich that the poor Negro sharecropper does not dare to say, even to himself, that he will take a part of his country for himself. Garvey spoke in glowing terms, that it was

beautiful and that here all would be wonderful. Any psychoanalyst
will say that the real content of this dream was to have their own
home. It is not an argument in favour of injecting the idea. It is
only an argument by which we can foresee the possibility of their
giving their dream a more realistic form.

Under the condition that Japan invades the United States and
the Negroes are called upon to fight – they may come to feel
themselves threatened first from one side and then from the other,
and finally awakened, may say, 'We have nothing to do with either
of you. We will have our own state.'

But the black state could enter into a federation. If the American
Negroes succeeded in creating their own state, I am sure that
after a few years of the satisfaction and pride of independence,
they would feel the need of entering into a federation. Even if
Catalonia which is very industrialised and highly developed
province, had realised its independence, it would have been just
a step to federation.

The Jews in Germany and Austria wanted nothing more than
to be the best German chauvinists. The most miserable of all
was the Social Democrat, Austerlitz, the editor of the *Arbeiter-
zeitung*. But now, with the turn of events, Hitler does not permit
them to be German chauvinists. Now many of them have become
Zionists and are Palestinian nationalists and anti-German. I saw a
disgusting picture recently of a Jewish actor, arriving in America,
bending down to kiss the soil of the United States. Then they will
get a few blows from the fascist fists in the United States and they
will go to kiss the soil of Palestine.

There is another alternative to the successful revolutionary
one. It is possible that fascism will come to power with its racial
delirium and oppression and the reaction of the Negro will be
toward racial independence. Fascism in the United States will
be directed against the Jews and the Negroes, but against the
Negroes particularly, and in a most terrible manner. A 'privileged'
condition will be created for the American white workers on the
backs of the Negroes. The Negroes have done everything possible
to become an integral part of the United States, in a psychological
as well as a political sense. We must foresee that their reaction
will show its power during the revolution. They will enter with a
great distrust of the whites. We must remain neutral in the matter

and hold the door open for both possibilities and promise our full support if they wish to create their own independent state.

So far as I am informed, it seems to me that the CP's attitude of making an imperative slogan of it was false. It was a case of the whites saying to the Negroes, 'You must create a ghetto for yourselves.' It is tactless and false and can only serve to repulse the Negroes. Their only interpretation can be that the whites want to be separated from them. Our Negro comrades of course have the right to participate more intimately in such developments. Our Negro comrades can say, 'The Fourth International says that if it is our wish to be independent, it will help us in every way possible, but that the choice is ours. However, I, as a Negro member of the Fourth, hold a view that we must remain in the same state as the whites', and so on. He can participate in the formation of the political and racial ideology of the Negroes.

Johnson: I am very glad that we have had this discussion, because I agree with you entirely. It seems to be the idea in America that we should advocate it as the CP has done. You seem to think that there is a greater possibility of the Negroes wanting self-determination than I think is probable. But we have a 100 per cent agreement on the idea of which you have put forward that we should be neutral in the development.

Trotsky: It is the word 'reactionary' that bothered me.

Johnson: Let me quote from the document: 'If he wanted self-determination, then however reactionary it might be in every other respect, it would be the business of the revolutionary party to raise that slogan.' I consider the idea of separating as a step backward so far as a socialist society is concerned. If the white workers extend a hand to the Negro, he will not want self-determination.

Trotsky: It is too abstract, because the realisation of this slogan can be reached only as the 13 or 14 million Negroes feel that the domination by the whites is terminated. To fight for the possibility of realising an independent state is a sight of great moral and political awakening. It would be a tremendous revolutionary step. This ascendancy would immediately have the best economic consequences.

5

BRACING FOR THE STORM

The approach of the Second World War was evident to Trotsky by the early 1930s. It would obviously be far more devastating than the First. He was convinced that the dominant forces in the organised working-class movement, the Social Democrats and the Stalinists, were politically bankrupt. Trotsky laboured tirelessly, relentlessly, to draw together revolutionary activists into a new world party of socialist revolution, the Fourth International, so that the decades-long accumulation of revolutionary Marxist insight and experience would not be lost. He knew that the coming war posed innumerable dangers and horrors, but – just as had been the case with the worldwide imperialist slaughter of 1914–18 – also a very profound radicalisation in countries throughout the world, a crisis of the old order, and immense revolutionary opportunities. The Fourth International was formally established in 1938, before the tidal wave of total war washed over so much of the world. The hope was that the handfuls of dedicated men and women committed to the new International's revolutionary socialist perspectives would be able to unfurl 'a stainless banner' that would be able to attract masses of other men and women radicalised by the upcoming experiences.[1]

Those who gathered at the founding conference of the Fourth International were influenced not simply by the immense defeats generated by Social Democracy and Stalinism, referred to in earlier pages of this volume, and not simply by the initial victories won by the Bolsheviks of 1917–21, but also by recent class-struggle victories – partial victories, to be sure, but no less vibrant for that – that had blocked the rise of fascism in France and that had resulted in the might triumphs of the Congress of Industrial Organizations (CIO) in the United States.[2] All of these lessons found reflection in the central document of the founding conference, 'The Death Agony of Capitalism and the Tasks of the Fourth International', more popularly known as the Transitional Programme. Excerpts of the Transitional Programme are presented as the initial reading of this section. Sketched here is a methodological approach toward the development of a socialist strategy. Within the context of actual struggles, revolutionaries must develop 'a system of transitional demands, stemming from today's conditions and today's consciousness of wide layers of the working class' and yet in fundamental conflict with the actual dynamics of the capitalist economy, therefore 'unalterably leading to one final conclusion: the conquest of power by the proletariat'.

Trotsky's thought, however, was not characterised simply by drawing on 'the lessons of the past' (important as these might be) to make sense of current realities and future possibilities. Essential to his approach to Marxism and to reality is the understanding that qualitatively *new* realities come into being – especially in the context of the most expansive and dynamic economic system in human history, capitalism – which may call for tactical and strategic innovations. Alert to persistent patterns calling for new theorisations, he began working, shortly before his death, on the second reading in this section, 'Trade Unions in the Epoch of Imperialist Decay', which remained unfinished at the time of his assassination. It begins with a thought that has ominous implications for those inclined to base themselves on the programmatic orientation of the *Communist Manifesto*, with its focus on the building of trade unions as a central feature of building a revolutionary workers' movement. 'There is one common feature in the development, or more correctly the degeneration, of modern trade unions organisations throughout the world: it is their drawing closely to and growing together with state power.'

The final months of Trotsky's life in his Mexican exile were marked not only by an engagement with world events or analysing broad political and socio-economic trends. He was facing the certainty of imminent death either by assassination (one failed attempt clearly indicated that there would be another) or by his own rising blood pressure.[3] Aspects of the way he coped with this are indicated in the final reading here – his testament. It is a simple, powerful text that has moved many of his critics as well as followers.

Notes

1. On Trotsky's efforts, see George Breitman, 'The Rocky Road to the Fourth International, 1933–38', in Anthony Marcus, ed., *Malcolm X and the Third American Revolution: The Writings of George Breitman* (Amherst, NY: Humanity Books, 2005), 299–352. Valuable reflections can be found in Ernest Mandel, 'Reasons for Founding the Fourth International and Why They Remain Valid Today', in Ernest Mandel, *Revolutionary Marxism and Social Reality in the 20th Century, Collected Essays*, ed. Steve Bloom (Atlantic Highlands, NJ: Humanities Press, 1994), 143–78. Also see: Pierre Frank, *The Fourth International: The Long March of the Trotskyists* (London: Ink Links, 1979); Robert J. Alexander, *International Trotskyism, 1929–1985: A Documentary Analysis of the Movement* (Durham, NC: Duke University Press, 1991); Daniel Bensaïd, *Strategies of Resistance and 'Who Are the Trotskyists?'* (London: Socialist Resistance, 2009). See also the invaluable Encyclopedia of Trotskyism On-Line (ETOL): www.marxists.org/history/etol/index.htm.
2. See Jacques Danos and Marcel Gibelin, *June '36, Class Struggle and the Popular Front in France* (London: Bookmarks, 1986), and Art Preis, *Labor's Giant Step, Twenty Years of the CIO* (New York: Pathfinder Press, 1972).
3. A careful reconstruction of Trotsky's final exile, strong in historical detail though weaker in its understanding of Trotsky's politics, is Bertand M. Patenaude, *Trotsky: Downfall of a Revolutionary* (New York: HarperCollins, 2009). A very fine, slim volume, rich in photographs, is Alain Dugrand, *Trotsky in Mexico 1937–1940* (Manchester: Carcanet, 1992).

The Transitional Programme: The Death Agony of Capitalism and the Tasks of the Fourth International* (1938)

The Objective Prerequisites for a Socialist Revolution

The world political situation as a whole is chiefly characterised by a historical crisis of the leadership of the proletariat.

The economic prerequisite for the proletarian revolution has already in general achieved the highest point of fruition that can be reached under capitalism. Mankind's productive forces stagnate. Already new inventions and improvements fail to raise the level of material wealth. Conjunctural crises under the conditions of the social crisis of the whole capitalist system inflict ever heavier deprivations and sufferings upon the masses.

---

* From Trotsky Internet Archive (www.marxists.org/archive/trotsky/1938/tp/index.htm), with revisions by the editors.

Growing unemployment, in its turn, deepens the financial crisis of the state and undermines the unstable monetary systems. Democratic regimes, as well as fascist, stagger on from one bankruptcy to another.

The bourgeoisie itself sees no way out. In countries where it has already been forced to stake its last upon the card of fascism, it now toboggans with closed eyes toward an economic and military catastrophe. In the historically privileged countries, that is, in those where the bourgeoisie can still for a certain period permit itself the luxury of democracy at the expense of national accumulations (Great Britain, France, United States, etc.), all of capital's traditional parties are in a state of perplexity bordering on a paralysis of will.

The 'New Deal', despite its first period of pretentious resoluteness, represents but a special form of political perplexity, possible only in a country where the bourgeoisie succeeded in accumulating incalculable wealth. The present crisis, far from having run its full course, has already succeeded in showing that 'New Deal' politics, like Popular Front politics in France, opens no new exit from the economic blind alley.

International relations present no better picture. Under the increasing tension of capitalist disintegration, imperialist antagonisms reach an impasse at the height of which separate clashes and bloody local disturbances (Ethiopia, Spain, the Far East, Central Europe) must inevitably coalesce into a conflagration of world dimensions. The bourgeoisie, of course, is aware of the mortal danger to its domination represented by a new war. But that class is now immeasurably less capable of averting war than on the eve of 1914.

All talk to the effect that historical conditions have not yet 'ripened' for socialism is the product of ignorance or conscious deception. The objective prerequisites for the proletarian revolution have not only 'ripened'; they have begun to get somewhat rotten. Without a socialist revolution, in the next historical period at that, a catastrophe threatens the whole culture of mankind. The turn is now to the proletariat, that is, chiefly to its revolutionary vanguard. The historical crisis of mankind is reduced to the crisis of the revolutionary leadership.

The Proletariat and its Leadership

The economy, the state, the politics of the bourgeoisie and its international relations are completely blighted by a social crisis, characteristic of a prerevolutionary state of society. The chief obstacle in the path of transforming the prerevolutionary into a revolutionary state is the opportunist character of proletarian leadership: its petty bourgeois cowardice before the big bourgeoisie and its perfidious connection with it even in its death agony.

In all countries the proletariat is racked by a deep disquiet. The multimillioned masses again and again enter the road of revolution. But each time they are blocked by their own conservative bureaucratic machines.

The Spanish proletariat has made a series of heroic attempts since April 1931 to take power in its hands and guide the fate of society. However, its own parties (Social Democrats, Stalinists, Anarchists, POUMists) – each in its own way acted as a brake and thus prepared Franco's triumphs.

In France, the great wave of 'sit down' strikes, particularly during June 1936, revealed the wholehearted readiness of the proletariat to overthrow the capitalist system. However, the leading organisations (Socialists, Stalinists, Syndicalists) under the label of the Popular Front succeeded in canalising and damming, at least temporarily, the revolutionary stream.

The unprecedented wave of sit down strikes and the amazingly rapid growth of industrial unionism in the United States (the CIO) is the most indisputable expression of the instinctive striving of the American workers to raise themselves to the level of the tasks imposed on them by history. But here, too, the leading political organisations, including the newly created CIO, do everything possible to keep in check and paralyse the revolutionary pressure of the masses.

The definite passing over of the Comintern to the side of bourgeois order, its cynically counterrevolutionary role throughout the world, particularly in Spain, France, the United States, and other 'democratic' countries, created exceptional supplementary difficulties for the world proletariat. Under the banner of the October Revolution, the conciliatory politics practiced by the 'People's Front' doom the working class to impotence and clear the road for fascism.

'People's Fronts' on the one hand – fascism on the other: these are the last political resources of imperialism in the struggle against the proletarian revolution. From the historical point of view, however, both these resources are stopgaps. The decay of capitalism continues under the sign of the Phrygian cap* in France as under the sign of the swastika in Germany. Nothing short of the overthrow of the bourgeoisie can open a road out.

The orientation of the masses is determined first by the objective conditions of decaying capitalism, and second, by the treacherous politics of the old workers' organisations. Of these factors, the first, of course, is the decisive one: the laws of history are stronger than the bureaucratic apparatus. No matter how the methods of the social betrayers differ – from the 'social' legislation of [French Socialist prime minister Leon] Blum to the judicial frame-ups of Stalin – they will never succeed in breaking the revolutionary will of the proletariat. As time goes on, their desperate efforts to hold back the wheel of history will demonstrate more clearly to the masses that the crisis of the proletarian leadership, having become the crisis in mankind's culture, can be resolved only by the Fourth International.

The Minimum Programme and the Transitional Programme

The strategic task of the next period – prerevolutionary period of agitation, propaganda, and organisation – consists in overcoming the contradiction between the maturity of the objective revolutionary conditions and the immaturity of the proletariat and its vanguard (the confusion and disappointment of the older generation, the inexperience of the younger generation). It is necessary to help the masses in the process of the daily struggle to find the bridge between present demand and the socialist programme of the revolution. This bridge should include a system of *transitional demands*, stemming from today's conditions and from today's consciousness of wide layers of the working class and unalterably leading to one final conclusion: the conquest of power by the proletariat.

Classical Social Democracy, functioning in an epoch of progressive capitalism, divided its programme into two parts

---

* The liberty cap, symbol of the French Revolution. – Editors

independent of each other: the *minimum programme* which limited itself to reforms within the framework of bourgeois society, and the *maximum programme* which promised substitution of socialism for capitalism in the indefinite future. Between the minimum and the maximum programmes no bridge existed. And indeed Social Democracy has no need of such a bridge, since the word *socialism* is used only for holiday speechifying. The Comintern has set out to follow the path of Social Democracy in an epoch of decaying capitalism: when, in general, there can be no discussion of systematic social reforms and the raising of the masses' living standards; when every serious demand of the proletariat and even every serious demand of the petty bourgeoisie inevitably reaches beyond the limits of capitalist property relations and of the bourgeois state.

The strategic task of the Fourth International lies not in reforming capitalism but in its overthrow. Its political aim is the conquest of power by the proletariat for the purpose of expropriating the bourgeoisie. However, the achievement of this strategic task is unthinkable without the most considered attention to all, even small and partial, questions of tactics. All sections of the proletariat, all its layers, occupations and groups should be drawn into the revolutionary movement. The present epoch is distinguished not for the fact that it frees the revolutionary party from day-to-day work but because it permits this work to be carried on indissolubly with the actual tasks of the revolution.

The Fourth International does not discard the program of the old 'minimal' demands to the degree to which these have preserved at least part of their vital forcefulness. Indefatigably, it defends the democratic rights and social conquests of the workers. But it carries on this day-to-day work within the framework of the correct actual, that is, revolutionary perspective. Insofar as the old, partial, 'minimal' demands of the masses clash with the destructive and degrading tendencies of decadent capitalism – and this occurs at each step – the Fourth International advances a system of *transitional demands*, the essence of which is contained in the fact that ever more openly and decisively they will be directed against the very bases of the bourgeois regime. The old 'minimal programme' is superseded by the *transitional programme*, the task of which lies in systematic mobilisation of the masses for the proletarian revolution ...

[*Trotsky goes on, at this point, to discuss possible transitional demands – a sliding scale of wages and hours to keep pace with inflation while providing full employment – that would seem quite reasonable to the majority of people but would come into conflict with the continued existence of capitalism. He follows this with a discussion of building a class-struggle left-wing in the unions, and also developing democratic working-class committees in the workplaces to establish greater workers' control, and also the elimination of 'business secrets' used to cheat the workers – advancing the demand 'open the books!' Also posed are the questions of the workers expropriating capitalist enterprises and industries (though factory occupations), nationaliszing banks and the credit system, putting all of this under the control of the working class.*

Trotsky's discussion outlines a tactical escalation that includes massive picket-lines, defence guards to protect mass picketing and other workers' actions, the development of workers' militias and the general arming of the working class – all within the context of mass struggles carried out by a radicalising labour movement, which would be forced to confront attacks by the government, by armed thugs hired by the employers, fascist gangs, etc. All of this reflects actual struggles in which Trotskyists of various countries had participated. Since Trotsky saw this as posing the question of political power, he continued with a discussion of a workers and farmers alliance, the struggle against imperialism and war, and the call for 'a workers' and farmers' government', which Trotsky defined as a popularisation of the concept of working-class political rule (or 'dictatorship of the proletariat'), based on democratic councils in workplaces and communities.

Reference points in the foregoing discussion are to realities in the industrially advanced capitalist countries. The document then goes on to discuss at length realities of colonialism and imperialism, and the fight for the interests of workers and peasants in the oppressed regions of Asia, Africa, and Latin America. This is followed by substantial sections discussing struggles in fascist countries and also in the Soviet Union. After the critical discussion of left-wing political currents deemed to be either succumbing to 'opportunism and unprincipled revisionism' on the one hand, or to 'sectarianism' on the other, the document calls for connecting with fresh radicalising forces, especially to women workers and the youth. – Editors]

Under the Banner of the Fourth International!

Sceptics ask: But has the moment for the creation of the Fourth International yet arrived? It is impossible, they say, to create an International 'artificially'; it can arise only out of great events, etc., etc. All of these objections merely show that sceptics are no good for the building of a new International. They are good for scarcely anything at all.

The Fourth International has already arisen out of great events: the greatest defeats of the proletariat in history. The cause for these defeats is to be found in the degeneration and perfidy of the old leadership. The class struggle does not tolerate an interruption. The Third International, following the Second, is dead for purposes of revolution. Long live the Fourth International!

But has the time yet arrived to proclaim its creation? ... The sceptics are not quieted down. The Fourth International, we answer, has no need of being 'proclaimed'. It exists and it fights. It is weak? Yes, its ranks are not numerous because it is still young. They are as yet chiefly cadres. But these cadres are pledges for the future. Outside these cadres there does not exist a single revolutionary current on this planet really meriting the name. If our international be still weak in numbers, it is strong in doctrine, program, tradition, in the incomparable tempering of its cadres. Who does not perceive this today, let him in the meantime stand aside. Tomorrow it will become more evident.

The Fourth International, already today, is deservedly hated by the Stalinists, Social Democrats, bourgeois liberals, and fascists. There is not and there cannot be a place for it in any of the People's Fronts. It uncompromisingly gives battle to all political groupings tied to the apron strings of the bourgeoisie. Its task – the abolition of capitalism's domination. Its aim – socialism. Its method – the proletarian revolution.

Without inner democracy – no revolutionary education. Without discipline – no revolutionary action. The inner structure of the Fourth International is based on the principles of *democratic centralism*: full freedom in discussion, complete unity in action.

The present crisis in human culture is the crisis in the proletarian leadership. The advanced workers, united in the Fourth International, show their class the way out of the crisis. They offer a programme based on international experience in the struggle of the proletariat and of all the oppressed of the world for liberation. They offer a spotless banner.

Workers – men and women – of all countries, place yourselves under the banner of the Fourth International. It is the banner of your approaching victory!

Trade Unions in the Epoch of Imperialist Decay[*]
(1940)

There is one common feature in the development, or more correctly the degeneration, of modern trade union organisations in the entire world: it is their drawing closely to and growing together with the state power. This process is equally characteristic of the neutral, the Social Democratic, the Communist and 'anarchist' trade unions. This fact alone shows that the tendency towards 'growing together' is intrinsic not in this or that doctrine as such but derives from social conditions common for all unions.

Monopoly capitalism does not rest on competition and free private initiative but on centralised command. The capitalist cliques at the head of mighty trusts, syndicates, banking consortiums, etcetera, view economic life from the very same heights as does state power; and they require at every step the collaboration of the latter. In their turn the trade unions in the most important branches of industry find themselves deprived of the possibility of profiting by the competition between the different enterprises. They have to confront a centralised capitalist adversary, intimately bound up with state power. Hence flows the need of the trade unions – insofar as they remain on reformist positions, that is, on positions of adapting themselves to private property – to adapt themselves to the capitalist state and to contend for its cooperation. In the eyes of the bureaucracy of the trade union movement the chief task lies in 'freeing' the state from the embrace of capitalism, in weakening its dependence on trusts, in pulling it over to their side. This position

*   From Trotsky Internet Archive (www.marxists.org/archive/trotsky/1940/xx/tu.htm), with revisions by the editors.

is in complete harmony with the social position of the labour aristocracy and the labour bureaucracy, who fight for a crumb in the share of super-profits of imperialist capitalism. The labour bureaucrats do their level best in words and deeds to demonstrate to the 'democratic' state how reliable and indispensable they are in peace-time and especially in time of war. By transforming the trade unions into organs of the state, fascism invents nothing new; it merely draws to their ultimate conclusion the tendencies inherent in imperialism.

Colonial and semi-colonial countries are under the sway not of native capitalism but of foreign imperialism. However, this does not weaken but on the contrary, strengthens the need of direct, daily, practical ties between the magnates of capitalism and the governments which are in essence subject to them – the governments of colonial or semi-colonial countries. Inasmuch as imperialist capitalism creates both in colonies and semi-colonies a stratum of labour aristocracy and bureaucracy, the latter requires the support of colonial and semi-colonial governments, as protectors, patrons and, sometimes, as arbitrators. This constitutes the most important social basis for the Bonapartist and semi-Bonapartist character of governments in the colonies and in backward countries generally. This likewise constitutes the basis for the dependence of reformist unions upon the state.

In Mexico the trade unions have been transformed by law into semi-state institutions and have, in the nature of things, assumed a semi-totalitarian character. The statisation of the trade unions was, according to the conception of the legislators, introduced in the interests of the workers in order to assure them an influence upon the governmental and economic life. But insofar as foreign imperialist capitalism dominates the national state and insofar as it is able, with the assistance of internal reactionary forces, to overthrow the unstable democracy and replace it with outright fascist dictatorship, to that extent the legislation relating to the trade unions can easily become a weapon in the hands of imperialist dictatorship.

Slogans for Freeing the Unions

From the foregoing it seems, at first sight, easy to draw the conclusion that the trade unions cease to be trade unions in the imperialist epoch. They leave almost no room at all for workers' democracy which, in the good old days, when free trade ruled on the economic arena, constituted the content of the inner life of labour organisations. In the absence of workers' democracy there cannot be any free struggle for the influence over the trade union membership. And because of this, the chief arena of work for revolutionists within the trade unions disappears. Such a position, however, would be false to the core. We cannot select the arena and the conditions for our activity to suit our own likes and dislikes. It is infinitely more difficult to fight in a totalitarian or a semi-totalitarian state for influence over the working masses than in a democracy. The very same thing likewise applies to trade unions whose fate reflects the change in the destiny of capitalist states. We cannot renounce the struggle for influence over workers in Germany merely because the totalitarian regime makes such work extremely difficult there. We cannot, in precisely the same way, renounce the struggle within the compulsory labour organisations created by fascism. All the less so can we renounce internal systematic work in trade unions of totalitarian and semi-totalitarian type merely because they depend directly or indirectly on the workers' state or because the bureaucracy deprives the revolutionists of the possibility of working freely within these trade unions. It is necessary to conduct a struggle under all those concrete conditions which have been created by the preceding developments, including therein the mistakes of the working class and the crimes of its leaders. In the fascist and semi-fascist countries it is impossible to carry on revolutionary work that is not underground, illegal, conspiratorial. Within the totalitarian and semi-totalitarian unions it is impossible or well-nigh impossible to carry on any except conspiratorial work. It is necessary to adapt ourselves to the concrete conditions existing in the trade unions of every given country in order to mobilise the masses not only against the bourgeoisie but also against the totalitarian regime within the trade unions themselves and against the leaders enforcing this regime. The primary slogan for this struggle is: *complete and unconditional independence of the trade unions in relation to the capitalist state*. This means a struggle to turn the trade unions into the organs of the broad exploited masses and not the organs of a labour aristocracy.

* * *

The second slogan is: *trade union democracy*. This second slogan flows directly from the first and presupposes for its realisation the complete freedom of the trade unions from the imperialist or colonial state. In other words, the trade unions in the present epoch cannot simply be the organs of democracy as they were in the epoch of free capitalism and they cannot any longer remain politically neutral, that is, limit themselves to serving the daily needs of the working class. They cannot any longer be anarchistic, that is, ignore the decisive influence of the state on the life of peoples and classes. They can no longer be reformist, because the objective conditions leave no room for any serious and lasting reforms. The trade unions of our time can either serve as secondary instruments of imperialist capitalism for the subordination and disciplining of workers and for obstructing the revolution, or, on the contrary, the trade unions can become the instruments of the revolutionary movement of the proletariat.

* * *

The neutrality of the trade unions is completely and irretrievably a thing of the past, gone together with the free bourgeois democracy.

* * *

From what has been said it follows quite clearly that, in spite of the progressive degeneration of trade unions and their growing together with the imperialist state, the work within the trade unions not only does not lose any of its importance but remains as before and becomes in a certain sense even more important work than ever for every revolutionary party. The matter at issue is essentially the struggle for influence over the working class. Every organisation, every party, every faction which permits itself an ultimalistic position in relation to the trade union, that is, in essence turns its back upon the working class, merely because of displeasure with its organisations, every such organisation is destined to perish. And it must be said it deserves to perish.

*   *   *

Inasmuch as the chief role in backward countries is not played by national but by foreign capitalism, the national bourgeoisie occupies, in the sense of its social position, a much more minor position than corresponds with the development of industry. Inasmuch as foreign capital does not import workers but pro-letarianises the native population, the national proletariat soon begins playing the most important role in the life of the country. In these conditions the national government, to the extent that it tries to show resistance to foreign capital, is compelled to a greater or lesser degree to lean on the proletariat. On the other hand, the governments of those backward countries which consider inescapable or more profitable for themselves to march shoulder to shoulder with foreign capital, destroy the labour organisations and institute a more or less totalitarian regime. Thus, the feebleness of the national bourgeoisie, the absence of traditions of municipal self-government, the pressure of foreign capitalism and the relatively rapid growth of the proletariat, cut the ground from under any kind of stable democratic regime. The governments of backward, that is, colonial and semi-colonial countries, by and large assume a Bonapartist or semi-Bonapartist character; and differ from one another in this, that some try to orient in a democratic direction, seeking support among workers and peasants, while others install a form close to military-police dictatorship. This likewise determines the fate of the trade unions. They either stand under the special patronage of the state or they are subjected to cruel persecution. Patronage on the part of the state is dictated by two tasks which confront it: first, to draw the working class closer, thus gaining a support for resistance against excessive pretensions on the part of imperialism; and, at the same time, to discipline the workers themselves by placing them under the control of a bureaucracy.

*   *   *

Monopoly Capitalism and the Unions

Monopoly capitalism is less and less willing to reconcile itself to the independence of trade unions. It demands of the reformist bureaucracy and the labour aristocracy who pick the crumbs from its banquet table, that they become transformed into its political police before the eyes of the working class. If that is not achieved, the labour bureaucracy is driven away and replaced by the fascists. Incidentally, all the efforts of the labour aristocracy in the service of imperialism cannot in the long run save them from destruction.

The intensification of class contradictions within each country, the intensification of antagonisms between one country and another, produce a situation in which imperialist capitalism can tolerate (that is, up to a certain time) a reformist bureaucracy only if the latter serves directly as a petty but active stockholder of its imperialist enterprises, of its plans and programmes within the country as well as on the world arena. Social reformism must become transformed into social-imperialism in order to prolong its existence, but only prolong it, and nothing more. Because along this road there is no way out in general.

Does this mean that in the epoch of imperialism independent trade unions are generally impossible? It would be fundamentally incorrect to pose the question this way. Impossible are the independent or semi-independent reformist trade unions. Wholly possible are revolutionary trade unions which not only are not stockholders of imperialist policy but which set as their task the direct overthrow of the rule of capitalism. In the epoch of imperialist decay the trade unions can be really independent only to the extent that they are conscious of being, in action, the organs of proletarian revolution. In this sense, the programme of transitional demands adopted by the last congress of the Fourth International is not only the programme for the activity of the party but in its fundamental features it is the programme for the activity of the trade unions.

(Translator's note: At this point Trotsky left room on the page, to expound further the connection between trade union activity and the Transitional Program of the Fourth International. It is obvious that implied here is a very powerful argument in favour of military training under trade union control. The following idea is implied: either the trade unions serve as the obedient recruiting sergeants for the imperialist army and imperialist war or they train workers for self-defence and revolution.)

The development of backward countries is characterised by its combined character. In other words, the last word of imperialist technology, economics, and politics is combined in these countries with traditional backwardness and primitiveness. This law can be observed in the most diverse spheres of the development of colonial and semi-colonial countries, including the sphere of the trade union movement. Imperialist capitalism operates here in its most cynical and naked form. It transports to virgin soil the most perfected methods of its tyrannical rule.

*   *   *

In the trade union movement throughout the world there is to be observed in the last period a swing to the right and the suppression of internal democracy. In England, the Minority Movement in the trade unions has been crushed (not without the assistance of Moscow); the leaders of the trade union movement are today, especially in the field of foreign policy, the obedient agents of the Conservative Party. In France there was no room for an independent existence for Stalinist trade unions; they united with the so-called anarcho-syndicalist trade unions under the leadership of Jouhaux and as a result of this unification there was a general shift of the trade union movement not to the left but to the right. The leadership of the CGT is the most direct and open agency of French imperialist capitalism.

In the United States the trade union movement has passed through the most stormy history in recent years. The rise of the CIO is incontrovertible evidence of the revolutionary tendencies within the working masses. Indicative and noteworthy in the highest degree, however, is the fact that the new 'leftist' trade union organisation was no sooner founded than it fell into the steel embrace of the imperialist state. The struggle among the tops between the old federation and the new is reducible in large measure to the struggle for the sympathy and support of Roosevelt and his cabinet.

No less graphic, although in a different sense, is the picture of the development or the degeneration of the trade union movement in Spain. In the socialist trade unions all those leading elements which to any degree represented the independence of the trade union movement were pushed out. As regards the anarcho-syndicalist unions, they were transformed into the instrument of the bourgeois republicans; the anarcho-syndicalist leaders became conservative bourgeois ministers. The fact that this metamorphosis took place in conditions of civil war does not weaken its significance. War is the continuation of the self-same policies. It speeds up processes, exposes their basic features, destroys all that is rotten, false, equivocal and lays bare all that is essential. The shift of the trade unions to the right was due to the sharpening of class and international contradictions. The leaders of the trade union movement sensed or understood, or were given to understand, that now was no time to play the game of opposition. Every oppositional movement within the trade union movement, especially among the tops, threatens to provoke a stormy movement of the masses and to create difficulties for national imperialism. Hence flows the swing of the trade unions to the right, and the suppression of workers' democracy within the unions. The basic feature, the swing towards the totalitarian regime, passes through the labour movement of the whole world.

We should also recall Holland, where the reformist and the trade union movement was not only a reliable prop of imperialist capitalism, but where the so-called anarcho-syndicalist organisation also was actually under the control of the imperialist government. The secretary of this organisation, Sneevliet, in spite of his platonic sympathies for the Fourth International was as deputy in the Dutch parliament most concerned lest the wrath of the government descend upon his trade union organisation.

* * *

In the United States the Department of Labor with its leftist bureaucracy has as its task the subordination of the trade union movement to the democratic state and it must be said that this task has up to now been solved with some success.

* * *

The nationalisation of railways and oil fields in Mexico has of course nothing in common with socialism. It is a measure of state capitalism in a backward country which in this way seeks to defend itself on the one hand against foreign imperialism and on the other against its own proletariat. The management of railways, oil fields, etc., through labour organisations has nothing in common with workers' control over industry, for in the essence of the matter the management is effected through the labour bureaucracy which is independent of the workers, but in return, completely dependent on the bourgeois state. This measure on the part of the ruling class pursues the aim of disciplining the working class, making it more industrious in the service of the common interests of the state, which appear on the surface to merge with the interests of the working class itself. As a matter of fact, the whole task of the bourgeoisie consists in liquidating the trade unions as organs of the class struggle and substituting in their place the trade union bureaucracy as the organ of the leadership over the workers by the bourgeois state. In these conditions, the task of the revolutionary vanguard is to conduct a struggle for the complete independence of the trade unions and for the introduction of actual workers' control over the present union bureaucracy, which has been turned into the administration of railways, oil enterprises, etc.

* * *

Events of the last period (before the war) have revealed with especial clarity that anarchism, which in point of theory is always only liberalism drawn to its extremes, was, in practice, peaceful propaganda within the democratic republic, the protection of which it required. If we leave aside individual terrorist acts, etcetera, anarchism, as a system of mass movement and politics, presented only propaganda material under the peaceful protection of the laws. In conditions of crisis the anarchists always did just the opposite of what they taught in peace times. This was pointed out by Marx himself in connection with the Paris Commune. And it was repeated on a far more colossal scale in the experience of the Spanish Revolution.

* * *

Democratic unions in the old sense of the term, bodies where in the framework of one and the same mass organisation different tendencies struggled more or less freely, can no longer exist. Just as it is impossible to bring back the bourgeois democratic state, so it is impossible to bring back the old workers' democracy. The fate of the one reflects the fate of the other. As a matter of fact, the independence of trade unions in the class sense, in their relations to the bourgeois state can, in the present conditions, be assured only by a completely revolutionary leadership, that is, the leadership of the Fourth International. This leadership, naturally, must and can be rational and assure the unions the maximum of democracy conceivable under the present concrete conditions. But without the political leadership of the Fourth International the independence of the trade unions is impossible.

Trotsky's Testament*
(1940)

My high (and still rising) blood pressure is deceiving those near me about my actual condition. I am active and able to work but the outcome is evidently near. These lines will be made public after my death.

I have no need to refute here once again the stupid and vile slander of Stalin and his agents: there is not a single spot on my revolutionary honour. I have never entered, either directly or indirectly, into any behind-the-scenes agreements or even negotiations with the enemies of the working class. Thousands of Stalin's opponents have fallen victims of similar false accusations. The new revolutionary generations will rehabilitate their political honour and deal with the Kremlin executioners according to their deserts.

I thank warmly the friends who remained loyal to me through the most difficult hours of my life. I do not name anyone in particular because I cannot name them all.

However, I consider myself justified in making an exception in the case of my companion, Natalia Ivanovna Sedova. In addition to the happiness of being a fighter for the cause of socialism, fate gave me the happiness of being her husband. During the almost 40 years of our life together she remained an inexhaustible source of love, magnanimity, and tenderness. She underwent great

---

* Trotsky Internet Archive (www.marxists.org/archive/trotsky/1932/11/oct.htm# poincare), with revisions by the editors.

sufferings, especially in the last period of our lives. But I find some comfort in the fact that she also knew days of happiness.

For 43 years of my conscious life I have remained a revolutionist; for 42 of them I have fought under the banner of Marxism. If I had to begin all over again I would of course try to avoid this or that mistake, but the main course of my life would remain unchanged. I shall die a proletarian revolutionist, a Marxist, a dialectical materialist, and, consequently, an irreconcilable atheist. My faith in the communist future of mankind is not less ardent; indeed it is firmer today than it was in the days of my youth.

Natasha has just come up to the window from the courtyard and opened it wider so that the air may enter more freely into my room. I can see the bright green strip of grass beneath the wall, and the clear blue sky above the wall, and sunlight everywhere. Life is beautiful. Let the future generations cleanse it of all evil, oppression, and violence, and enjoy it to the full.

L. Trotsky
27 February 1940
Coyoacán

FURTHER READING AND REFERENCES

For many the most easily accessible source for information about and writings of Leon Trotsky will be the magnificent Marxist Internet Archive (www.marxists.org/index.htm), with its special Trotsky section (www.marxists.org/archive/trotsky/index.htm) and its Encyclopedia of Trotskyism On-Line (ETOL – www.marxists.org/history/etol/index.htm). Among the most interesting brief introductions to Trotsky are the graphic biographies – the most recent one by Rick Geary, *Trotsky: A Graphic Biography* (New York: Hill and Wang, 2009) is quite good, though it lacks the delicious humour of the older one by Tariq Ali and Phil Evans, originally entitled *Trotsky for Beginners* and reissued as *Introducing Trotsky and Marxism* (Cambridge: Icon Books, 1998/New York: Totem Books, 2000). Other short and sympathetic introductions are Dave Renton's lively and nicely illustrated *Trotsky* (London: Haus Publishing, 2004) and Esme Choonara's very succinct *A Rebel's Guide to Trotsky* (London: Bookmarks, 2007). The definitive book of Trotsky and Trotsky-related photographs, also giving a sense of his life, is David King, *Trotsky: A Photographic Biography* (Oxford: Blackwell, 1986).

It is also reasonable, in seeking an understanding of Trotsky, to give attention to the historical context in which he lived and struggled. In regard to the Russian revolutionary context, one could hardly do better than David King, *Red Star Over Russia: A Visual History of the Soviet Union from the Revolution to the Death of Stalin* (New York: Abrams, 2008). A good academic survey is provided in Ronald G. Suny, *The Soviet Experiment: Russia, the USSR, and the Successor States*, second edition (New York: Oxford University Press, 2010); shorter, but also good, is Peter Kenez, *A History of the Soviet Union from the Beginning to the End*, second edition (Cambridge: Cambridge University Press, 2006). For the worldwide historic context, see Eric Hobsbawm, *The Age of Empire, 1875–1914* (New York: Vintage, 1989) and *The Age of Extremes: The History of the World, 1914–1991* (New York: Vintage, 1996); and Chris Harman, *A People's History of the World* (London: Verso, 2008). Trotsky's place in a general context of Marxism is indicated in Paul Le Blanc, *From Marx to Gramsci: A Reader in Revolutionary Marxist Politics* (Amherst, NY: Humanity Books, 1996). A broader revolutionary context is covered in the *International Encyclopedia of*

Revolution and Protest, 8 vols, ed. Immanuel Ness et al. (Boston, MA/ Oxford: Wiley-Blackwell, 2009).

Trotsky's Life

Trotsky tells his own story, up to the beginning of his years in exile, in the beautifully-written classic *My Life: An Attempt at Autobiography* (Mineola, NY: Dover, 2007). A valuable account by Trotsky's widow, Natalia Sedova, produced with assistance from Victor Serge, is also worthwhile – *The Life and Death of Leon Trotsky* (New York: Basic Books, 1972). The outstanding biography in English continues to be Isaac Deutscher's three-volume work – *The Prophet Armed, Trotsky: 1879–1921* (London: Oxford University Press, 1954), *The Prophet Unarmed, Trotsky: 1921–1929* (London: Oxford University Press, 1959), and *The Prophet Outcast, Trotsky: 1929–1940* (London: Oxford University Press, 1963) – although Pierre Broué's much-praised *Trotsky* (Paris: Fayard, 1988) cries out for translation from the French.

An especially useful memoir by Jean van Heijenoort, one of Trotsky's secretaries and aides, provides an abundance of insights and details regarding Trotsky's life, from a highly responsible participant-observer who offers some useful corrections of Deutscher's work – *With Trotsky in Exile: From Prinkipo to Coyoacán* (Cambridge, MA: Harvard University Press, 1978). Also see Tony Cliff, *Trotsky*, four vols (London: Bookmarks, 1989–93), containing much information and distinctive interpretations.

There has been a recent avalanche of Trotsky studies fluctuating between the critical and the absolutely hostile. The best of these – Bertrand M. Patenaude's *Trotsky: Downfall of a Revolutionary* (New York: HarperCollins, 2009) – covers Trotsky's final exile and assassination, combining fine writing and serious research with a partial garbling of Trotsky's actual ideas. Joshua Rubenstein's *Leon Trotsky: A Revolutionary Life* (New Haven, CT: Yale University Press, 2011) is also critical while striving for scholarly balance. The work that has been treated to special and widespread praise, however, is Robert Service's *Trotsky, A Biography* (Cambridge, MA: Harvard University Press, 2009), which badly suffers from shockingly flawed scholarship and politically-motivated bias – documented in Paul Le Blanc, 'Trotsky Lives', *Revolutionary History*, vol. 10, no. 2, 2010, 390–413 – which has also been made available online at multiple sites (for example: www.internationalviewpoint.org/ spip.php?article1786, and also – with some follow-up discussion – at http://links.org.au/node/1440#nb29). Additional inaccuracies are noted in a review by Tom Twiss and Paul Le Blanc, 'Revolutionary Betrayed', *International Socialist Review*, no. 71, May–June 2010, online at www. isreview.org/issues/71/featrev-trotsky.shtml.

Perhaps the most balanced short biography from a critic, and erstwhile follower, is Irving Howe's *Leon Trotsky* (New York: Viking Press, 1978). Other longer biographies – with varying levels of reliability and hostility – include: Joel Carmichael, *Trotsky: An Appreciation of His Life* (New York: St. Martins, 1975); Robert Payne, *The Life and Death of Trotsky* (New York: McGraw-Hill, 1977); Robert S. Wistrich, *Trotsky: Fate of a Revolutionary* (New York: Stein and Day, 1982); Dmitri Volkogonov, *Trotsky, The Eternal Revolutionary* (New York: The Free Press, 1996). Ronald Segal offers a much friendlier account in *Leon Trotsky* (New York: Pantheon, 1979).

Surveying and Analysing Trotsky's Life and Ideas

The two most substantial surveys of Trotsky's thought, neither entirely uncritical, can be found in the left-liberal critique by Baruch Knei-Paz, *The Social and Political Thought of Leon Trotsky* (Oxford: Oxford University Press, 1978), and Kunal Chattopadhyay's Marxist alternative, *The Marxism of Leon Trotsky* (Kolkata [Calcutta]: Progressive Publishers, 2006). Ernest Mandel provided two intelligent, sympathetic shorter surveys, *Trotsky: A Study in the Dynamic of His Thought* (London: New Left Books, 1979), and *Trotsky as Alternative* (London: Verso, 1995), both worth consulting, as is Duncan Hallas's somewhat more critical *Trotsky's Marxism* (Chicago: Haymarket, 2003). A more critical commentary is advanced in John Molyneux, *Leon Trotsky's Theory of Revolution* (New York: St. Martin's Press, 1981).

A classic discussion of Trotsky's central contribution has been reissued and merits attention – Michael Löwy's *The Politics of Uneven and Combined Development: The Theory of Permanent Revolution* (Chicago: Haymarket Books, 2010). A new and magnificent contribution focused on another central aspect of Trotsky's thought can be found in Thomas M. Twiss's meticulously researched 'Trotsky and the Problem of Soviet Bureaucracy' (doctoral dissertation, University of Pittsburgh, 2009), a version of which will be published by Brill and Haymarket Books. Trotsky's analysis of the Soviet bureaucracy – in comparison to other Marxist and Marxist-influenced analysis – finds intelligent consideration in Marcel van der Linden's helpful survey *Western Marxism and the Soviet Union* (Chicago: Haymarket Books, 2009).

Ian Thatcher's *Trotsky* (London: Routledge, 2003) and Geoffrey Swain's *Trotsky* (Harlow: Pearson, Longman, 2006) both provide biographical synopses with provocative critiques seeking to 'cut Trotsky down to size'. Especially Thatcher, but also Swain, make dramatic claims insufficiently corroborated by the historical evidence. Less hostile or iconoclastic are the collections of scholarly essays, some also critical, provided in: Hillel

Ticktin and Michael Cox, eds, *The Ideas of Leon Trotsky* (London: Porcupine Press, 1995), Terry Brotherstone and Paul Dukes, eds, *The Trotsky Reappraisal* (Edinburgh: Edinburgh University Press, 1992), and Bill Dunn and Hugo Radice, eds, *100 Years of Permanent Revolution, Results and Prospects* (London: Pluto Press, 2006).

Fiction and Documentaries

Sometimes fictional accounts can provide insights and a 'feel' for things that seem to elude even the most careful historian. Some such efforts are far more successful than others. Bernard Wolfe – a former Trotskyist, and a guard helping to protect Trotsky in Mexico – strips down the realities in *The Great Prince Died* (New York: Scribners, 1959) to a morality play in orbit around the author's 1950s perceptions of the flaws and failure of Communism.

Far more complex and satisfying is Meaghan Delahunt's fascinating and panoramic novel, *In the Casa Azul* (New York: Picador, 2001) – in the UK going by the title *In the Blue House* (making reference to the home of Mexican artist Frida Kahlo, in which Trotsky lived for a time). Delahunt places us in the minds of Trotsky and his wife Natalia, Frida Kahlo, Trotsky's assassin, Stalin as a young boy and as a dying man, Stalin's wife who committed suicide, and others. Barbara Kingsolver's very fine work, *The Lacuna* (New York: HarperCollins, 2009) employs greater artistic licence, while capturing important aspects of Trotsky's nature and context, also extending the story – through her fictional hero – into the period of McCarthyite persecutions in 1950s America.

In some ways, the most interesting novel – partially autobiographical – was written by Lillian Pollak, like Wolfe a follower during the 1930s of Trotsky who also spent some time in his Mexican household. Pollak was in her early nineties when offering her novel *The Sweetest Dream: Love, Lies, Assassination,* New York: iUniverse, 2008; second printing 2009, with some corrections and retitled *The Sweetest Dream: Love, Lies, Assassination & Hope.* Of all the novelists, she offers perhaps the most careful picture of the Trotsky household in Coyoacán, blending a number of historical figures with fictional ones, also giving a critical but sympathetic sense of the US radical movement.

Of the fictional Trotskys provided by the movie industry, it can be argued that Richard Burton – in the somewhat dubious *The Assassination of Leon Trotsky* (1972, directed by Joseph Losey) – is outclassed by Geoffrey Rush's more subdued performance in the delightful *Frida* (2002, directed by Julie Taymor). The young Trotsky, when he first allies himself with and then breaks with Lenin in 1903, is portrayed convincingly by Michael Kitchen (opposite Patrick Stewart's very convincing Lenin) in segment six ('Absolute Beginners') of the 1974 BBC mini-series *The Fall of Eagles*. The challenging 1970 play by Peter Weiss, *Trotsky in Exile* (New York: Atheneum, 1972), captures many aspects of Trotsky's story and deserves a revival and film version.

Fewer depictions can be found in the documentary films. There is an excruciatingly long, rambling three-hour French production dubbed in English, which should be avoided by all but the most dedicated – which utilises valuable footage gathered by the late US film-maker David Weiss (which other US film-makers are hoping to craft into a more worthwhile product). Easier to sit through is *Trotsky: Rise and Fall of a Revolutionary*, created by Daniel Ast and Jürgen Ast, and available in English, which runs for 53 minutes (DVD – West Long Branch, NJ: Kultur, 2007). It gets much of the factual history right (hardly all), and offers some splendid original footage, but treats Trotsky as Heroic Individual with minimal connection to organised movements and struggles and comrades (indeed, his years of exile are presented as if he alone – utterly alone – is standing up against Stalinism). Not surprisingly, it concludes, this imperious individual contributed mightily to the creation an authoritarian order in the USSR before losing in a power struggle to an even nastier authoritarian.

Trotsky y Mexico (2006), made under the direction of Mexican film-maker Adolfo Garcia-Videla, is graced with English subtitles and runs for 90 minutes. The focus is on Trotsky's life especially as it intersects with Mexico, which naturally means that attention is given to two popular revolutions of the early twentieth century: the Russian and the Mexican. Trotsky's life is contextualised not only with the sweep of history and headlines, but also with the interplay of historians, eyewitnesses, and participants. Trotsky's ideas come through in ways that would not be possible if he were presented as the Great Solitary One.

A remarkable full-length documentary of Trotsky, begun by the late David Weiss, is presently being completed by film-maker Lindy Laub, with assistance from historian Susan Weissman.

Trotsky's Writings in Exile

While Trotsky's writings before his exile more or less fall beyond the purview of this volume, there are his many writings before joining Lenin's party, ranging from his 1904 critique of Lenin, *Our Political Tasks* (London: New Park, no date), his first elaboration of the theory of permanent revolution in *Results and Prospects* (1906), and his account of the 1905 revolution – *1905* (New York: Vintage Books, 1972). No less important are his writings of 1917–29, including materials gathered in *How the Revolution Armed 1918–1923*, five vols, ed. Brian Pearce

(London: New Park, 1979–81) and the three-volume *Challenge of the Left Opposition, 1923–1929*, ed. George Shriver and Naomi Allen (New York: Pathfinder Press, 1975–81). This is far from a complete accounting of his pre-exile writings. Listed below, however, are major works produced during his 1929–40 exile.

George Breitman and various co-editors have gathered together the writings of the exile period in *The Writings of Leon Trotsky, 1929-1940*, 14 vols. (New York: Pathfinder Press, 1973-1979). There is general agreement that Trotsky's most substantial contributions include:

- *My Life, An Attempt at Autobiography* (Mineola, NY: Dover, 2007);
- *The History of the Russian Revolution* (Chicago: Haymarket Books, 2008);
- *The Permanent Revolution and Results and Prospects* (London: Socialist Resistance, 2007); also an Indian version ed. K. Chattopadhyay, A. Banerjee and S. Sarkar (Delhi: Aakar Books, 2005);
- *The Revolution Betrayed: What is the Soviet Union and Where is it Going?* (Mineola, NY: Dover, 2004); also an Indian version ed. S. Sarkar (Delhi: Aakar Books, 2005).

Unfortunately, Trotsky was never able to complete his biographies of Lenin and Stalin. Only a fragment of the former has been published – *The Young Lenin* (Garden City, NY: Doubleday, 1972). The latter was almost completed – *Stalin* (New York: Stain and Day, 1967). A rich collection of Trotsky's literary pen-portraits can be found in *Portraits Political and Personal*, ed. George Breitman and George Saunders (New York: Pathfinder Press, 1977).

Collections focusing on specific countries – predominantly made up of writings from exile – include: *Struggle Against German Fascism in Germany*, ed. George Breitman and Merry Meisel (New York: Pathfinder Press, 1971); *The Spanish Revolution, 1931–39*, ed. Naomi Allen and George Breitman (New York: Pathfinder Press, 1973); *Leon Trotsky on France*, ed. David Salner (New York: Monad/Pathfinder, 1979), and *The Crisis of the French Section, 1935–36*, ed. Naomi Allen and George Breitman (New York: Pathfinder Press, 1977).

Once again, we must confess that this listing is far from complete. Interested readers are encouraged to consult Louis Sinclair's magnificent compendium, *Trotsky: A Bibliography* (Aldershot: Scolar Press, 1989), and also the online Trotsky bibliography of Wolfgang and Petra Lubitz at www.trotskyana.net.

INDEX